The Psych 101 Series

James C. Kaufman, PhD, Series Editor

Department of Educational Psychology

University of Connecticut

David C. Devonis, PhD, received his doctorate in the history of psychology from the University of New Hampshire's erstwhile program in that subject in 1989 with a thesis on the history of conscious pleasure in modern American psychology. Since then he has taught virtually every course in the psychology curriculum in his academic odyssey from the University of Redlands in Redlands, California, and the now-closed Teikyo Marycrest University (formerly Marycrest College in Davenport, Iowa) to—for the past 17 years—Graceland University in Lamoni, Iowa, alma mater of Bruce Jenner and, more famously for the history of psychology, of Noble H. Kelly (1901–1997), eminent contributor to psychology's infrastructure through his many years of service to the American Board of Examiners in Professional Psychology. Dr. Devonis has been a member of Cheiron: The International Society for the History of Behavioral and Social Sciences since 1990, a contributor to many of its activities, and its treasurer for the past 10 years. Currently he is on the editorial board of the American Psychological Association journal *History of Psychology* and is, with Wade Pickren, coeditor and compiler of the online bibliography *History of Psychology* in the *Oxford Bibliographies Online* series.

History of Psychology

101

David C. Devonis, PhD

SPRINGER PUBLISHING COMPANY
NEW YORK

Springer Publishing Company, LLC
11 West 42nd Street
New York, NY 10036
www.springerpub.com

Acquisitions Editor: Nancy S. Hale
Composition: Amnet Systems

ISBN: 978-0-8261-9569-2
e-book ISBN: 978-0-8261-9571-5

14 15 16 / 5 4 3 2 1

The author and the publisher of this Work have made every effort to use sources believed
to be reliable to provide information that is accurate and compatible with the standards
generally accepted at the time of publication. The author and publisher shall not be li-
able for any special, consequential, or exemplary damages resulting, in whole or in part,
from the readers' use of, or reliance on, the information contained in this book. The
publisher has no responsibility for the persistence or accuracy of URLs for external or
third-party Internet websites referred to in this publication and does not guarantee that
any content on such websites is, or will remain, accurate or appropriate.

Library of Congress Cataloging-in-Publication Data

Devonis, David C.
 History of psychology 101 / David C. Devonis.
   pages cm.—(Psych 101 series)
 Includes bibliographical references.
 ISBN 978-0-8261-9569-2 (print)—ISBN 978-0-8261-9571-5 (e-book)
 1. Psychology—Study and teaching (Higher)—United States—History. I. Title.
 BF80.7.U6D49 2014
 150.973—dc23

                                                                    2013050799

Special discounts on bulk quantities of our books are available to corporations, professional associations, pharmaceutical companies, health care organizations, and
other qualifying groups. If you are interested in a custom book, including chapters
from more than one of our titles, we can provide that service as well.

For details, please contact:
Special Sales Department, Springer Publishing Company, LLC
11 West 42nd Street, 15th Floor, New York, NY 10036-8002
Phone: 877-687-7476 or 212-431-4370; Fax: 212-941-7842
E-mail: sales@springerpub.com

Printed in the United States of America by Gasch Printing.

Contents

CONTENTS

Preface

n 1989, I finished my graduate studies and took a job at a college in Southern California as a replacement for a faculty member who was moving back East. It had always been my dream to live in California, and when I got there I set about becoming a Californian right away. The first stop was the Department of Motor Vehicles to change my New Hampshire license plates for new California ones—number 2NZB642—and the next was the local office of the Automobile Club of Southern California (ACSC). There they gave me a membership card and a fat, dark-blue plastic envelope full of information, including the one thing most essential to existence in Southern California then and now: the ACSC map of the Los Angeles freeway system. This was before GPS. Maps were printed on paper and were stored, badly refolded, in the glove compartment, and hauled out to be consulted with one eye while looking ahead with the other; an early version of texting while driving.

A couple of months later I was sitting by the pool at my apartment complex, on an 80-degree day in January, faced with teaching, the next week, the history of psychology for the first time. I had just received my doctorate in that area from the University of New Hampshire, but had never before taught the course to an undergraduate group. How would I be able to present simply the complex past of psychology? While thinking over this question, my eyes fell on the freeway map, and the result is the following drawing.

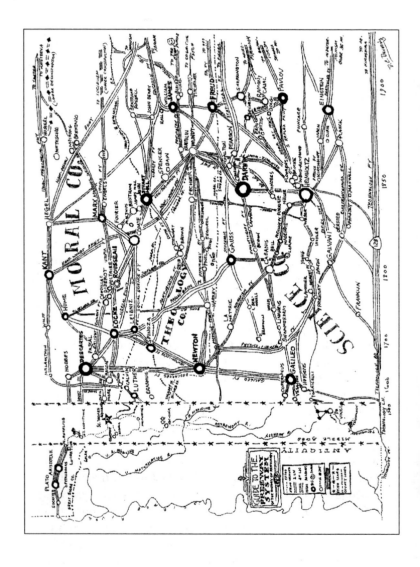

In the upper half of the map, I tried to illustrate a chronological sequence showing how modern psychology emerged from philosophy, converging over time with science, coming up from the lower half, compressing religion down to a thin stream that eventually went underground. As far as I could, I marked the main cities and towns (theorists, inventors, scientists, and other intellectual ancestors) and tried to map them so that plausible paths of influence connected them. Once my students and I got over the initial shock, we found it answered our purposes well. It expresses what I think about the past, which is that it is always there and we can always travel around in it easily, on good roads constructed by historians, translators, and others who have kept the past alive. Not only can we drive wherever and for however long we like, but we can also return to the present with whatever we find useful on our travels.

Of course, as the general semanticists told us, the map is not the territory, and maps are notoriously incomplete. I still wonder how I left out all the imaginative writers and artists that have informed not only psychology but all that has preceded it. Many of the relative distances between thinkers and even some of the connections are, I am sure, inaccurate if not plain wrong. But as a heuristic device for finding individuals and ideas in psychology's ancient past, it works well. When I drew it, in 1990, courses in the history of psychology were often based on textbooks in which the histories of individuals marked on the map, and the ideas associated with them, made up well over half of the course. That was the case for the first history of psychology course I took in 1981. By 1990, though, it was already clear that a map such as I had drawn had more than a little irony to it, leaving out as it did at least 80 years of development since the point at which it stopped. I suppose that drawing it was, for me, at some unconscious level a way of asserting that the recent past is the interesting one, the one that needs our attention, interest, and research.

Twenty-five years of teaching and writing about the history of psychology have convinced me that the past 80 years in psychology, in the United States and in the world at large, is at least as interesting a historical period as any comparable period in the past, and that it can stand on its own with any of them. So, think of this book as the continuation of my 1990 freeway map, as a sketch or a conceptual map of the routes that psychology, mainly in the United States, has taken since 1930 to reach our present time.

Attending to the recent rather than the ancient past has several advantages for those approaching the history of psychology for the first time. For one thing, much of the story will be new enough that the events will be somewhat familiar, both from other modern history courses and also from family and personal histories. Another advantage is that the issues that have arisen in times nearer to our own are not only historical but in most cases still lively in psychologists' thinking. Connecting them to their origins will help provide what one eminent historian called a "usable past." I have tried to show as many continuities between psychology's past and present as I could, given the limitations of a basic treatment of the subject. I have also tried to present the story in a way that will give you a framework for placing yourself and your experiences into the larger story of this vitally necessary field, psychology. I hope you will find as much enlightenment and enjoyment reading it as I have in writing it. Have a good trip!

Creativity 101
James C. Kaufman, PhD

Genius 101
Dean Keith Simonton, PhD

IQ Testing 101
Alan S. Kaufman, PhD

Leadership 101
Michael D. Mumford, PhD

Anxiety 101
Moshe Zeidner, PhD
Gerald Matthews, PhD

Psycholinguistics 101
H. Wind Cowles, PhD

Humor 101
Mitch Earleywine, PhD

Obesity 101
Lauren Rossen, PhD
Eric Rossen, PhD

Emotional Intelligence 101
Gerald Matthews, PhD
Moshe Zeidner, PhD
Richard D. Roberts, PhD

Personality 101
Gorkan Ahmetoglu, PhD
Tomas Chamorro-Premuzic, PhD

Giftedness 101
Linda Kreger Silverman, PhD

Evolutionary Psychology 101
Glenn Geher, PhD

Psychology of Love 101
Karin Sternberg, PhD

Intelligence 101
Jonathan A. Plucker, PhD
Amber Esping, PhD

Depression 101
C. Emily Durbin, PhD

History of Psychology 101
David C. Devonis, PhD

History of Psychology

101

Prologue

This history of psychology focuses solely on the modern period and begins in 1927. From a historical standpoint this is an important date, because that is the year in which Percy Bridgman's *The Logic of Modern Physics* (Bridgman, 1927) was published. Psychology took the term "operationalism" from

Percy Bridgman (1882–1961, USA) Physicist specializing in the behavior of materials under high pressure.

that book and made it the primary defining characteristic of the field. Since then, psychology has striven to become not just the "hope of a science" that in 1892 William James said it was (James, 1892, p. 335), but an actual science based on quantification and reproducibility of results. Arguably, operationalism (also often spelled and pronounced "operationism"), the idea that terms in a science are understood only through the means available to measure them, was the first and the most enduring term from the modern philosophy of science adopted by psychology. It permeates all aspects of the psychological enterprise.

Since 1927, three main divisions of psychology have coexisted more or less independently of each other in an unstable coalition. These divisions are, for the purposes of this narrative, theoretical psychology, applied psychology, and clinical psychology. By 1927 each was clearly discernible and each had practitioners. In that year about 80% of psychology was theoretical, devoted to proposing theories about psychological phenomena and experiments to test

1

them. About 15% of psychologists were employed in translating the results of theoretical studies into practical use, in a way similar to the way that engineers convert physics into processes and products. Also, about 5% of psychologists were forging an alliance with medicine—specifically with psychiatry—that would eventually have far-reaching consequences for the field.

Since then, those proportions have changed substantially: Today, about 25% of psychologists are theorists, and the other 75% are divided between a range of applications in education, law, and business, on the one hand (another 25%), and a version of nonmedical or paramedical psychiatry (about 50%). The beginning student and the interested citizen alike properly understand psychology as a type of advice giving. Its counseling and consulting roles have become prominent and embedded in U.S. culture. The consequences of psychology's gradual shift from theory to practice, and to a medical/health orientation rather than a strictly biophysical one, is the single most important feature of the modern era. While a short account of the history of modern psychology cannot resolve all the issues connected with the shift to a medical and health stance, it can at least foreground them and serve as a reminder to seek the primary sources of energy and conflict in the field in that shift.

In one sense, the history of modern psychology since 1927 can be understood as the attempt to bring all aspects of psychology's coalition into a unified whole, linked by a common language of operationalization and quantification. In the case of theoretical and applied psychology, this is a workable scheme and can account for the pattern of progress in each area since that time. However, clinical practice, whether in psychiatry or psychology, has proven quite resistant to quantification and operationalization, even though some of the best scientific minds in the field have occupied themselves with that problem for over half a century. The current demand for "evidence-based" clinical interventions is a sign of both the impetus to create a unified psychology with a shared operationalized base of terms and the difficulty of achieving that goal. The fault line between clinical practice and psychological science is still an active volcanic and seismic site:

The best historical evidence for this is the split in the American Psychological Association (APA), a quarter century ago, of the "scientific" psychologists from those perceived as clinicians, thus forming the American Psychological Society. This group later changed its name to the Association for Psychological *Science* to emphasize the core element of its difference.

A comprehensive history of the field cannot ignore this primary rift, and accordingly part of the following narrative will be organized by decades to present parallel brief histories of these three main divisions of psychological activity: theoretical, applied (nonclinical), and clinical. The plan is to choose three or four representative aspects of each of the coalition partners' activities and show, decade by decade, the theories and practices that have had the longest-lasting effects on psychologists' thoughts and behaviors. As it happens, before 1945 it is relatively easy to tell three separate histories of each coalition partner. Each was autonomous and self-contained. However, in 1945 a great move toward unification of psychology occurred with the inclusion of both applied and clinical psychology in a new, enlarged, and reorganized APA. While the APA is not and never was the sole organization of psychologists, its history will be the schematic framework on which the story will be built. The APA—founded in 1892, incorporated in 1925, and still in existence today—is a conceptual space in which all of these streams of psychology have, for a time, flowed together. Thus, after 1940, it becomes difficult to separate the interacting coalition elements: The change in style at that point of the summaries of coalition activity will reflect their developing interactivity. The aim of the whole book is to orient the reader to continuing themes in the field and to also point any future historian to unresolved historical questions as these appear at present (in 2014). Such connections as can be made between the coalition partners will be noted. Psychology has literally thousands of theories and applications, and no claim to completeness is made for what will follow. Fortunately, there are many specialized histories of both scientific and practical aspects of psychology that can be consulted for more detail and these are listed in Appendix II.

3

So far what is projected is not different from what would be encountered in any textbook survey of psychology's history: a succession of theories and practices arranged chronologically by specialty area. The choice of problem and method, from the scientific side, and of area of application, societal or therapeutic, on the applied and clinical sides, is often governed by the principle of "theory (or practice) for theory's (or practice's) sake." While this is a sound principle that is followed in many areas of human activity, including art, it does result in a history that becomes a record of what one art historian said was characteristic of contemporary art activity, a sequence of great individual performances. This is mirrored in another, world-historical event from 1927, Charles Lindbergh's solo flight across the Atlantic. Much of the history of psychology focuses on "firsts" and on distinct individual achievements associated with particular names (e.g., Maslow's hierarchy of needs, Bandura's social learning theory). Since psychology has not yet adopted a set of universal core theoretical principles or even agreed on a shared vocabulary (cf. Takasuna, 2013), a history that appears to be an accumulation of disparate theories in widely divergent areas (vision, development, psychopathy) seems to be inevitable. Solo flights are great achievements and they are a large part of what "makes history."

Yet, for psychology, there is a nagging sense that, beyond its activity in generating theories and styles of practice, the field has functioned as a force, and moreover as a unified force, influencing human affairs in a collective way through the gravity of its influences. Two examples, one from 1927 and one from 27 years later, exemplify this. In 1927, the Supreme Court of the

Oliver Wendell Holmes, Jr. (1841–1935, USA) American jurist: Associate Justice of the U.S. Supreme Court 1902–1932. Friend of William James.

United States decided the case *Buck v. Bell*, and the then 86-year-old Associate Justice Oliver Wendell Holmes, Jr., delivered the opinion of the court. Based on social science evidence, including the writings and teachings of some psychologists, the decision was that sterilization of the "feeble-minded" was constitutionally justified. "Three generations," Holmes wrote, "of imbeciles

4

is enough" (Holmes, 1927, p. 208). In 1954, the Supreme Court, again relying on testimony from social scientists, psychologists prominent among them, decided in *Brown v. Board of Education* (1954) that segregation by race in public schooling—and by implication, in all public places—was unconstitutional. These are prominent examples of the way in which psychological theory and practice became embodied in society as a whole. Still, there are many other examples of psychologists' activities that, taken as a whole, contribute to the shaping of social practice and, in the words of contemporary psychologists, to "helping those who help others" (Olson-Buchanan, Koppes Bryan, & Thompson, 2013). Through their effects on individuals, families, localities, and institutions, psychologists have contributed to many initiatives that have helped to build lasting changes into society.

This activity often occurs at the "grass-roots" level—in schools, courts, workplaces, public meetings, the press, through religious activity, and by word of mouth. To capture completely this rhizomatic influence of psychology on its surrounding society in all of its complexity is, compared with trying to chart the accumulation of styles of theory and practice, even more challenging. Yet even a basic history of psychology today would be incomplete without an attempt to capture the ways in which psychology intervenes in lives, individually and collectively. Accordingly, alongside the accounts of the development of the coalition of theory and practice, an account of some of the effects of psychology on society will be presented via the account of a fictional family—the Blacks—whose several generations were impacted by the development of psychology from the 1920s to the present. The episodes in their lives, arranged also chronologically by decade, will chart not only typical events that occurred at the intersection of individuals and psychology over the last century, but will also help organize a conception of the collection of ways in which psychology has influenced social practice and policy through the period. The areas of influence to be considered are education, criminal law (specifically juvenile justice), social activism, the workplace, peace studies, negotiation, and civil rights

5

(including issues connected to segregation, gender equity, sexual identity, and intercultural awareness).

It is fair to state at the outset some of the limitations of the history to follow. The necessary incompleteness of the history of technical theory and practice has already been mentioned. To this must be added the restriction, for the most part, of the story told here to the development of psychology in North America and Western Europe, and to the United States in particular. Part of the reason for this is that this book is aimed at readers in the United States and the cultural references need to be specific to them, and part of the reason is that there is a preponderant bias toward the United States and Western culture in general that pervades psychology. It is fair to say that the most serious criticisms of psychology, worldwide, are aimed at exactly that style of psychology that developed in the United States, since that sort of psychology has been one of America's chief exports during the period. That this bias is problematic not only for this history of psychology but for the field as a whole has been amply demonstrated over the past 30 years, and as far as possible in the limited compass of this work, points at which redress might be attempted are suggested. A further limitation that some may see as a grave omission is the lack of direct reference to psychology's history before 1927. Conventionally, many historians of psychology tend to interpret the familiar statement attributed to Hermann Ebbinghaus (1850–1909), a German psychologist who conducted important research on memory and who also wrote a well-regarded history of psychology published in 1909, "Psychology has a long past but a short history," as a demand for a long examination of psychology's ancient philosophical roots. Even current histories of modern psychology begin, usually, with references to the 18th and early 19th centuries in an attempt to convince the reader that psychology has a long scientific pedigree. However, today it is generally conceded that psychology has achieved independence from philosophy and that it has become a science in its own right, and so, its philosophical past can be examined in the various histories of psychology, classic and modern, brief and lengthy, that currently exist and that appear in Appendix II. This is not to say that psychology itself is a nonphilosophical endeavor. Far from it! Supposing the fundamental problem—the "constitutive problem," as George Miller (1985) termed it—of psychology is conscious experience, then there is a vibrant current discussion of that quintessential philosophical idea occurring in many areas of psychology today. However, the history of psychology is not coterminous with any particular philosophy and should not be confused with the philosophy of psychology. This is also not to say that the history of psychology at present is uninterested in philosophical questions regarding the status of narrative, the question of reflexivity, the nature of the good life, and other philosophical ideas that bear directly on the reading and writing of history as well as on psychological practice. The essentials of the history of psychology, however, may be adequately understood without total immersion in either the ancient past or the philosophical present of philosophy, and, accordingly, only such philosophical ideas as are necessary to understand the history will be introduced. Some of psychology's persisting philosophical problems will be discussed in the epilogue.

The plan of organization is, as mentioned, by decade. Each chapter will open with a summary—a "test boring"—of the primary developments in each of the areas of the theory-applied-psychotherapy coalition, and will be followed by a narrative of the social effects of psychology as exemplified by the experiences of the Blacks during that decade. The remainder of this chapter sets the stage for what follows in Chapters 1 through 8 by introducing both psychology and the Black family as they were in 1909, the year that the Black family immigrated to the United States. The accounts of the coalition in the first part of each chapter can be read separately from the narrative of social influence. Much of the development of psychological theory has proceeded fairly independently of the effects of psychology in society at large, as is the case with the development of theoretical sciences generally. Such connections as there are will be pointed out. Alternatively, the sections that discuss the ways in which psychological theory and practice affected members of the Black family may also be read as a separate narrative. In fact, I recommend reading the family story as a separate entity. At the end, an epilogue addresses some of the questions of science, history, and culture that have been raised in both narratives.

PRELUDE IN 1909

The World in 1909

The world opened 1909 with a population of about 1.7 billion people (it would reach 2 billion for the first time in 1927). China's population was about 420 million; Great Britain's, about 400 million; Russia, about 150 million; the U.S. population was about 90 million; France, about 83 million; Germany, about 78 million; Japan, about 50 million; Austria-Hungary, about 42 million; Brazil, about 20 million; Mexico, about 12 million; Ireland about 4 million; Denmark about 2 million; Cuba about 1.5 million; and El Salvador, about a million. The leaders among the European and American countries had their numbers swelled by the population of the countries in their empires, colonies, or protectorates. European, Britain, and France together had about 80 million people, and Germany the same.

U.S. Naval Captain Alfred Thayer Mahan (1840–1914) published a book in 1890 that gathered wide readership: *The Influence of Sea Power Upon History, 1660–1783*. Its central tenet was that the strength of navies determined national dominance. This book's seed fell on fertile ground: Between 1890 and 1900 navies all over the world increased greatly in size. In 1905, the Japanese Navy, hardly visible in statistical tables 20 years before, crushed the Russian Far East Fleet at the battle of the Tsushima Strait, an event that was one of the precipitating causes of the instability in Russia that led, 12 years later, to the victory of the Bolshevik faction of the Russian Social-Democratic Workers' Party in the Russian Revolution.

World commerce traveled by ship. Air power as a military force was only a visionary gleam in the eye of younger officers, a few of whom dared to ascend in the new airships. The world progressed from the air age to the jet age to the space age within a span of about 60 years. In 1909, powered flight was officially only 5 years old, but in that year Louis Bleriot crossed the English Channel alone in a single-engine monoplane and opened an era of aviation distance challenges that continued through Charles Lindbergh's solo flight across the Atlantic, to Amelia Earhart's duplication of that feat in May, 1932, to Howard Hughes's record-breaking 91-hour circumnavigation of the earth in 1938, to the first human flights into space at the beginning of the 1960s.

Across the world, the same variation in human living conditions existed in 1909 as it does today. The rich lived in luxury. Their houses, worldwide, had electric lights and telephones, and some even had primitive air conditioning systems using ice and fans. Central heating and indoor plumbing with toilets and shower baths were standard features of upper-class life in Europe and the Americas. They were immersed in familiar modern technology, differing from ours today only in detail. Cars populated the streets of Cairo, Berlin, Milan, and London—but not yet Tokyo: Automobile production in Japan would begin only about a dozen years later. Phonographs scratched out tunes; the first primitive transmission of images for long distances via the Nipkow disc (a mechanical scanner) and cathode ray tubes had occurred. On January 23, 1909, the first successful radio rescue call was made by the Marconi radio operators on the steamship *Republic* off of Nantucket. Railroads allowed comparatively rapid travel, for a price, between almost any two points on the globe, except in western China and Afghanistan, where railroad building was banned. Police and fire departments could be found in all major cities and towns worldwide. By 1915 a telephone call could travel from New York to San Francisco; by 1927, a call could cross the Atlantic.

The poorest of the poor lived much as they do today, on the streets, in ramshackle slums constructed out of the waste from building more elaborate dwellings, and in the shelter of transportation infrastructures. The merely poor lived in close proximity to each other in cities, often in buildings five to seven stories high without running water or toilet facilities. But the discoveries of the 19th century about the sources of contamination and disease in water and air had their effect: Even the poorest of the poor benefited from great improvements in public water purification and sewer systems that were made after the 1870s. Medical care varied very widely depending on economics: The world's centers of medical and surgical knowledge were in Europe's great cities. In country villages, especially as one traveled farther east, medicine became more medieval: One of the most dangerous ages to be alive was to be under 1 year of age.

The United States in 1909

In 1909, Teddy Roosevelt finished the second of his two terms as president. He signed measures dismantling large industrial combinations—"trusts"—that exerted monopolies on trade (though of course he didn't abolish corporations!) and also ensuring that food and drugs would be manufactured under strict sanitary conditions. His navy, one of the largest in the world, rostered 187 ships at the end of 1909, among them 25 battleships and 27 cruisers. Painted white, 16 of the battleships circled the globe between December 1907 and February 1909, a convincing demonstration of the military strength of the United States at a time when European nations were engaged in an escalation of tensions and an arms-building race.

In the United States, the same divide that existed in Europe could be seen between the rich and the poor. Elaborate mansions dotted the eastern and western coasts; tall skyscrapers rose in New York, Chicago, and other cities to symbolize the concentration of wealth in the corporations that built them. Those who could afford it might even pull a picnic tender, a forerunner of the modern camping trailer, behind their cars when on vacation. Private schools and elite universities existed, then as now. But the promise of America, in the early 20th century, was the ability to amass as much wealth as possible on the one hand, and on the other, that everyone in America might share in its apparently limitless prosperity. These two contradictory aims had resulted, in the decades before 1909, in the concentration of wealth in comparatively few hands and a palpable difference between the lifestyles and opportunities available to upper echelons of society and the workers who supported them. Social unrest and ultimately active violence against inequality and perceived greed resulted in the formation of strong unions of workers and also in the enactment of laws to regulate and restrict wealth acquisition. By 1913, the 16th Amendment, authorizing a federal income tax, passed. The income tax, in fact, was the result of an attempt by business interests to kill the idea of taxing corporations and wealthy individuals by proposing an amendment that they thought could never be ratified. Surprisingly, it was (U.S. National Archives, 2013).

Medicine in the United States in 1909 was, like elsewhere in the world, variable in availability and quality. Not only economics but also geography affected the quality of care. Top surgeons plied their trades in New York, Baltimore, Boston, Philadelphia, and other large cities. In rural areas, doctors with any sort of medical education were often hard to come by, and those with medical education may have received it in medical schools, for three fourths of which the educator and social reformer Abraham Flexner (1866–1959), who began his tour of examination of American medical practices in 1909, recommended immediate closure the next year. In November 1909, the American Academy of Medicine held a 2-day conference at Yale University on the subject of "Prevention of Infant Mortality"—in America, also, a leading cause of death. In 1909, Clifford Beers (1876–1943), who had, by the efforts of powerful friends, been able to escape from a life sentence of confinement in dehumanizing insane asylums, founded, saying "I must fight in the open," the National Committee on Mental Hygiene.

For most immigrants, arrival in America meant starting at the bottom. Or rather, at the top—at the top of a five- or six-floor walk-up brick tenement house built to house 18 or more families. Only since 1879 had it been the law in New York that every room should have an outside window for air. Only since 1901 was there a requirement for sewage disposal and for indoor plumbing. Before that—and for some time thereafter, as not

11

all landlords complied immediately—outdoor privies were the norm. A sink in an apartment approached luxury: The mandated toilets, gas lit as were all of the apartments, were shared among three and six families per floor. Still, great strides had been made in combating the scourges of tenement life. Tuberculosis was much less common due to better sanitation and ventilation. The public water supply was more copious and cleaner. Eventually, electricity arrived, and forward-looking tenement owners began to increase the availability of plumbing. Some even provided hot water in pipes—a true luxury. Families still bathed, once a week, in galvanized tubs in their kitchens.

Work was hard, but available. Wages were low, but there were avenues for recourse. Unions agitated for better working conditions, and were sometimes successful. Sometimes it took more extraordinary events to improve the lot of workers. In March, 1911, a spark started a fire in the Triangle Shirtwaist Factory in lower Manhattan, which led to the gruesome deaths of 146 workers, most of them young immigrant women. The fire incited action: A social worker from Boston, Frances Perkins—eventually to become the U.S. Labor Secretary—was a central figure in the institutional and legislative response of the city and the State of New York to the tragedy (Roberts, 2011). The outcome was the passing of dozens of new laws mandating safety features such as sufficient fire extinguishers and also limiting hours of work.

Immigrants started at the bottom of the social caste ladder in America as well. Before 1910, a medical examination was required: Gradually, during the next decade, anti-immigrant citizens succeeded in mandating examinations for mental defects and literacy as well. Those lucky enough to have a relative already established to vouch for them, who could speak and write well, both in their native language and in English, and who carried some money, were at an advantage.

Immigration was not easy. But compared to the conditions that many immigrants left, including those from the Russian empire where violent anti-Semitism was an everyday evil, America, with its free public schools, its fantastic richness coupled with its public-spiritedness and individual philanthropy, was truly a Paradise that allowed even the poorest to enjoy parks and fountains; fresh-air camps for the children in the summer and free concerts; and enough work and enough food to eat. And ball games: baseball was at its zenith of popularity as America's Pastime, and the song "Take Me Out to the Ball Game" was 1 year old and a big national hit. Gradually, from coast to coast, the nation that had always been a nation of immigrants expanded and prospered, as always, at the expense of those at the very bottom of its social scale—the descendants of its African slaves and of its original native populations.

Psychology in 1909

Sigmund Freud's first and only visit to the United States took place in the summer of 1909. Freud observed that, since the publication of his *Interpretation of Dreams* 10 years previously, it had sold only 251 copies. Nonetheless, he was already the most famous psychologist in the world, a position he still holds today. This was possibly due to the way that his theories about the role of sexuality in the development of neuroses were translated into the popular idiom. Possibly, also, it was because Freud was not only a psychologist but also had a background in neurology and medicine. Psychology in 1909 was already respectable as a science. It had spread across the United States from coast to coast and from border to border. Along with the members of Freud's inner circle of psychoanalysts, Ernest Jones, Carl Jung, and Sandor Ferenczi, in the formal photograph taken at

Ernest Jones (1879–1958, England) A member of Freud's early circle of acolytes: best known as Freud's "official" biographer.

Sandor Ferenczi (1873–1933, Hungary). A close associate of Freud's from the beginning of psychoanalysis.

Bird Baldwin (1875–1928, USA) An early developmental psychologist based at the University of Iowa: He initiated the field of rehabilitation psychology during and after the First World War.

the Clark University conference that September were Joseph Jastrow of the University of Wisconsin, Bird Baldwin, and Carl

Emil Seashore of the University of Iowa. Frederic Lyman Wells, one of the earliest clinical psychologists in Boston, was there, as was Adolf Meyer, the most influential psychiatrist in America at the time. Also present was H. H. Goddard of the Vineland Training School in Vineland, New Jersey.

Carl Emil Seashore (1866–1949, Sweden–USA) Important second-generation psychologist long associated with the University of Iowa. He articulated one of the first visions of psychology as a combined experimental and applied science.

Frederic Lyman Wells (1884–1964, USA) One of the first U.S. clinical psychologists and an early theorist of personality, he published Pleasure and Behavior *in 1924.*

Adolf Meyer (1866–1950, Switzerland–USA) Psychiatrist instrumental in forging a bond between psychology and medicine at the turn of the 20th century; supported the endeavors of many early U.S. psychologists.

Herbert Henry Goddard (1866–1957, USA) Director of Research at the Vineland Training School in New Jersey and the earliest promoter of the Binet-Simon intelligence test as a means of determining "feeble-mindedness" and fitness.

In September 1909, the school year was opening at universities and colleges across the United States, and psychology departments were receiving new students in many of them. At Drake University in Des Moines, Iowa, Florence Richardson, 24 years old, was preparing for a new semester as an assistant professor of psychology: The previous year, she had received her PhD from the University of Chicago and, like many psychologists at the time, had spent the summer in Würzburg, Germany, with some of the world's leading psychologists. Later, in the 1920s, she would become influential in the new League of Women Voters: In 1909, she was still, along with many other women, agitating for the vote, which women would not have until 1920.

Jastrow, Baldwin, Robinson, and Seashore were excellent representatives of psychology's diffusion outward from the east coast as well as of its experimental activity at the time. The center of gravity of world psychology had shifted to America's Atlantic coast by 1909. The field that had originated in several European countries simultaneously between 1830 and 1880 had acquired its most avid

14

practitioners in America and, though the psychologists of 1909 did not know it yet, America would be the place that in 30 years would become the center of most of the world's scientific psychological activity for the next 70 after that. Psychology had already diffused widely in the U.S. Midwest. Among the articles published with a Wisconsin byline in 1909 were those of E. A. Ross, a well-respected sociologist, who wrote a contribution to a discussion titled "What Is Social Psychology?" (Ross, 1909). Michael Vincent O'Shea, an influential early contributor to child and educational psychology (Weizmann & Harris, 2012), wrote on, naturally enough, "Progress in Child and Educational Psychology" (O'Shea, 1909). And Daniel Starch, soon to become a central figure in the development of industrial psychology and the psychology of advertising, reviewed the work of F. G. Bruner, a graduate of Columbia University in anthropology and psychology, on the differences in auditory ability among 7 African Pygmies, 7 Vancouver Indians, 137 Filipinos, 10 Cocopa Indians, 63 Indians from Government School, and 156 Whites, among others. The journal in which they published, the *Psychological Bulletin*, then 6 years old, was one of the first of several dozen psychology journals that would emerge over the next 50 years. Also published in the *Bulletin* that year were the first reports, by Robert Yerkes and Serge Morgulis of Harvard, of the work of Ivan Pavlov on conditioning of dogs (Yerkes & Morgulis, 1909). In an even newer journal,

E(dward) A(lsworth) Ross (1866–1951, USA) Progressive-era sociologist long associated with the University of Wisconsin: authored Sin and Society *in 1907.*

Michael Vincent O'Shea (1866–1932, USA) Educational psychologist with a degree from Cornell University in 1892; supervised several surveys of state educational systems in the 1920s.

Daniel Starch (1883–1979, USA) An influential applied psychologist working in the areas of advertising and marketing.

F(rank) G. Bruner (1874–1965, USA) Graduate student of Robert S. Woodworth who assisted at the anthropological–psychological exhibition at the St. Louis World's Fair in 1904; later employed as a clinical psychologist in the Department of Child Study, Chicago Board of Education. He wrote on both racial differences and intelligence testing.

15

the *Journal of Abnormal Psychology*, an article appeared by Tom A. Williams, neurologist and consulting psychiatrist at the Freedmen's Hospital and Epiphany Free Dispensary in Washington, titled "Mental Causes in Bodily Disease: The Most Frequent Cause of the Origins of 'Nervous Indigestion'" (Williams, 1909). Psychology was already widely interested in not only the elemental scientific basis of behavior in conditioning but also in anthropology, abnormal psychology, and psychotherapy. It was as diverse in interests then as it is now.

Robert Mearns Yerkes (1876–1956, USA) Leading comparative psychologist. Arguably the most influential early U.S. psychologist in terms of aligning psychologists with governmental initiatives.

Serg(ius) Morgulis (1885–1971 Russia–USA) Physiologist and translator, in 1924, of Aleksandr I. Oparin's "The Origin of Life."

Tom A(lfred) Williams (1870–? Scotland–USA) Neurologist and psychiatrist based in an African American hospital in Washington, D.C.

In the front row of the 1909 Clark conference photo, standing with Freud, are the three most eminent American psychologists of that time. Edward B. Titchener (1867–1927), who had been trained both in Germany and England, came to America in the early 1890s and founded the psychology laboratory at Cornell University. His style of psychology emphasized the contents of the mind; the ability of humans to observe their own feelings, perceptions, and thoughts; precise experimental procedures; and a strict division between learning about the mind in the laboratory and applying knowledge about the mind outside of it. G. Stanley Hall (1844–1924) was one of the earliest students of psychology in America and received the first doctorate in psychology, awarded in the United States in 1878. After postgraduate study in Germany, he moved to Johns Hopkins University (where he trained Joseph Jastrow, among others) and then to Clark University in Worcester, Massachusetts, where 20 years later he hosted Freud. Earlier, in 1892, Hall gathered together 30 other men—psychologists were virtually all men at that time, even in the 1909 conference photo—and formed the APA, which elected him its first president. His psychology, in contrast to Titchener's, emphasized observation and careful narrative recording; the importance of child study in the understanding of behavior; and the relation of and application of psychology to practical problems of life in education, child and adolescent development, and religion, among many other areas of interest.

The third of these, William James (1842–1910), is acknowledged by every historian of psychology as the source of modern American psychology as we know it today. James was raised in an atmosphere of liberal mystic theology with a scientific bent (Swedenborgian). His brother, Henry James (1843–1916), became an eminent novelist. His sister Alice (1848–1892) was a diarist of note. Another brother, Robertson James (1846–1910), was an artist, a vagabond, and a florid alcoholic. Another brother, Garth James (1845–1883), distinguished himself in the Civil War but did not live up to the expectations of success that were expected of him. And success was expected of all the James siblings by their demanding, extremely rich father. The James children had educational advantages well beyond the norm, even for rich Americans of the time. William James met Darwin personally and was one of the earliest proponents of the Darwinian theory of evolution in the United States.

William James originally followed a path toward a career in art, but though he exhibited some talent in his studies with some of the leading American artists of the time, his father pressured him toward a scientific career. He studied medicine during the Civil War and did not participate in the battles, which were for many American men the defining events of their lives and their generation. But medicine left him cold, and though he obtained an MD in 1869, by the end of that course of study he was so deeply depressed that he entertained serious thoughts of suicide. He brought himself back from the brink by a course of reading and thought. Troubled by the implications of the conception of life as mechanism, which were taking hold all around him, James asserted that his will was indeed free and that his first freely willed act would be to believe in free will. Aided by good connections to Harvard, he was appointed an instructor of anatomy and physiology in 1873. By 1876 he had added courses in psychology to his repertoire, and by 1880 was teaching a

17

combination of physiology and hygiene, philosophy of evolution, physiological psychology, psychology of the intellect, and contemporary philosophy, a mix which evolved around this core over the next 27 years.

In 1890 James published a book that gathered wide readership: the two-volume *Principles of Psychology*. Like our psychology today, it covered the brain and the senses, perception, the self, emotion, and motivation. James had already written on the concepts of mind and emotion during the 1880s, formulating the well-known theory of emotion that bears both his and Carl Lange's names, the James-Lange theory. Perhaps its greatest chapter is the one on the will, which also contains many anecdotal connections to James's own experience with his brother's addiction to alcohol and the effect of addictions on people. Though it set a standard for completeness and vivacity in writing, James perceived his text to be incomplete. So, over the next 20 years, he supplemented it with two other texts that have also become standard works in American intellectual culture. The first of these is *The Varieties of Religious Experience*. Though not formally religious himself, James undertook to examine all the dimensions of religious life, from belief through ecstasy through existential despair. In that work, and in an 1896 predecessor series of lectures on exceptional mental states, James established the theoretical justification for discussing abnormality, including addiction, anxiety, and depression, in the context of a comprehensive psychology. In his last book, James outlined a philosophical theory based on the idea that belief can instantiate reality. If a belief is useful, it is real: That is the gist of *Pragmatism: A New Name for Some Old Ways of Thinking*. So James was equally a scientist, a philosopher, and a religious theorist. This attitude of acceptance influenced his view of the content of psychology, which could even encompass beliefs in parapsychological experience. This ecumenical approach found resonance in many of those who studied with him and with those who were his students and colleagues in psychology

Carl Lange (1834–1900, Denmark) Danish physician and physiologist.

philosophy at Harvard. Among those were Ralph Barton Perry, who was a mentor to Henry Nelson Wieman; E. B. Holt, who mentored J. J. Gibson; and Herbert S. Langfeld, who mentored Gordon Allport as well as E. C. Tolman. All of these individuals will be encountered several times in the narrative that follows.

Ralph Barton Perry (1876–1957, USA) Philosopher, biographer of William James.

Henry Nelson Wieman (1884–1975, USA) American philosopher and theologian, student of, among others, Ralph Barton Perry. He conceived of the idea of "creative interchange" as a means of integrating the diverse aims and interests of individuals into a socially beneficial whole.

In 1909, at the Clark conference, James was very sick. Today he would have already had extensive heart surgery: In his day, medicine was hardly that advanced. He lived long enough to complete an article, "The Moral Equivalent of War," which would have great resonance in the history of psychology in America. In that article, James contrasted the improvements that war makes not only in technology but in the attitudes of humans toward life. War focuses the intellect and demands the utmost in energy and endurance from all its participants. Yet war, so essential to progress, is a horror in its present state. James, a committed pacifist, had followed the changes in American weaponry from the time of the Civil War

Edwin Bissell Holt (1873–1946, USA) Student of William James and one of James's successors at Harvard, author in 1915 of The Freudian Wish and Its Place in Ethics. *Most influential as the mentor of J. J. Gibson at Princeton University in the 1920s. One of the few psychologists of his era openly identified as gay.*

Herbert Sidney Langfeld (1879–1958, USA) Psychologist and aestheticist: a very well-connected psychologist who was in the background of most of the important developments of psychology as an academic field during the first decades of the 20th century.

to 1909: By that time, ultra-high explosives, the machine gun, and aerial bombardment were realities. (Though James probably did not know it at the time, the seeds of atomic warfare were already growing steadily.) Against this carnage, James proposed

19

that humans, if they could never abandon war, should harness it to peaceful purposes, engaging the energies of youth to combat the age-old enemies of humans—disease, famine, and poverty. As we will see, this message continued to animate much of psychology over the next hundred years, a history to which we now turn.

THE BLACK FAMILY HISTORY: A COLLECTIVE BIOGRAPHY

The Black family's roots are in Eastern Europe, and the earliest and only surviving record of the family is that of the members who decided, in 1909, to emigrate to America. Jacob (1884–1918) and Lyuba (1885–1918) Schwartz lived in Ternopol in the Ukraine (all records of earlier generations were destroyed in the Holocaust). Immediately after arriving, Jacob went to work in the clothing industry in New York, employed by a cousin who had emigrated 17 years earlier. One of the first things that Jacob did was change his name to the American translation of "Schwartz"—"Black." Lyuba delivered her first child, Rosa (1909–1999), soon after arriving. Rosa was followed by Harry (1911–1986) and by Helen (1918–). Lyuba died in childbirth in 1918, and Jacob succumbed to the epidemic influenza shortly afterward. The children were taken in by Jacob's cousin, who had in the meantime become a prosperous business owner and had moved to a newly built neighborhood in Queens, New York.

Rosa had a reasonably happy childhood and graduated from high school in 1927. Recognized for her talent in writing while in school, she attended New York University for 2 years and then, wishing to be independent and to live on her own, embarked on a journalistic career with a variety of Yiddish and radical papers and magazines. She eventually became a successful freelancer for a wide variety of publications. Though she broke with Communism early in the 1940s, she was accused of un-American activities during the McCarthy era. This, however, did not appreciably hinder her from making a living, as she had skills as an editor, an occupation very much in demand. In 1939 she began a long-term relationship with Francine Miller (1905–1994), with whom she shared an apartment and life from 1943 until her death. She retired from active writing in 1974 but wrote a memoir of her life and relationship in 1986.

Harry had a less happy experience growing up. Loss of his father affected him severely and he became truant and eventually got involved with a gang. With them, he participated in several burglaries and was eventually caught and brought to trial in 1927. Intervention by juvenile probation services and other social agencies arranged for his conditional release on probation, requiring him to complete high school, which he did in 1930. At that time he was employed by a bookbindery, but when that business failed during the Depression in 1932, Harry took to the road. After traveling throughout America, he settled down with Joan Harris, an artist and poet who had been a student at the Black Mountain College in North Carolina. Harry worked several jobs to support Joan, whom he married in 1939. Their son, Donald, was born in 1940. Harry joined the army in 1941 and served in Europe during the Second World War. When he finished his service in 1946, he attended the University of Tennessee, studying psychology. Following graduation with an MA in psychology in 1950, he worked as a clinical psychologist associated with a Veterans Administration (VA) hospital in North Carolina. He obtained his PhD from the University of Tennessee in 1952, was licensed to practice clinical psychology in Tennessee in 1953, and practiced in a North Carolina university town from 1955 until his retirement in 1982. He wrote a memoir of his career in 1983.

Even though her adolescence coincided with the Great Depression, Helen was shielded from its effects, as her father's cousin remained employed and became even more successful during the 1930s. Helen graduated from high school in 1936 and attended City College of New York, graduating in 1940. She met Eddie McConnell (1915–1965), an engineering student at Columbia, at a dance in 1939 and married him right after graduating. Eddie and Helen moved to Los Angeles, California, where Eddie was employed by a large aircraft maker as an engineer and designer. Eddie was drafted in 1943, 2 months after Carolyn, their daughter, was born. Helen worked in an aircraft factory during the war years and returned to homemaking when Eddie returned from the service in 1945. They moved to Van Nuys, California, in 1953. After Eddie's death in 1965, Helen returned to school, obtaining an MA in social work from the University of California, San Francisco, in 1967. She was a consultant to the Los Angeles schools on cross-cultural mental health issues, and retired in 1990.

The 1920s

THEORETICAL PSYCHOLOGY IN THE 1920s

In 1920, in America, psychology was dominated by two main currents. The first was a tendency to reduce life to habit, and the second was to establish differences between humans by test. Typifying the first tendency was John B. Watson's (1878–1958) behaviorism, which tended to reduce life to its simplest terms of action and reaction. "You may maintain," Watson wrote in his popular textbook *Behaviorism* in 1924, "that we never play with situations and stimuli as I have here suggested. Go then to real life. We increase our employees' salaries. We offer a bonus— we offer them homes at nominal rental so they can get married. We put in baths—playgrounds. We are constantly manipulating stimuli, dangling this, that, and the other combinations in front of the human being in order to determine the reactions they will bring forth, hoping the reaction will be 'in line with progress,' 'desirable,' 'good.' (And society really means by "desirable," "good," and "in line with progress", reactions that will not disturb its recognized and established traditional order of things.)" (Watson, 1924, pp. 19–20).

The second tendency, toward testing, had burst suddenly on the scene with the coming of the Binet tests to America in 1905. By 1917 there were dozens of tests in use in business and industry, in psychiatry, and in schools (Devonis, 2013). With the coming of the First World War, tests were introduced into the U.S. Army, and the corresponding publicity, by psychologists and in the press, ensured that psychological testing would be a permanent part of the U.S. economy. By 1921 the Psychological Corporation was founded to distribute, for a profit, tests that since that time have been one of the essential elements of psychological activity in the United States.

It is tempting to write history in terms of struggles between opposites, and from some perspectives the three theoretical perspectives that form the framework of this story (theoretical, applied, and clinical psychology) could be seen then, and still can be seen today, as reactions against the simplistic conceptions of life that behaviorism and testing promoted. And each of these three connected with other tendencies in psychology that were present at the time and that have also had a continuous existence. The first of these, Gestalt psychology, appeared to some to be an exotic import. It is true that its major practitioners were all German. But where psychologists in America before 1920 went to Germany to learn their craft, here the German psychologists were coming to America to expand their horizons and reach, for already it was plain that psychology's future as an applied science would be centered in America, which was providing rich funding and supportive academic environments for the endeavor (Sokal, 1994). Kurt Koffka's (1886–1941) appointment at Smith College in 1927 was a portent for the inrush of psychologists from Germany over the next decade. A claim could be made that Adolf Hitler simultaneously destroyed German psychology and advanced it in America.

There wasn't a great deal of similarity between the experimental interests of the major Gestalt psychologists. Wolfgang Koehler (1887–1967) had established himself as a primatologist interested in problem solving in apes; Kurt Koffka was interested in the ways in which the mind becomes organized developmentally; and Max Wertheimer (1880–1943) and Karl Duncker (1903–1940) were most interested in perception and cognition—why is it that incomplete series, for instance, seem to demand completion? Why do people develop mental blocks to seeing the solution to seemingly simple problems? Why do two lights flashing separately give rise to a perception of unitary motion?

Behind all of these surface differences of practice was the ethos of the Gestalt movement. We remember it today, not mistakenly, as "the whole is more than the sum of its parts." In terms of the human cognitive system, the active, inquisitive mind takes in the raw material of environmental stimulation and individual neurons and assembles it into complex, contextualized combinations that are recognized as wholes. A set of behaviors becomes perceived as a relationship, either of actions or between humans. The idea of contextualized relationships determined by perceptual interpretation challenged the notions that had sprung up around behaviorism that the brain was empty, functioning only as a router between environmental stimulus and motor response. The idea, still vivid in American psychology during the 1920s, that psychology was "the science of mental life" (as William James had termed it in 1890 and as the title of R. S. Woodworth's textbook, the most popular

Robert Sessions Woodworth (1869–1962, USA) Early generalist psychologist associated with Columbia University.

psychology textbook of the 1920s, called it) was reinforced and extended by the diffusion of Gestalt psychology through American psychology over the coming decades, as the rest of these reviews of theory and practice will show.

Another way to show relationships between environment and behavioral output is to study the organ—the brain—that mediates that relationship. Most behaviorists—most psychologists in 1920, really—had little to go on besides the knowledge of brain anatomy and the rudiments of neural organization. Karl S. Lashley (1890–1958) was a student of John B. Watson and learned his trade in the rat maze lab, establishing habits and measuring the correlation between environmental manipulations—feeding, obstacles, and injury—and the acquisition and maintenance of habits. He also accompanied Watson on expeditions off Key West to study the behavior of nesting terns in the wild. Both he and Wolfgang Koehler had a background in behavior in naturalistic settings. During the 1920s, first at the University of Minnesota, then at Chicago, and eventually at Harvard University, Lashley began a series of studies designed to discover the representation of the maze habit in the brain. Enough was known about the brain at the time to localize the probable site of any such representation in the cortex and, fortunately enough, Lashley's preferred experimental species, the rat, was at least minimally cortical. After training rats in maze problems, Lashley began systematically extirpating cortex, varying in location and amount, by suction and cautery. The outcome of these studies, which Lashley presented to the 9th International Congress of Psychology at Yale University in 1929—the first time that the conference had been held in the United States—demonstrated that if there were a connection between a neural representation of the maze and the motor behavior, it was distributed throughout the brain, since while the relative amount of cortex left after the operations determined the speed and skill of tracing the maze, the location of the lesions had no effect (Lashley, 1929). Why this should be the case is still not fully determined today (we see a similar situation in the recovery of functions after brain damage in humans). The effect of his findings was twofold. It provided evidence for the complexity of cortical coordination and integration and against the simple "telephone switchboard" model of stimulus response connection prevalent at the time, and it also reinforced the idea that the brain functioned the brain functioned holistically. This was a conclusion in accord with the findings of Kurt Goldstein (1878–1965), an unsung Gestaltist who had studied brain injuries for two decades in Germany and, after resettling to America, published in 1940 the very influential books *The Organism* and *Human Nature in the Light of Psychopathology*, which many American psychologists of that time had on their shelves.

The third lasting theoretical contribution of the 1920s was the result of the organizational skills of an immigrant from Sweden, Martin Luther Reymert (1883–1953), who in 1925 had accepted a post as an assistant professor of psychology at Wittenberg College, a Lutheran institution in Springfield, Ohio. For the ceremonies surrounding the dedication of the psychological laboratories in the new Chemistry–Psychology building in 1927, Reymert arranged for over 30 leading psychologists from Europe and America to convene in Springfield that October to present on the topic of emotion at the First Wittenberg Symposium on Emotion. In the usual telling of psychology's history, emotion doesn't find a niche. Some historians might even see some symbolism in the death, in August, of one of the symposium's featured speakers, Edward B. Titchener. Titchener, one of the most well-known of the second generation of psychologists in America, was associated with a psychology that at the time was thought out of date—the last survivor, some thought, of the older introspective method in modern, objective, behaviorist times. Nonetheless, the conference went off as planned and was well attended. As it turned out, the symposium's summary volume, *Feelings and Emotions* (Reymert, 1928), sold well and became, for many years until Reymert organized a second symposium in 1950, the main reference source for those psychologists who carried on with research on emotion. Though in 1933, Max Meyer, one of the original behaviorists (his 1911 text *The Fundamental Laws of Human Behavior* is considered by some to mark the start of behaviorism in the United States), pronounced emotion "that whale among the fishes" and thought that any psychologist studying it might be competing selfishly with "ministers of religion" in

Max Meyer (1873–1967, Germany–USA) Migrated to the United States and was associated for a long time with the University of Missouri. A pioneer in psychoacoustic and music research; dismissed from his academic position in 1930 due to a controversy over a student survey concerning sexual behavior.

what they might offer as science (Meyer, 1933), today it is difficult to imagine a psychology that doesn't center around the role of emotion in life. Emotions, their definition, experience, and proposals for their management, have been central to psychological theory and practice from B. F. Skinner advising, in a filmed interview in 1987, those who are depressed to "change how you feel" with a drug, to recent theories of the role of the feeling of terror in modifying perceptions. The ancient triads of perception–brain–emotion and thought–feeling–behavior persisted in the infrastructure of the field as the elements out of which all of psychology to come was constructed.

APPLIED PSYCHOLOGY IN THE 1920s

American prosperity in the 1920s was, like it is today, most visible in the tall towers of its institutions of financial management (or financial manipulation, as it was viewed in the following decade) and, like today, was grounded in its workforce. The classic photographs of work from the 1920s show mostly men: In 1920 women made up less than 25% of the U.S. workforce and were mostly employed in office/clerical, domestic service, or manufacturing, especially in what were then called the "needle trades", the manufacture of cloth and clothing. Most work was done by men, and most men were employed in the manufacturing or transportation sectors. Work in a typical manufacturing setting, for both men and women, was typically dirty, monotonous, stressful physically and mentally, and actually dangerous. Streetcar drivers, for example, mostly men, stood for 8 to 12 hours either in a cramped, unventilated cab or on a semi-exposed platform in all weathers. Psychology had already been applied to the streetcar rider by Raymond Dodge, the first psychologist to identify and measure saccadic eye movements in 1896, when he recommended that riders facing

Raymond Dodge (1871–1942, USA) Studied with Benno Erdmann at the University of Halle, Germany: discovered saccadic eye movements. President of the American Psychological Society (1916) and a model for the development of experimental psychology in the United States.

outward not fix their gaze on the scenery streaming by in order to avoid disorienting nystagmus (Dodge, 1902). It was Hugo Münsterberg, William James's German successor at Harvard, who conducted and published the first studies on streetcar drivers' perceptual and motor skills, and it was Morris Viteles, employed by the Philadelphia Transit Company, who in 1924 inaugurated the first comprehensive program of employee selection, training, evaluation, and safety education, a prototype of the integrated human relations departments found in all large corporations today (Viteles, 1932). The founding

Hugo Münsterberg (1863–1916, Germany–USA) William James's hand-picked choice to lead the Psychology Laboratory at Harvard, Münsterberg, holder of doctorates in both psychology and medicine, was one of the most potent forces in developing an applied experimentalism, especially in the areas of industry and forensics.

Morris Viteles (1898–1996, Russia–USA) Influential American industrial–organizational psychologist whose 1932 book Industrial Psychology *defined the modern dimensions of the field.*

and expansion of psychology programs in universities large and small coast to coast resulted in a growing number of psychologists seeking employment themselves, as psychologists, naturally. The marketing of the new tests and programs for managing employees for greater efficiency and productivity caught on and became, during the 1920s, integral to the work process in the United States. As a side note, industrial consulting work was one of the areas that attracted many women psychologists and gave them their start in the field at this time (Koppes, 1997). Another collateral benefit of involvement with workplaces for psychologists was that they provided mass laboratories with vast numbers of experimental participants. The Hawthorne Works in Chicago, a massive factory producing electric switching apparatus for telephones, was the site of the "Hawthorne Studies," demonstrating that simple knowledge of being observed could have a measurable effect on performance—often cited as the most salient example of experimenter effects in research (Hsueh, 2002).

That said, most work still remained unexamined by psychologists, and work in steel mills, mines, and other factories was no less dangerous and monotonous as before. Nor was work usually found by walking into a psychologist's office in a human relations department, but by searching the "help wanted" ads in newspapers or on office or factory doors, a haphazard process that, however, worked fairly well when the skill levels for most jobs were low. However, as industry mechanized and as manufacturing and distribution processes became more technical and complex, finding a job became correspondingly more complicated. Along with the development of industrial psychology came the development of psychological intervention at the point of induction into the workforce. Much as psychology had gotten involved with the induction and classification of military personnel during the First World War, it saw in the hiring lines of the burgeoning American economy another opportunity for employing its tests. Donald Paterson (1892–1961), son of deaf parents who studied psychology with Rudolf Pintner (1884–1942), an early pioneer of mental testing at The Ohio State University, moved to the University of Minnesota in 1921 and began a long career there as a trainer of applied psychologists who put psychological principles to use in all areas of life. He was committed to the dissemination of psychology, sponsoring 88 dissertations and 300 master's theses. Paterson studied the science of revealing human differences via testing, but alongside this, during the 1920s he began a program of student counseling aimed at identifying and improving all aspects of the fit of student and college environment. Paterson's original work emphasized vocational counseling and career direction. But it evolved, for example through the efforts of one of his students, Leona Tyler, interested in psychology that would further the cause of peace, into the profession of counseling, providing advice and guidance in all areas of life (Held, 2010). Thus, as an offshoot of psychologists' involvement with industry, the 1920s saw the beginning of the "counseling" area of "clinical-counseling" psychology so prominent today.

Psychologists in industrial and industrial-related consulting and counseling were the main promoters of applied psychology, for this decade and beyond, along with those psychologists employed in educational settings and in settings such as advertising (including John B. Watson, who became a vice president of a major New York ad firm after being censured and removed from his academic position in 1920). Their absolute numbers were small—probably only a thousand or so nationwide—but they came into contact with many more people via massive programs of testing, or as teachers or other education professionals in classroom or training settings. Gradually, psychology became well disseminated in culture, perceived as a source of guidance, counseling, and testing. Another channel that psychologists put to use to disseminate the new field was the media. In the 1920s there were hundreds of newspapers published daily, dozens of weekly magazines, along with books. Print media was the primary means of communication of information and ideas. Into this world came radio, which revolutionized communication virtually overnight. The first commercial radio broadcast occurred in 1920. By 1930, there were hundreds of radio stations, and by 1935, it could be confidently stated that every American household could be reached by radio.

Psychologists already had a public that hungered for advice about all aspects of their lives. How to choose mates, how to resolve marital disagreements, how to raise or discipline children, how to manage sex relations—all of these were areas where popular advice-givers including clergy, politicians, and "experts" of varying credibility and honesty had proliferated for decades. Now, psychologists, in possession of new knowledge about learning and memory, job prospecting, child development, and all other aspects of life realized that they had an opportunity to do more than share their findings with their colleagues in journals and conferences. The 1920s was a boom market for popular psychology treatments. In fact, Joseph Jastrow (1863–1944), long a faculty member at the University of Wisconsin, when he gave the keynote speech after the banquet at the Wittenberg Symposium in 1927, railed against those psychologists who would allow you to "acquire a permanent wave of your psychic head-gear" while pocketing what he implied might be ill-gotten gains (Jastrow, 1928b, p. 435). Someday, he said, a psychologist will emerge with the qualities of Newton and Darwin, and

31

"may he be greeted—Lo! The Great Psychologist!" (Jastrow, 1928b, p. 438). Anyone who didn't know Jastrow would have taken him for a disgruntled academic psychologist, despairing over the perversion of science by commerce. In fact, Jastrow had a long pedigree as a popularizer of psychology. He had administered mental tests to all comers at a booth on the Midway of the World's Columbian Exposition in 1893, and by 1927 was already the author of several books of popular psychology, including *Keeping Mentally Fit* (Jastrow, 1928a). There, he punned on the current fad for purgatives by advising the stressed and stale worker to "Take a Relaxative!" When Jastrow left the podium, he headed back not to Wisconsin where he had been a faculty member for over 30 years, but to New York City and his syndicated newspaper column, and later his radio program, one of the first of its type among psychologists, and one that soon had many imitators. Psychology's advance was guaranteed by the alliances its practical applicators forged with industry and the media during the 1920s, alliances that have continually strengthened since that time.

PSYCHOTHERAPY IN THE 1920s

This was the era of the mental hospital in all its grimness. The American population exploded, life had become more complex and stressful, and new forms of diagnosis—"feeblemindedness," determined by low scores on IQ tests—came into use. The building of the architectural monstrosities called the "Kirkbrides,"

Thomas Kirkbride (1809–1883, USA) Psychiatrist influential in determining the design of mental hospitals from the 1850s onward.

after their principal architect, the forbidding monitory asylums that rose up menacingly from otherwise placid rural landscapes, had determined that there would be ample spaces in which to house, and little more, those whom society could not manage or accept. In 1925, commitment to a mental hospital meant, whether for an elderly woman experiencing dementia, a young man experiencing a first-time schizophrenic episode, a middle-aged manic woman, or even an obstreperous colleague or relative, an easy admittance and often a life sentence in what was for all intents and purposes a place of incarceration.

There were some signs of hope: Rationally organized clinics such as that of the Menninger brothers in Topeka, Kansas, adequately staffed and with well-trained psychiatrists adept at relating to patients, were in place, but they were very few in number. For the most part, the role of psychiatrist in a mental hospital, even for those who still maintained their skills, was, because of the sheer number of admittances and the nearly complete lack of effective ways to manage patient behavior, a daunting and eventually crushing task.

Some forms of what would later be called clinical psychology had taken root in a few places: By 1927, books were available outlining the role of the clinical psychologist in taking histories, administering personality and other mental tests, and other tasks in support of diagnosis and treatment (e.g., Wells, 1927). Psychologists, however, were only infrequently found in mental hospitals, and when they were, they were often kept strictly separate from the medical staff. Autonomy and authority within a medical setting were yet to be achieved. But during this period, psychiatrists sympathetic to psychology—William Alanson White and Adolf Meyer—fostered collaboration between psychiatrists and psychologists that would eventually lead to a hybridization of psychiatry

William Alanson White (1870–1937, USA) Eminent psychiatrist based St. Elizabeth's Hospital and at George Washington University in Washington, DC, from 1903 until his death.

and psychology, though without full admittance to medical privileges such as prescribing drugs, which would become more and more a point of contention as pharmacology—primitive in the 1920s—became more important in therapy in the coming decades.

For those who could afford it and who were not institutionalized, some small amount of psychotherapy was available.

Psychotherapy, as distinct from institutional psychiatry, had emerged from a confluence of religious and intellectual sources, mostly in New England toward the end of the 19th century (Taylor, 2009). A consensus was beginning to form around the idea that there were forms of mental illness that were tractable to being relieved, and possibly even cured, by some form of interpersonal interaction between the patient and doctor—the "psychotherapist," so called because the process of cure occurred in the mind through talk. There were a few such practitioners by 1920, and also a larger number of Freudian-trained or influenced individuals who offered Freud's more formalized system of psychotherapy. For the next 20 years, Freud's system was the most prominent and well-documented system. An alliance had been formed between psychoanalysis and the medical establishment, ensuring that the practice of psychoanalysis would for a long time afterward be contingent on the possession of an MD, and effectively cut psychologists out of the practice of psychotherapy unless other pathways to it could be found. One pathway was to find alternate means of delivering psychotherapy systematically. Like contemporary automobile makes, psychotherapy brands began to proliferate in the 1920s. Henry Murray, a larger-than-life psychological adventurer, returned from Europe having made the acquaintance of Carl Jung and eager to introduce Jung's *Psychological Types* to America—

Henry Murray (1893–1988, USA) Successor to Morton Prince at the Harvard Psychological Clinic. Developed, with his partner Christiana Morgan, the Thematic Apperception Test and published, in 1938, with many collaborators, a now-classic book, Explorations in Personality.

though Jung's ideas had already been in circulation in artistic and feminist circles in New York for at least a decade (Sherry, 2012). Alfred Adler (1870–1937), ostracized and exiled from Freud's inner circle, began lecturing in America in the 1920s. He was included in the Wittenberg Symposium. Witty and urbane, his down-to-earth realism about human affairs made him a popular speaker and helped him acquire many followers, who began to found Adlerian Institutes that would put some of his principles into practice. Also during the 1920s, Harry Stack Sullivan (1892–1949) developed his empathic style of psychotherapy, which, while it owed something to all of its predecessors, had at its core the intimate interpersonal relationship between psychotherapist and client. Sullivan had the ability to communicate with those clients who were unreachable by other means, and was able to pass this technique on to others who would fuse it, along with what they gleaned from the other psychotherapeutic systems and the accumulated experience of their own and others' practices, into the eclectic individualized therapeutic styles characteristic of mid- and late-20th century psychotherapy.

Yet, even though many of the elements that would combine to produce clinical psychology were present, it was not born yet. Even if all the psychotherapists in America in 1927 had a full caseload weekly for the full year, the total number of clients served would have been in the low thousands. Psychotherapy was rare, and a person who was depressed, anxious, or otherwise troubled mentally would have to seek solace, during this decade, by traditional means, through religion or through self-medication.

THE FAMILY STORY: TWO TEENAGERS

Both Rose and Harry were lucky to have encountered psychology that made a real difference in their lives. For Rose, though she was bright, was a reserved and sometimes stubborn child that didn't let many people get too close to her. Her immigrant status, especially in her new school in Queens, where she stood out from her peers by contrast, was another problem that could have resulted in a less-than-favorable school experience. Harry, on the other hand, was an obviously troubled young person. He had, by the time he was 15, several encounters with the police, and had begun hanging around with a gang in his old lower Manhattan neighborhood. It was only a step upward to real crime from petty youth vandalism and loitering, and it was one that was easy for Harry to take, since he had developed a hard toughness while trying to deal with the loss of his father.

They were lucky to each encounter helpful adults who had some psychological understanding of adolescence and education. They lived in New York, and the probability of encountering a teacher with psychological training from a teacher's college—in each of their cases, Columbia University—was higher there than in other places in the United States, though by 1927 education schools were the prime conduit for the diffusion of psychological knowledge across the United States. One estimate is that one third of the graduates of psychology master's and PhD programs at that time became employed in education, with a large proportion of those entering public education systems as teachers or guidance personnel (school guidance had developed rapidly as an ancillary profession by this time.)

In Rose's case, the person who helped her was her high school English teacher, who had attended Columbia University for his master's degree and became a teacher in order to have a steady income to get married. Columbia's master's education program, one offshoot of the Progressive Era in America, which led to the development of programs to advance literacy, health, and education, had long been a center for psychological interest in education, with John Dewey and Edward L. Thorndike as its most prominent leaders. By 1917, when Rose's teacher entered Columbia, Leta Stetter Hollingworth (1886–1939) was there promoting her plan to institute programs for gifted and talented students in selected New York schools. Hollingworth was not the first to observe that schools were often doing a disservice to their most talented students: Before 1905, Alfred Binet (1857–1911) and Theodore

John Dewey (1859–1952, USA) One of the most visible and influential American philosophers of the early 20th century, best known for his theories of education.

Edward Lee Thorndike (1874–1949, USA) Advanced an influential early view of learning as a trial-and-error process, based on experiments with cat escape behavior. Later a theorist of education and values.

Simon (1872–1961) in France had asserted, along with Ovide Decroly (1871–1932) in Belgium, that students at all levels of ability needed education tailored to their specific needs, and an American movement to develop gifted and talented education was under way in several places across America by 1914. Her plan bore fruit with the establishment of five such programs in New York between 1918 and 1922 (Pritchard, 1951).

Rose, however, was not in one of the relatively small groups of students who participated in these laboratory school programs for the gifted and talented. It was because her teacher had an interest in psychology that he took extra elective psychology credits and encountered one of the other progressive educators interested in the psychological needs of gifted students in a lecture course in 1920. Impressed by what he heard, he was sensitized, when he came to work in the classroom, to the signs of creativity in his students, and Rose was an early beneficiary of his acumen. He recognized right away the degree of writing talent Rose had, and encouraged her not only to excel in the classroom but also to begin to contribute to newspapers and magazines. Rose noted in a 1986 memoir that she was "hooked" on writing when she had letters published in the *Jewish Daily Forward* and the *New York Times* the same week in 1926. Her teacher encouraged her to apply to New York University and they both celebrated in May 1927, when she learned of her acceptance there.

Harry was lucky in different ways. One reason that he didn't go "up the river" to Sing Sing or Dannemora was that his guardian was wealthy and could have access to both legal and judicial advice, which he engaged immediately after Harry's burglary arrest in January 1927. These contacts led to Harry being examined in a pretrial diversionary program that was empowered to recommend lesser sentences for adolescents with mitigating circumstances. The counselor whom Harry saw was actually a social worker, much as would happen today. She had obtained her degree in Social Work at Indiana University and had moved to New York in 1925 with her husband, who took a job there in banking and securities management. Her training at Indiana was highly influenced by both the traditions of social work education

37

that had evolved in the Midwest as social work developed as a profession in the years after Hull House was founded by Jane Addams (1860–1935) in 1889, and by the long-standing tradition of psychology that had been established by the person who was currently Indiana University's president, William Lowe Bryan. She, and Harry through her, was the beneficiary of 30 or more years of the development of child and adolescent psychology both in Europe and America. The social worker was able to convincingly present Harry's case to the presiding judge of the Juvenile Court as one of a troubled boy still trying to deal with the grief and loss connected with his father's death. She was able to call Harry's sister as a witness, and Rosa corroborated the social worker's impressions that Harry was highly intelligent (she had tested him on the Stanford-Binet—then 10 years old and in wide practical use—on which he scored 133). The decision was ultimately made, the same week that Rosa graduated from high school, to sentence Harry to probation contingent on finishing high school and staying out of trouble until then.

William Lowe Bryan (1860–1955, USA) One of the earliest American experimental psychologists who published, with Noble Harter in 1897, a definitive work on the time course of learning. Eventually became President of the University of Indiana, 1902–1937.

That there was a juvenile court in which this could take place was another lucky break that would not have been available to Harry 15 years earlier. It was through the combined efforts of psychologist Augusta Bronner (1881–1966) and psychologist-neurologist–criminologist William Healy (1869–1963), along with many others in the legal and social science communities, that the first juvenile courts were established during the preceding decade (Boyd, 2004; Young, 2010). Programs such as mandatory counseling for first-time offenders, conditional release, programs of community service, and other programs appropriate to developing adolescents at the stage before they entered an irreversible course toward a life of crime and imprisonment became widely available over the next decades. Although not every case had as favorable an outcome, in Harry's case the experience halted his slide toward crime and turned him inward to search for ways to control himself. He had missed enough school that he had to graduate a year late, but graduate he did, in May 1930.

There was no connection between the neuropsychology of Lashley and the theorizing of the Wittenberg Symposium on either Rose's or Harry's experience. A connection could have possibly been made between the developmental and organic theories of the Gestalt psychologists, but these were just coming into view: Kurt Koffka's *The Growth of the Mind* (Koffka, 1925), one of the first comprehensive theories of development, had been published only 2 years earlier and was circulating only among academics, while Kurt Goldstein's *The Organism* didn't appear until 1939. Nor did vocational counseling or the advice-giving aspect of applied psychology come into play, although the well-established technology of testing did impact both Rose and Harry. Rose took the very first version of the College Entrance Examination Board's test in conjunction with her college applications in the fall of 1926, and Harry's high score on the Stanford-Binet was one factor in his favor when his case came before the judge. Although there was little if any clinical psychology as such at that time, both Rose's teacher and Harry's advisor in the judicial process practiced what we now know are counseling skills informed by knowledge of development, learning, and socialization. Had either Rosa's teacher or Harry's counselor been familiar with Alfred Adler—neither was, as Adler was just beginning to make his way in America as a popular lecturer in 1927—Adler could have certainly suggested ways to conceptualize Harry's maladjustment and perhaps predict, based on Harry's ability to compensate for his anger and loss, his future successes.

Here, in the effects of psychology on Rosa and Harry in this decade, are points in the development of several large streams of psychological activity that have continued to influence generations of people. Child development and adolescent psychology have become mainstays of the curriculum for students of psychology and education alike. Programs for nurturing talent evolved from the 1920s through the 1960s with Project Zero at

Harvard and Julian Stanley's (1918–2005) programs for identifying talent at Johns Hopkins University. Attention to the "gifted and talented" is a permanent part of the educational landscape. The question of how to adjudicate adolescents and how to apportion rights and responsibilities to them is as lively now as it was in 1927, when it informed the thinking of those concerned with Harry's welfare. Both talent recognition programs and legal advisory programs for adolescents are parts of the permanent social infrastructure that psychology—along with social work, sociology, criminology, and the established professions of education and law—helped create and maintain.

The 1930s

THEORETICAL PSYCHOLOGY IN THE 1930s

Gordon Allport (1897–1967), addressing the American Psychological Association (APA) as its president in September 1939, observed that psychology, over the preceding 50 years, had divided into its pure and applied aspects (the theoretical/applied division represented in this book). He disapproved of the tendency he saw for psychologists to become immured in their methodology and their individual research programs. "An increasing number," he wrote, "of investigators now pin their faith upon experimentation with animals. Our program (1939) tells us that 25% of the papers delivered at this year's meetings are based upon animal research. In 1914, twenty-five years ago, the corresponding percentage was 11" (Allport, 1940, p. 14).

Psychology in the 1930s was preeminently characterized theoretically by the behavioristic systems of E. C. Tolman (1886–1959), Clark Hull (1884–1952), and B. F. Skinner (1904–1990), all of whom were based on animal models. Of these, Tolman's

41

has had the most lasting effect on psychology today. That Tolman was a behaviorist and a "rat man" there is no doubt: He dedicated his major theoretical work, *Purposive Behavior in Animals and Men* (Tolman, 1932) to "Mus Norvegicus," the Norway Rat. Like most behaviorists of the 1930s, Tolman became interested in psychology because of almost anything else other than rats and habits. He had considered, for a time, becoming a Unitarian minister, and his 1915 doctoral thesis concerned memory and sensory imagery. But he realized, on his move to the University of California, that he would have to address the issues raised by the evidential truth that human behavior, whether imagistic, religious, emotional, or irrational, and whether or not it seemed to be the result of free choice, was ultimately determined, and rested on the foundation of Pavlovian conditioning and associative learning. The "law of effect"—the measurable strengthening of behavior as a result of reinforcing consequences defined by E. L. Thorndike 30 years previously—was then, as now, an article of scientific faith in psychology.

Clark Hull (1884–1952, USA) One of the triumvirate of behaviorists, along with Skinner and Tolman, who were central figures from the 1920s through the 1950s. Hull was one of the first psychological theorists to suggest a general mathematical account of all behavior.

Allport continued in his address, "A colleague, a good friend of mine, recently challenged me to name a single psychological problem not referable to rats for its solution. Considerably startled, I murmured something, I think, about the psychology of reading disability. But to my mind came flooding the historic problems of the aesthetic, humorous, religious, and cultural behavior of men [*sic*]. I thought how men build clavichords and cathedrals, how they write books, and how they laugh uproariously at Mickey Mouse; how they plan their lives five, ten, or twenty years ahead; how, by an elaborate metaphysic of their own contrivance, they deny the utility of their own experience, including the utility of the metaphysic that led them to this denial. I thought of poetry and puns, of propaganda and revolution, of stock markets and suicide, and of man's despairing hope for peace." (Allport, 1940, pp. 14–15) Further, he asked, "(M)ight we not for profit hold a symposium for the purpose of discovering to what extent infrahuman analogues have given us power to predict, understand, and control human behavior?" (Allport, 1940, p. 15). He continued, "We need to ask ourselves point-blank whether the problems we frame with our rats are unquestionably of the same order as the problems we envisage for human kind . . . and if we are forced to verify our principles by a separate study of man, whether we have the right to inveigh against the psychologist who prefers to study human manners and morals, since it is upon his work that the validation of our own will ultimately rest" (Allport, 1940, p. 15).

As it turned out, all the major behaviorists, Tolman, Hull, and Skinner, addressed the peculiarly human conditions mentioned in Allport's challenge to them. Hull's attempt was stillborn, because he started late and was overtaken by ill health. Skinner, as will be seen in later chapters, became convinced that only through cultural change would human problems be solved. But because he resisted including a mind—rational or irrational—in the process, and because he insisted too strongly on the seemingly paradoxical idea that humans have no free choice in the process, he was misunderstood, vilified, and at least as of now temporarily forgotten as a cultural critic. It was Tolman who managed to weld the mind to behavior, who produced the synthesis between cognition and behavior that characterizes our current psychology.

How he did this was partly due to his background in cognitive issues; it was due partly to international travel; partly to Adolf Hitler; partly to his influential and visible academic position; and above all it was due to the friends he made across all of psychology. As mentioned, Tolman was no stranger to the language of mentalism. He was able to carry on a debate with one of the forgotten geniuses of American psychology, Leonard Troland, on mentalistic terms in the opening pages of *Purposive Behavior*. Troland was a contemporary, a younger graduate classmate of Tolman's at Harvard who had already achieved much in the sciences of chemistry and vision, and was evolving a complex account of mind and behavior based on physical principles.

Troland was also a socialist, and proposed that a "technology of behavior" be devised to maximize human happiness. In his comprehensive psychological system, Troland proposed a hedonic theory of motivation: Behavior depends on the quantity of pleasure to which it is related. For the early behaviorists, the slogan for habit formation was "pleasure stamps in; unpleasure stamps out." But as many commentators observed then and still observe now, "pleasure" is a nebulous term and can mean, as William James noted, anything from happiness to "interest," which was the term that James settled on as the driving force of human motivation. Troland, however, conceived of a palpable and quantifiable amount of pleasure that could be achieved in one of three ways—as a pleasure of the past (meaning a stored association between a pleasurable outcome and a behavior); as a pleasure of the present (meaning an immediate sensory gratification); and as a pleasure of the future (meaning an anticipation, based on cognitive or emotional calculations, of the expected yield of pleasure from an activity, used as a means of weighting decisions about action). To this, Tolman opposed the view, very similar to that of William James, that pleasure was only an aftereffect of behavior: value added, as it were, but not necessary to carry out actions.

That Tolman consented to carry on this debate showed the extent to which he took pleasure—and by extension, the existence of mental events such as emotions or feelings—seriously, and it was only because of Troland's early death (at age 43) in the same year that *Purposive Behavior* was published that their dialogue about pleasure did not continue. Tolman's preservation of mind in behavioral psychology also rested on his being the last American psychologist to go to Germany for new ideas. Formerly, in the generations before 1920, Germany was one of the main European sources of psychological ideas. Thanks to Herr Hitler, after 1930 the relevant Germans were exiled, mainly in America; inducted into the Nazi race-and-war machine (Geuter, 1992); silenced in their own country; or dead. Before the First World War, Tolman had studied in Germany and made many contacts and friends among the Gestalt psychologists. (Later, to one in particular, Egon Brunswik, he became a specific benefactor in making it possible for him to come to America to escape the Nazi regime.)

Tolman once wryly observed that in mazes, American rats ran determinedly and rapidly in all directions, exhibiting ceaseless activity, while German rats sat and thought about what to do next. While it did not start from this cultural observation, Tolman's most well-cited experiment from 1930, coauthored with Charles Honzik (1897–1968), who later became a counseling psychologist, showed that rats implicitly formed what for all intents and purposes were ideas about their environment (Tolman & Honzik, 1930). Tolman and Honzik allowed rats to explore a complex maze freely, feeding one group at the conclusion of the route, not feeding one group, and feeding one group but only after 10 days of nonfeeding. They found that the last group, which had traversed the maze without food reward, became more error-free and faster than the constantly reinforced group. This led Tolman and Honzik to conclude that learning was taking place during the period when no food was available at the maze terminus—learning that implied an internalized representation of the maze, which allowed the rats to select the most efficient path once their end incentive was increased. Many variables were in play in this study and the results were the subject of much debate at the time (Jensen, 2006). Many texts conclude that this study was the one that demonstrated the existence of hypothetical "cognitive maps" in rats, but it was a later study by Tolman and colleagues (Tolman, Ritchie, & Kalish, 1946) that was more influential in this regard. In that study, rats learned a path that led to a reinforcement "northeast" of their starting point in a right-angled maze that led them to proceed "north," then "east" to the goal. Then the path that they had learned was blocked, and instead a set of paths radiating out from the starting point in several directions was substituted. If the rats were, thought Tolman's group, really forming some conception of general spatial orientation of the goal along with learning a specific route to it, then, when confronted with choices that opened a more direct path to the goal, that one would be chosen. And that was the result (Lombrozo, 2013). Later, Tolman would generalize this finding in a paper titled "Cognitive Maps in Rats and Men" (Tolman, 1948), confirming the idea of cognition as central to psychology and providing a thread of theoretical continuity between the new cognitive science and the old behaviorism: If rats had mental representations, why not humans?

In 1933, the new right-wing extremist government of Germany summarily terminated the employment of many of Germany's leading psychologists who were liberals, Communists, or Jews. As mentioned, this included the Gestalt psychologists who had not already left, along with many psychoanalysts, personality theorists, developmentalists, and Kurt Lewin, who defied easy categorization. Tolman and his colleague in the Bay Area, Ernest Hilgard, would have liked to offer a position to a psychologist who came to complement their own mentalistic thinking as well as their prosocial attitudes. They both offered friendship and support to Kurt Lewin when he arrived in the United States, but it was a difficult proposition to fund new positions for theoretical psychologists during the 1930s. Brilliant and eminently likeable, Lewin personally appealed to so many people that it was comparatively easy for him to be re-employed first at Cornell University and, then, for 10 years between 1935 and 1945, at the University of Iowa's Iowa Child Welfare Research Station, where the influence of the Dean of Faculty, the august psychological pioneer of the second generation of American psychologists, Carl Seashore (1866–1949), who had been instrumental in arranging philanthropic support for the founding of the station 20 years earlier, paved the way for Lewin and many other émigré intellectuals to continue their work.

Ernest Ropiequet Hilgard (1904–2001, USA) A durable psychologist whose interests, over 7 decades of activity, changed from conditioning to hypnosis to history of psychology. He was a major architect of the reconfiguration of the APA in 1945.

Lewin, and especially his students (the most famous of which was Leon Festinger, who invented the idea of cognitive dissonance, one of the most enduring general psychological concepts), was outsized in his influence in all areas of American

46

psychology. Born in 1890 to a cultured Jewish family in Galicia, in the borderland between Germany and Russia, Lewin studied at the University of Berlin and served in the German army during the First World War. From the very start his work emphasized the importance of perception and interpretation: His first published paper, in 1917, *Kriegslandschaft*, described how different a landscape would look to an ordinary observer observing it during peacetime compared to a soldier at war who had the ability to discriminate the hidden perceptual clues that would make the difference between life and death (Lewin, 1917).

Lewin, though not usually grouped with the Gestalt psychologists, advanced ideas that were not different from those of the leading Gestaltists. For example, during the 1920s in Germany, he and his student Bluma Zeigarnik observed that incomplete tasks persist more in memory than completed ones—the well-known Zeigarnik Effect. Lewin's talent was in creating scientific metaphors that were intuitively accessible.

Bluma Zeigarnik (1901–1988, Lithuania–USSR) Soviet Russian psychologist who, after her early studies with Lewin, returned to the Soviet Union and was instrumental in the development of neuropsychiatry there.

Drawing on non-Euclidean geometry and topology (well beyond the mathematical capabilities of most psychologists then and now), Lewin fashioned a schematic of human behavior in which individuals were situated in a force field, acted on by vectors of social forces of differing magnitudes, and redirecting internal energies to overcome blockages toward goals. That was a schematic that, though it was ultimately metaphorical rather than quantitative, appealed not only to Tolman but also to Adlerians, who could see the redistribution of internal forces as a component of compensation. By 1938, drawing on both Jacques Loeb, who had theorized about the light tropisms of plants, and on Lewin, who theorized about similar interactive tropisms in humans in their "life spaces," Tolman invented a hypothetical

Jacques Loeb (1859–1924, Germany–USA) Leading biologist well known for his theories regarding tropisms and automatic behavior.

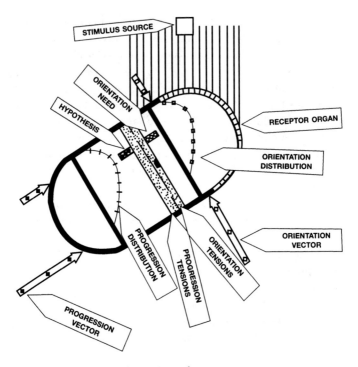

FIGURE 2.1 Tolman's schematic sowbug.

behavioral robot—the "schematic sowbug" (see Figure 2.1)—
that incorporated Lewin's language of behavioral vectors and
valences (Tolman, 1939).

But it was not just theoretical psychology that animated
Lewin. He had a commitment to social justice and was actively
political. Lewin had escaped to America not only to preserve his
life but to carry on his quest for an egalitarian and democratic
society. Allport, toward the close of his 1939 address, turned to
the idea of whether psychology ought to be involved in politics.
"Speaking on this very campus forty years ago, John Dewey, later
to become the eighth President of our Association, made what for
that time was a striking observation. Psychology, he held, cannot
help but be politically conditioned. He had in mind, for example,

that the doctrines of the fixedness of human nature flourish in an aristocracy and perish in a democracy. The privileges of the elite in ancient Greece, and the doctrines of the Church in mediaeval times, provided the setting for psychological theories of their day. Under modern conditions theories of statehood play a major role" (Allport, 1940, p. 25). In saying this, Allport was directly addressing German psychology, which proclaimed that its role would henceforth be, officially, to promote the racial and national doctrines of German National Socialism.

Lewin, and much of American psychology as will shortly be seen, was the antithesis of autocratic fascism and militarism, against which America was soon to go to war. In 1939, for one example, one of his students, Alex Bavelas (1920–), began a long-term research project in a field setting, a clothing factory in Virginia, the Harwood Manufacturing Company, which was owned by a close friend of Lewin, Alfred Marrow. Marrow, a psychologist in his own right (PhD New York University, 1937), wanted to see if the principles of group dynamics being developed by Lewin would lead to improvements in employee productivity and morale. Completely at variance with the majority contemporary view in industrial psychology of the worker as a malleable, manageable subordinate with little say in the process, Bavelas and others from Lewin's group of students and colleagues came to show that the introduction of democratic processes in production goal setting, for example, would lead not only to improved morale but also to increased production (Marrow, 1970).

Another leading theory from 1939 was proposed by a group of researchers at Yale, at least one of which, John Dollard, had already had extensive experience with the way that different racial groups related to each other in the segregated American South. The theory, the "frustration–aggression" hypothesis, had then and still has

John Dollard (1900–1980, USA) Sociologist who contributed substantially to the literature on race prejudice during the 1930s; eventually professor of psychology at Yale from 1942 to 1969.

intuitive appeal. Individuals frustrated in an aim act aggressively against the agent of frustration, against the situation, and against the environment (Miller, 1941). As Allport was speaking at the University of California at Berkeley on September 7, 1939, a frustrated, racist individual adept at awakening frustrations sleeping in many humans, and skilled at manipulating the levers of political power, had only 6 days earlier fabricated a pretext for invading Poland and unleashing the Holocaust and the Second World War.

APPLIED PSYCHOLOGY IN THE 1930s

Leonard Troland died on May 27, 1932, while being photographed on Mt. Wilson in Los Angeles. He backed over the side of a sheer drop of 350 feet, some say because he was careless, others, because he was depressed. He died in Los Angeles because he was there in his capacity not as a professor of psychology at Harvard but as the chief engineer of the Technicolor Corporation, which had progressed to the color mixing process that let audiences enjoy Mickey Mouse in vivid color later in the decade. When Troland spoke of technology, he did so from a position of personal craft knowledge. He and his partners had been working on the process for over 13 years (Zegarac, 2007). The Technicolor process was the practical realization of the practical possibilities of most of the activities of 19th-century psychology, which concentrated almost exclusively on problems of how physical quantities were translated into sensation, and how sensation was converted into perception in the nervous system and the brain. As such, Technicolor stands as the prototype of the physical devices that have evolved from psychological research.

Troland was no mere technological tinkerer: He had studied philosophy and won an undergraduate prize in chemistry; he advocated, as mentioned in the theoretical section, for a reorganization of society along technologically determined lines; and he even, like many other great psychologists of the 20th century, researched parapsychology (Devonis, 2012a). Walter Miles, on the other hand, nearly the same age as Troland, was no utopian or mystic, but a practical scientist who was inducted into psychology by the same Carl Seashore whose largesse supported Kurt Lewin. Miles got his start in science working on the question of how alcohol affected the psychological characteristics of humans, a study that was undertaken with the support of the Carnegie Foundation starting in 1913, one of the earliest examples of psychological foundation patronage and a major source of its support thereafter. He joined

Walter Miles (1885–1978, USA) American experimentalist, protégé of Carl Seashore and Raymond Dodge: He left voluminous papers that are a primary record of the activity of psychologists between 1920 and 1960 in the United States.

the biologist Francis Benedict and the psychologist Raymond Dodge, already well known for his work in vision, and for the next several years conducted a meticulous series of studies on the effects of measured small doses of alcohol (Goodwin, 2003). The earlier studies of Dodge and Benedict were part of the evidence introduced in support of a constitutional amendment to prohibit the sale of alcoholic beverages, an amendment that went into legal force in 1920. Through the 1920s Miles continued to study alcohol, eventually focusing on the effects of alcohol on driving (Miles, 1934). But like psychology itself, Miles was eclectic and responsive to popular culture. Since experimental psychology's start 50 years before, psychologists had been involved in measuring athletic performance. Also during that period, football began its upsurge to becoming America's most popular sport: The first National Football League postseason championship game took place in December 1933. During the late 1920s, Miles and his Stanford graduate student B. C. Graves designed an apparatus that could record the reaction times of charging linemen en masse, which, along with other psychologists' efforts to measure the speed and skill of baseball players, boxers, and other athletes, led to psychology finding a niche in sports (Green & Benjamin, 2009; Joyce & Baker, 2008).

Taken together, Troland and Miles represent the flowering, during this decade, of two persisting areas of psychological applications: consultation on the design of technologies in which human sensory and perceptual characteristics interact with equipment and devices, and the study of the effects of drugs of various kinds on human performance. Along with these, the 1930s brought several advances in measurement. Allport, in his 1939 presidential address, observed the rapid increase over the preceding decade in the amount and complexity of statistical treatments of experimental data. Factor analysis and the analysis of variance replaced simple frequency counts and correlations. The development of that time with the most far-reaching effects was the creation of the Minnesota Multiphasic Personality Inventory (MMPI) by Starke Hathaway and J. Charnley McKinley in 1936. McKinley was an eminent neurologist and psychiatrist and head of the Department of Medicine at the University of Minnesota; Hathaway was a young graduate of The Ohio State University with expertise in psychometrics. McKinley wanted a more accurate diagnostic instrument than what was then available. At that time, personality inventories existed, but they were dependent on the personal predilections and theoretical outlooks of their authors

Starke Hathaway (1903–1984, USA) American clinical psychologist most often associated with his activity, along with J. Charnley McKinley (1891–1950), in developing the Minnesota Multiphasic Personality Inventory. He was also an early promoter of the idea of the Doctor of Psychology (PsyD) degree.

and were useful only as aids to descriptive psychiatry since they were not generally normed. It was Hathaway's signal achievement to design a test that would sort out psychiatrically interesting personality types by contrasting their test performances with the performances of a group selected for its representative normality—the famous "Minnesota Normals," 750 friends and relatives of inpatients in the psychiatric unit of the University of Minnesota Hospitals. No preconceptions were held about the pattern of answers to 504 questions about thoughts, emotions, and behavior that would distinguish abnormal from normal personality: The distinctions between scoring patterns evolved in use, empirically, and were subsequently keyed to yield profile scores on 11 scales. Paul Meehl (1920–2003) began his career as a theorist of clinical psychology by analyzing the accuracy of profile scores for the first published version of the MMPI from 1943, demonstrating their efficacy at identifying psychiatric syndromes, and even being able to discover pathology that was not immediately evident (Hathaway & Meehl, 1951). It was fateful for psychology that its first psychometrically stable and reliable personality test would be one that differentiated people along clinical psychiatric lines. Thus the MMPI was crucial to the development of psychometric theory and practice, but even more so to reinforcing the idea that psychology's development was linked to psychiatry's.

Today, Americans are far away from an era in which strong and consistent governmental intervention in everyday social life was greeted mostly with enthusiasm and relief. The people of the United States were appalled by the effects of the universal economic stall that collapsed the U.S. economy in 1932. The election of 1932 delivered a new administration that was prepared to address the general anxiety of the American people: "We have nothing to fear," said Franklin Roosevelt in his inaugural address in 1933, one day before Hitler became the official leader of Germany, "but fear itself." The anxieties of Americans centered around the lack of employment and around other issues as well. People were living longer and there was no reliable way for them to save for the future. Health insurance was rudimentary, and if there were pensions for old age, those were small. At any rate, the depression had depleted what little retirement security individuals had. Labor unions and other organized labor-related groups had been agitating for provisions for pensions along with their other demands for fair treatment in wages, hiring, hours, and retention, and had paid for their efforts in blood and imprisonment. The Great Depression brought these issues to a head and for the first time the complaints of labor found a responsive individual who had the power to make significant changes in social policy. Frances Perkins (1882–1965), who had a background in economics but was also well versed in social work, having been associated with early "settlement" social work and its many meliorative activities, was instrumental in the passage of the Social Security Act of 1935, a governmental intervention that had the effect of relieving a structural cause of anxiety, and served as a model for future interventions that would have significant mass psychological effects (Social Security Administration, 1979).

Though the established theoretical psychologists, almost entirely residents in universities, did not lack employment during the 1930s (at the worst they took pay cuts of 15% or 20% in 1933 and 1934), younger psychologists just finishing their degrees or who had been hired toward the end of the 1920s boom to work in industry or other consulting areas found themselves unemployed and adrift in the early depression years. By 1933, the general U.S. unemployment rate had reached 25%. In those days, an acceptable response to economic hardship was to organize and to demonstrate for economic justice, and many young people did just that, joining one of the many social and political movements, most of them liberal tending to socialist in outlook, some even more radically communist. Gradually, during the 1930s, psychologists who sensed that John Dewey was right in his statement that there was no psychology that was not political began to coalesce. Psychologists active in the "Social Gospel" movement, a loose federation of religiously oriented individuals who sought to implant liberal religious principles in secular society, psychologists who had been frankly radicalized, and psychologists whose research had led them to question the injustices and inequalities inherent in pre-Depression American society, including institutionalized poverty, racism, child maltreatment, and other social ills, came together in 1936 to form the Society for the Psychological Study of Social Issues (SPSSI; Finison, 1986). Their activity was not an applied psychology in the sense of inventing tests or physical devices, but rather a collective arena for disseminating ideas in support of liberal political and social causes. In 1939, for example, Mamie Phipps Clark and Kenneth Clark, working for their dissertations under the direction of early SPSSI member Otto Klineberg, who had been working for years assembling material to challenge the ideas of racial inferiority, collaborated on studies in which Black children in segregated nursery schools in Washington, DC, were offered a choice of line drawings of children differing only in skin color, and were asked which they thought was most like them (Clark & Clark, 1939). Their published results—that the Black children came to choose the darker-colored drawing by age 4—along with the results of other similar studies, became core components of the evidence on which federal laws regarding racial segregation were changed in the coming decades. By the close of the 1930s, then, psychology had expanded its already extensive activities in education and testing: From Technicolor to the fight for racial equality, psychologists were, as historian James Capshew put it, "on the march" (Capshew, 1999).

Mamie Phipps Clark (1917–1983, USA) and Kenneth Clark (1914–2005, USA) African American psychologists—a married couple—who were instrumental in advancing the cause of integration in the psychological profession.

Otto Klineberg (1899–1982, Canada–USA) Student of intelligence who advanced the idea of intellectual equality among races.

PSYCHOTHERAPY IN THE 1930s

By 1936, psychotherapy was common enough within psychology that Saul Rosenzweig, then a 29-year-old associate at Henry Murray's Psychological Clinic at Harvard University, could state with confidence that all psychotherapies worked because they share common factors of a strong client–therapist bond, that they involve a healing ritual, and that they engender hope (Rosenzweig, 1936). There was not only Freudian psychotherapy by this time, but Adlerian, Jungian, Kleinian, and Alexandrian, and others not derived from Freud: Harry Stack Sullivan's interpersonalism, Knight Dunlap's oppositional technique for stuttering and homosexuality, and even some attempts at politically influenced consciousness raising were all being practiced. Still, the absolute number of therapists

Saul Rosenzweig (1907–2004, USA) Clinician, experimentalist, personality theorist, and historian of psychology. He advanced a personality theory called idiodynamics.

was small. While psychologists were still shut out of the practice of strict medical psychiatry per se, the reported success of non-medical psychological treatments along with the hybridization of Freudian approaches and other hybrids such as "psychosomatic medicine" gradually weakened the boundary between medicine and psychology. New systems of diagnosis, including those supported by the new MMPI, led to the creation of grades of mental disorder ranging from mild to severe, acute to chronic, and most importantly, neurotic or psychotic. The class of neurotics was expanded to include many more individuals who, though functional, could, in the opinions of treating psychotherapists at least, improve aspects of their lives through therapy and counseling, and efforts developed to secure these "worried well" as a client base. Long-standing cultural norms of self-improvement aligned with changing views of medicine from horrific to helpful to lessen resistance to new forms of psychological medicine. While university clinics and occasional private practices were the first sites of these borderland clinical psychological/psychotherapy practices, functioning in a grey area relative to laws regarding the practice of medicine, psychotherapy as distinct from medical psychiatry had established a beachhead and was poised to expand.

Within psychology proper, transitional individuals were emerging who would further bridge the gap between psychiatry and clinical psychology. Laurence F. Shaffer, in 1936 at Columbia University, aligned psychology with the "mental hygiene" movement in his book *The Psychology of Adjustment* (Shaffer, 1936).

Laurence F. Shaffer (1903–1976, USA) Important figure in the integration of psychiatry and clinical psychology: APA President, 1953.

"Mental hygiene" (which can be literally translated as "mental health," of course) was conceived early in the 20th century as an amalgam of ideas drawn from the popular and clinical literature on health maintenance and health promotion with ideas about the ways in which individuals might cope, environmentally and socially, with conditions that might otherwise result in neurosis or psychosis. The idea of coping or adjustment was less threatening and invasive than treatment, and put responsibility in the hands of the client. This was far enough away from medicine, and yet therapeutic enough, to be successfully put into practice by all sorts of paramedical personnel, including nurses, social workers, pastoral and ministerial staff, and other individuals (for instance, prison counselors and school guidance staffs) and expanded the psychotherapeutic horizon widely.

Within psychiatry, psychology had long had allies, and during the 1930s some powerful ones became associated with psychology and supported its aims to develop a parallel nonmedical psychotherapy system. Most prominent among these were the Menningers, Karl and William, psychiatrists who had established a private psychiatric clinic in Topeka in 1919 similar to that established by the Mayo brothers for allopathic medicine in Minnesota some years earlier. Their methods were a return in some ways to the shared community approach that was a feature of earlier moral treatment, and the Menningers also invested in personnel, including students of psychology at the University of Kansas and elsewhere, who were willing to involve themselves in this therapeutic community. Karl Menninger's first book, *The Human Mind* (Menninger, 1930), was a series of case studies of individuals in turmoil who were helped by supportive psychotherapy. It sold thousands of copies and inspired, among others, the 12-year-old Paul Meehl, just recovering from his father's suicide. Others who worked with Menninger, such as David Rapaport, who emigrated from Hungary in 1938, became essential in ensuring the success of clinical psychology as an independent psychotherapeutic specialty.

Karl Menninger (1893–1990, USA) Psychiatrist who with his father Charles Frederick (1862–1952) and brother William (1899–1966) founded the Menninger Clinic in Topeka, Kansas, an institution that did for American psychiatry what the Mayo Clinic did for medicine at that time in modernizing medical care.

David Rapaport (1911–1960, Hungary–USA) Influential psychodynamic psychiatrist and director of the Menninger Foundation and the Austen Riggs Center in Stockbridge, Massachusetts; editor of a seminal comprehensive textbook, Organization and Pathology of Thought *(1951).*

However, on the eve of World War II, the situation of the mentally ill in America had changed very little from the previous decade. Schizophrenia occurred, then as now, with a 1:100 regularity and was acute and florid in about one third of those cases. In 1938, there would have been at least 200,000 florid schizophrenics in the general adult population of 129 million. In 1939, the total number of institutionalized mental patients in the United States was 467,000, with 44% (207,000) diagnosed with "dementia praecox" (schizophrenia). New York alone had 76,000 hospitalized patients, California 25,000 (U.S. Department of Commerce, 1943). Perhaps hospitalization was working well, at least in terms of catching the number of cases and providing beds for them. But even beds, to say nothing of individualized care and effective treatments, were in short supply: Overcrowding affected hospitals in virtually every state, and 27% of patients returned. That year, 31,451 patients died in state hospitals. It was 3 years since Walter Freeman and James Watts had performed the first lobotomy in America (El-Hai, 2005). In 1939, electroshock was added to insulin and metrazol convulsion-inducing treatments. It was the age of what Elliott Valenstein (1986) called "great and desperate cures."

In August 1939, Wilhelm Reich (1897–1957) arrived in America. Communist, irascible, driven, and manic, he was the personality antithesis of Kurt Lewin. He was unabashed about making physical contact with his patients. He saw mental illness in terms of armoring and the task of the therapist to break that armor. He brought with him the seeds of the idea that a general energy pervades the universe, and that the body, when it is harmonized with this energy, is whole and cured.

THE FAMILY STORY: ADJUSTING TO ADVERSITY

Rosa did well in college but was bored with it, and wanted to be on her own. She was still living with her father's cousin and his large family in Queens and wanted her own place, as many young people do. Finding that she could make a good living as a writer and editor for newspapers, she quit New York University in the spring of 1929 and began a long career as a freelancer. In those days, New York was home to the publishers of over 500 newspapers and magazines. She quickly developed a reputation as a speedy and accurate reporter as well as a first-class editor. She attended Harry's graduation in May 1930. They quarreled, and didn't write to each other for many years. She never saw him again. The Great Depression set in and lengthened, but Rosa gave it little thought except to work harder and for longer hours. Her client list ranged from *Underwear Daily* to the *New York Sun* to the *Forward* and the *Daily Worker*—a Communist newspaper. Rosa, however, remained almost apathetically apolitical until witnessing a particularly brutal attack of police on a protester during the textile workers' strike in 1934. After that time Rosa specialized in working for labor-related newspapers as well as other Communist-related papers, and briefly for the African American newspaper the *New York Amsterdam News*, until she obtained a regular position as a copy editor with a national weekly magazine in 1938. In October 1939, one month after World War II began in Europe with the invasion of Poland by Germany, Rosa fell in love with a colleague on the magazine, Francine Miller.

Harry, after graduation, went to work at a bookbindery that failed in 1932. Filled with curiosity and wanderlust and a sense that he had nothing to lose, Harry set out, as did many young men in those years, to travel the country. He saw it all, hitchhiking and riding freight trains (trains were slower and went to many more places than they do now) and eventually ended up in Raleigh, North Carolina, where he began to work on a tobacco farm. After a succession of jobs, he got steady work as a truck driver, carrying freight between Virginia and North Carolina for one of the early national freight carriers. Sometime around 1937 he met Joan Harris, a poet and artist who had studied at Black Mountain College, the experimental North Carolina school that had attracted many artists, playwrights, and other creative people and brought them together in an experimental, communal educational environment. Harry was passionately attracted to Joan's intellect, which ignited his own and started him on the way to realizing his intellectual potential. They married in 1939 and their son Donald was born the next year. After Donald's birth, Joan experienced the first of many episodes of depression. Harry was frightened and confused about this. He had come to rely on Joan and was made anxious by her new vulnerability and the added responsibility of caring for a child. It was in this frame of mind that he met, quite by accident in 1941, a member of the team of psychologists, one of Kurt Lewin's students, working at the Harwood Manufacturing Company in Virginia who was involved in implementing democratic practices into industrial management in that plant. Harry, who had a practical and scientific mind, was intrigued by the precision of the planned interventions and the neatly quantified results that had already been obtained. He was invited to join the team, but on the weekend before he was to go and be interviewed for a position there, Pearl Harbor was attacked, and the next week Harry, mindful of the need for steady employment and insurance for his wife and son and animated by a sense of responsibility and the need to pay back what the United States had offered his father, joined the U.S. Army.

Helen, by contrast, had an uneventful, one might say serene, childhood and adolescence, and a normal college experience. Her decision to marry Eddie McConnell was perceived as rash, it is true, and Helen and Eddie married quickly and left immediately for California. It was 1940, and already the United States realized that it was "The Arsenal of Democracy" and manufacturing was moving to a war footing. Eddie's training in engineering was a ticket to early security for his young family, soon to include Carolyn, born in the last week of 1942, 2 weeks before Eddie received an induction notice.

From the standpoint of the then-popular psychology of adjustment, all three of the Black siblings coped effectively with their circumstances and were able to make progress with their lives during this difficult decade in America. In their favor was their individual initiative, which the psychologists who came of age during this period also shared. Harry's experiences were fairly typical for a young man in the '30s: Rosa's less so for a woman, Helen's about average. Rosa and Harry had opposite reactions to the economic and social distress of the 1930s. Rosa, after coming to grips with the realities of social life in the bust phase of boom-and-bust capitalism, externalized her frustration and disgust by expressing her views publicly. This fed into the ferment of social change that typified the mid- and late 1930s in the United States. For the first time in America, massive governmental intervention occurred and brought with it a system designed to provide a cushion for economic shocks not only for the poor and elderly but for all Americans—Social Security and the other programs of the New Deal. By the late 1930s, organized labor had completed a long war for economic justice that culminated in the consolidation of worker bargaining power in the combined American Federation of Labor/Congress of Industrial Organizations (AFL-CIO), a war that had involved real bloodshed and real assertion of oppositional political power from the radical left against the conservative right. It was this ferment of activism, fueled by the radical press for which Rosa labored in those years, that animated many psychologists who sensed that psychology could be a force for social change, and which led them to establish organizations such as the SPSSI and other groups that incorporated radicalized Americans and recent refugees driven from Nazi Europe in a coalition demanding social justice. In 1939, the president of the APA, Gordon Allport, exhorted American psychologists to "pay [their] way in the civilization that is sustaining us" (Allport, 1940, p. 27): The drive to do this had been forged in the radical revisioning of American society's balance of individualism versus collectivism during this decade.

Harry's chance meeting with members of the Harwood team put him in contact with the research projects of one of the greatest exponents of engaging psychological science for social good, Kurt Lewin. The Harwood project was made possible by the friendship between Harwood's CEO, Alfred Marrow, and Lewin. As mentioned earlier, Lewin was a champion of the need to put theory into action in actual social situations, and Harwood was the first real test of a Lewinian intervention outside the confines of a university setting. It was a good example of psychologists taking seriously what Allport had also demanded in his 1939 address: that they take into account the "subject's point of view" and "frame of reference." Harry intuitively sensed that here was a way in which control could be achieved without violence to anyone involved. In contrast to his sister, Harry saw in the working out of Lewin's theory at Harwood a way of achieving a goal by changing perceptions, by internalizing, working from within the individual outward, rather than by attacking problems from the outside.

Yet, for Harry, and for most of the rest of the United States, calm and dispassionate implementation of workplace democracy would have to wait until the externalization of force was brought to bear on the greatest threat yet to world peace and stability, the combined military might of the Axis powers. The same week that Harry was assigned to his infantry unit was the week that Tolman's *Drives Toward War* (Tolman, 1942) was published. Harry, home on leave before his unit was shipped overseas, was able to read it in the "New Books" section of his library. In his decision to join the army, which may have seemed to anyone who knew Harry to be precipitate and unconsidered, he exemplified the outcome of the competing motives and drives that Tolman, now basing his conclusions on the evidence about social dominance that had emerged from the study of primates during the preceding 2 decades, described as acting to lead men to war (see Figure 2.2). Psychologically scarred and self-abasing after his father's death, Harry had turned to crime as a youth. He had the capacity, with the addition of motive displacement, to turn aggression against inferiors and outsiders: Propaganda and military indoctrination reinforced those tendencies.

Yet when Harry read the book and looked at another of Tolman's diagrams of the motivations to go to war (Figure 2.3), he could not readily connect himself to the war. He could not decide whether he was socialized to be more individualistic or collective, and could not readily place himself in Tolman's chart of motives—in fact, he was uncertain about why he was going to war at all. But he did agree when he read that, in the future for psychological man, a supranational state would be necessary to replace the hatreds of the individual nations

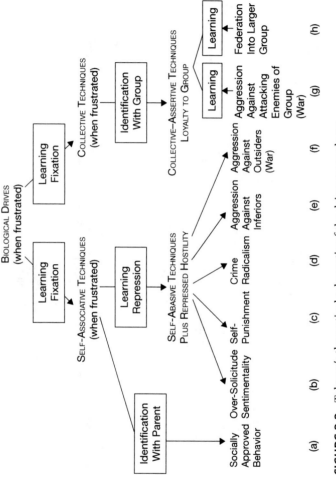

FIGURE 2.2 Tolman's theoretical schematic of the drives toward war.

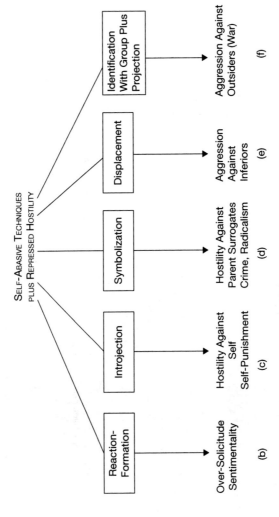

FIGURE 2.3 A detail of one aspect of Tolman's system of motivations toward war; self-abasement and its relation to warmaking.

now displayed on battlefields across the world. "This World-Federation, or superstate, or whatever we may want to call it, must command all our allegiances more strongly than our national states now do. Just as I am more loyal to the United States than I am to California, so in the future I must be more loyal to this World-Federation than I am to the United States. And not only I, but you, and the corner grocer, and the American Legionnaire, and the boys who return from this war, and the capitalist who now hates Russia, and the Russian himself who now scorns the 'backward' Chinese, and the Hindus, and the Africans, and the Indonesians, and the Germans, and the Italians, and the Japanese—all, all must then be made to adopt this one greater loyalty. All must feel that they belong to one such greater whole. For, if no such whole be consummated, then we may most certainly expect another and more terrible war when a fresh and unwitting generation shall have been raised to fighting age" (Tolman, 1942, pp. 108–109). In 1942, alone with his thoughts in his barracks, Harry only dimly intuited how much he would come to depend on Menninger, on the MMPI, and on all the other elements of psychotherapy that then were coming into alignment, both in his future profession and in his personal life.

For Rosa, for Harry, and for Helen, the 1930s were a formative decade, as they were for psychology, setting the stage for the events of the succeeding decades that led to the psychology we have today. The drives to war have not lessened in the intervening years. Though the participants and the venues have changed, many of the same elements that Tolman noted in 1942 are still in play. The momentum for governmentally mediated collectivism, established by the economic trials and radical politics of the 1930s, likewise has not lessened. The forces in society opposed to it, rationally and otherwise, are still with us also.

The 1940s

THE PSYCHOLOGICAL COALITION FORMS

The Second World War was the watershed world historical event of the 20th century. The power of war machines, proven in the First World War, was multiplied by several orders of magnitude. For the first time, whole populations of civilians were systematically taken to their deaths as if on factory conveyor belts or assembly lines. The war, which officially began for the United States on December 8, 1941 (though virtually everyone had seen it coming for 2 years), was likewise the preeminent defining event of most people's lives. Millions of men and smaller numbers of women were, within a very few months, uniformed and trained and formed into immense armies that were transported across the Atlantic and Pacific oceans to do battle in Africa, on both oceans, in Europe, and on the chains of Pacific islands leading toward Japan.

Inside America, major events occurred that would have lasting repercussions. Factories, mines, farms, and all methods of transportation were all enlisted in the production of armaments, clothing, food, and the other necessities of war. Unemployment vanished. Mass migrations occurred as people flocked to the new centers of industry. Millions of Southern Blacks and Whites converged in the industrial cities of the North. Millions more streamed west, to California and its aircraft and shipbuilding plants. The U.S. government forcibly interned citizens of Japanese ancestry living on the west coast in internment camps similar in form, though not in ultimate purpose, to those of Germany and Eastern Europe. Racial tension and violence replaced labor violence. In July, 1943, a riot broke out between Blacks and Whites on Belle Isle in Detroit that resulted in 33 deaths and 433 injuries. The National Guard had to be called in to quell the fighting: observers nationwide saw firsthand the racial violence that had existed covertly in the American South for years.

On the other hand, both all-Japanese and all-Black units were formed in the Armed Services, and displayed the highest levels of bravery and courage under fire. A squadron of fighter pilots, recruited partially from the students and staff of the Civilian Pilot Training Program of the all-Black Tuskegee Institute in Alabama, became one of the most celebrated and decorated of all of the groups serving on the front lines. By 1944 it was apparent that every American citizen would need to contribute to the war effort, and this had the effect of forcing racial groups together in a common cause for the first time since the Civil War. The publication, in 1944, of the Swedish economist Gunnar Myrdal's *An American Dilemma: The Negro Problem and Modern Democracy* (Myrdal, 1944) along with the continued efforts of groups such as the Society for the Psychological Study of

Gunnar Myrdal (1898–1987, Sweden–USA) Nobel Prize–winning economist who became a major contributor to antiracist initiatives.

Social Issues (SPSSI) psychologists, added intellectual weight to the practical demonstrations of the benefits of integration.

The First World War, it is often said, "put psychology on the map." Certainly it seemed to catch the psychologists of that time off guard, but after April 6, 1917—the date of the U.S. declaration of war on Germany—they acted rapidly. Virtually all academic psychologists traded their lecterns and laboratories for uniforms and, commissioned as officers, participated in applied activities, virtually entirely stateside. Raymond Dodge assessed pilots' and submariners' perceptual abilities under simulated battle conditions. Hundreds of other psychologists participated in programs of testing and assessment intended to match men to military jobs. In the post-World War I view of psychologists, at least, this burst of activity, which lasted for little more than a year between June 1917 and November 1918, was positive proof of the indispensability of psychology to the military (Yerkes, 1921). In the run-up to the Second World War, psychologists acted proactively and arranged to enter many areas of the war effort. By the first months of 1942, psychologists, including many who had fled Europe only a few years before, were engaged not only in administering tests for fitness and job assignment but also in code breaking, propaganda production and analysis, and the promotion of civilian morale. Civilian life changed radically as well. Automobile production was curtailed for the duration of the war and gasoline and tires were strictly rationed, as were foods. Systematic drives to reduce waste and collect scrap iron for the war effort were assisted by the work of, among others, psychologists who had formerly advised advertisers on sales technique. Kurt Lewin and his colleagues devised a program to convince housewives to change their perceptions of less desirable cuts of meat and other foods in order to support conservation efforts (Lewin, 1943). Other profound civilian effects occurred. Virtually all of the male population of military age—between 18 and 37—was in uniform or slated to be drafted into service: Few exemptions were permitted. Their places in the expanding industrial workplaces were filled by millions of women who for the first time were allowed full and equal participation in what had been until that time a sex-segregated region of American life, manufacturing (Gerken, 1949). While in the First World War no academic psychologist was exposed to much more danger than civilians, in the Second World War the majority of psychologists, younger and still in the

69

formative stages of their careers, got firsthand experience of the war overseas, many in combat. Those who were interested in self-education through reading could, on troopships or on furlough from the front lines, read *Psychology for the Fighting Man* (Boring, 1943). Its author, Edwin G. Boring (1886–1968), head of the Harvard Psychology Department at the time and a tireless promoter of psychology as well as its leading historian in the United States, had been designing textbooks for some time. This little paperback, published by the U.S. government for the troops, ran to hundreds of thousands of copies and contained much of the structure of psychology textbooks today, including advice on how to cooperate with different groups of people (Harris, 2013).

Gardner Murphy (1895–1979, USA) Psychologist with wide interests and a visionary spirit, he also authored an influential history of psychology in 1929 that went into several succeeding editions.

In 1945, many of the members of SPSSI collectively published a volume edited by Gardner Murphy, *Human Nature and Enduring Peace*, a collection of many speculative proposals about the role of psychology and behavioral science in forging a new postwar world, from recovery from urban devastation to improving collective human relations, and a harbinger of programmatic efforts that would soon be directed not only outward toward Europe and Asia, but inward toward the United States as well (Murphy, 1945). For, soon afterward, the United Nations was founded, and soon after that, two atomic bombs were dropped on Hiroshima and Nagasaki in Japan. The war was over and peace had suddenly begun.

The year 1945 saw the culmination of many developments in psychology since the 1920s, which led to two major coalitions being formed. The first of these was represented in the reorganization of the American Psychological Association (APA). The most important aspect of this reorganization was the consensus that theory, applications, and clinical activities, formerly represented by separate organizations and carrying on their affairs at a distance from each other, were indeed all parts of a unitary entity, psychology. The structure of APA divisions that today still forms the official taxonomy of psychological interests and activities in the United States emerged at this time by the incorporation, into one body, of several preexisting areas of theoretical interests (developmental psychology, teaching of psychology, psychology of measurement and statistics, general psychology, experimental psychology, social psychology [including SPSSI as a separate entity], aesthetics, and personality), several applied areas (including consulting psychology, industrial organizational psychology, educational psychology, school psychology, and military psychology), and two other divisions, abnormal psychology (Division 11) and clinical psychology (Division 12). The forces that combined to produce this structure were many. Research activities had increased gradually from 1900 onward. Likewise, applied areas had multiplied. In 1944, F. K. Berrien's applied psychology textbook, *Practical Psychology* (Berrien, 1944), whose title reflected the underlying pragmatism of psychologists making their way into American society, included sections on study efficiency, classroom learning, principles of mental health, guidance, adjustments in old age, employment psychology, production efficiency, morale and rewards for work, industrial and highway accidents, consumer and advertising research, factors contributing to crime, testimony and the courtroom, detecting deception, treatment of offenders, vocational guidance, and effective speaking and writing.

F(rederick) K(enneth) Berrien (1909–1971, USA) Applied psychologist who contributed to the systems theory of organizations.

Some of psychology's early academic founders resisted the inclusion of applied psychology into psychology proper, agreeing with Edward Titchener when he said, in 1910, that he saw little value in applied work. Yet there is precedent in science for theory emerging from work on practical problems. Pasteur's work on fermentation had its beginnings in the industries of wine and beer. In psychology, the preceding two decades had revealed many ways in which psychological knowledge interacted with commercial, industrial, and even entertainment interests, and the war had shown that practical problems, rather than being simply acted upon in ways determined by the results of laboratory science, could themselves be the source for discoveries otherwise unanticipated by theory not connected to real-world problems. For one example, James J. Gibson (1904–1979) was, before the war, a fairly conventional student of perception, perhaps best known for an experiment showing the effect of mental expectation on the perception and naming of ambiguous figures (Gibson, 1929), a psychologist apparently content to work in a laboratory setting on theoretical problems. Then came the war, and Gibson was posted to a unit devising tests to select and train flight personnel. Problems of how to land planes on runways in inhospitable environments surrounded by confusing terrain, of pilots being able to understand orientation from the array of perceptual inputs rushing in on them during flight, of gunners needing to predict when a fighter seen earlier might break out of an obscuring cloud, took the place of well-controlled studies of simple phenomena in a college lab. Aided by animators from Hollywood film studios, Gibson and his team developed film tests to assess judgment of moving objects as well as simulations of the perceptual conditions of landing and takeoff (Gibson, 1947). It was these studies that moved Gibson's thinking toward what his mentor E. B. Holt had called "molar stimuli"—complexes of physical forces impinging on the perceiving organism, whose task it would be to interpret them and act on them automatically, and toward what another mentor, Kurt Koffka, taught about the whole-field nature of perception and its function as an interpreter of relations. Gibson's later books, *The Perception of the Visual World* (1950), *The Senses Considered as Perceptual Systems* (1966), and *Ecological Perception* (1979), which had their roots in Gibson's work on applied problems, were recognized, in their time as now, as unanswered theoretical challenges to theories that see sensation as distinct from perception and separate from cognition.

Another area of wartime applications had the effect of raising interest in systems and systems theories, which before the 1940s had been either philosophical abstractions connected with speculations about the unity of science or visionary ideas of the interconnections between fields embodied in the theories of Count Korzybski and General Semanticists (Korzybski, 1941). The need to find ways to estimate how well messages could be understood through interference under battle conditions led to mathematical theories of the ratio of signal to noise. The need to develop mechanisms that could automatically lock antiaircraft weapons onto targets led to the perfection of computational systems, which had already been under development before the war. One particularly influential psychologist contributing to this development was the young British polymath, K. J. W. Craik (Collins, 2013). The complex arrangements needed to manage a modern world war, typified by the organizational chart of the newly built (in 1943) Pentagon, were a further impetus to thinking in terms of interconnected and interactive units. The idea of cybernetics, control via computation and programming, was extended into psychology by the work of the mathematician Norbert Wiener in his books *Cybernetics* (1948) and *The Human Use of Human Beings* (1950). In a later work, Wiener said, "The world of the future will be an even more demanding struggle against the limitations of our intelligence, not a comfortable hammock in which we can lie down to be waited upon by our robot slaves" (Wiener, 1964, p. 69). Psychologists advanced their own comprehensive views of behavioral science as a complex system (e.g., Miller, 1955). Taken all together, these currents converged on theories of communication and information systems, which, in combination with the development of similar systematic models in biology, strongly influenced psychological thinking over the next several decades.

Alfred Habdank Scarbek Korzybski (1879–1950, Poland–USA) Styled himself Count Korzybski and was the founder of the General Semantics movement; his 1933 book Science and Sanity *influenced several generations of psychologists.*

K(enneth) J. W. Craik (1914–1945, Great Britain) Wunderkind protégé of several early British psychologists, Craik made his mark early as a progenitor of information theory and cognitive psychology.

Norbert Wiener (1894–1964, USA) Mathematician and cybernetician.

James Grier Miller (1916–2002, USA) Psychologist and systems theorist, PhD Harvard 1943, coined the term "behavioral science."

While these massive theories of systematic interconnection of information and behavior may have been in the back of the minds of the organizers of the new coalition of psychologists represented by the APA, the organization really did not measure up to those standards. The authors of this organization of the field gave wide scope to their understanding of psychology's purposes, and they assembled the coalition of theory, applied, and psychotherapy as the optimal way of organizing psychology at the time. This was a tacit acknowledgment of the failure of psychology to unite behind a particular method, and a victory of sorts for the aim expressed by Gordon Allport in his APA Presidential Address in 1939 that psychology should not engage in a "bigotry" of method but should be friendly to all approaches to the understanding of human thought, perception, and behavior. This also allowed the continued blending of cognition and behavior, which has been the most typical psychological approach up to the present.

The new APA was a congeries of 19 separate interest groups, welded together by its organizers partly to maintain theoretical ecumenism in the field, and partly—here the influence of some of the veterans of earlier attempts to organize psychology after the First World War was felt—because it was sensed that, with major amounts of money being apportioned by the U.S. government to research in health, science, and medicine after the war, psychology would be in a better position to negotiate for a share of it if it presented a unified presence, ensuring that its members' voices would be heard in the apportionment of resources as well as in appointments to important areas controlling research directions and funding. After the war, economic support in the form of grants from philanthropic foundations such as the Rockefeller and Macy Foundations combined with the catalyst of the beginnings of the Cold War, which boosted defense spending on scientific research in all the sciences, including psychology. The consolidation of scientific research in the National Science Foundation and associated agencies, and the consolidation of medical research in the National Institutes of Health opened up more places for psychologists, who now had developed many connections between psychology and both biophysical and medical science, to engage in research. Along with this, the successful efforts of psychiatry and psychology combined to make "mental health" a nearly equal player in the health arena by the creation of the National Institute of Mental Health. This plethora of organization assured a funding infrastructure that industrialized the production of scientific knowledge, opening up what seemed to be a limitless source of public and private financial support for psychological activity. The perception that psychology was a united front continued to be a successful strategy, which further confirmed its presence within the spectrum of physical and social sciences.

Beyond those areas of psychological theory and research that evolved out of the involvement of psychologists with mechanized warfare, the '40s saw continuing influences from Gestalt psychology and, especially, from the influence of those psychologists from Europe who had managed to escape the debacle in their home countries and established themselves in the United States. Social psychology, which in previous decades was a mélange of crowd psychology and anthropological ideas, acquired a perceptual and cognitive focus. Fritz Heider (1896–1988), in particular, introduced the idea of attribution into the interpretation of social behavior, while other psychologists, notably Jerome Bruner, a 1941 graduate of Harvard who had worked with both Lewinians and with Gordon Allport, introduced what was called the "New Look" in perception. The "New Look" alluded to a term in the fashion world at the time. The French designer Dior had introduced, in 1947, a line of sweeping conical skirts combined with vivid striped blouses that, with its dash and color, replaced the drab women's clothing of the war years with a bright, modern look. In social perception, the New Look's central idea was that individual cognition, motivation, and expectations would interact to shape perceptions, not only of social relations but

Jerome Bruner (1915–, USA) One of the psychologists who defined cognitive psychology as a unique field within psychology: His 1956 book, coauthored with Jacqueline Goodnow (1924–) and G. A. Austin, A Study of Thinking, *was influential in this regard.*

even of physical objects. Bruner and Cecile Goodman conducted a study in which they asked children to adjust the aperture of a disc of light on a screen until the spot of light they saw corresponded with the memory of the size of various denominations of either coins or similar-sized plain discs (Bruner & Goodman, 1947). They found that while the estimates of the plain discs did not deviate greatly from the actual objects, the estimates of the coin sizes increased widely with the increase in actual value from 1 to 50 cents. (It is worth noting that, in 1947, for a normally intelligent 10-year-old child like those in Bruner and Goodman's study, a quarter represented a fairly substantial sum: This was a time when a Coke cost a nickel and when the average year's salary for a working adult was less than $3,000.) Another study from this time, from which the effects carried forward for several decades,

Leo Postman (1918–2004, Russia–USA). Influential theorist of interference in memory and also editor, in 1962, of a historical account of several contemporary research problems, Psychology in the Making.

was that of Gordon Allport and Leo Postman, published in their *Psychology of Rumor* (Allport & Postman, 1947). There, participants viewed a picture of two men arguing, one of whom (White) was pointing his finger at the other one (Black) while holding a razor in his other hand. Allport was, at the time, assembling the material that he would sum up in his influential book *Prejudice* in 1954, and the result of asking the viewers what they remembered after briefly seeing the picture was that the weapon migrated, in memory, into the hand of the threatened man. These studies set the tone for the turn, over the next few decades, toward an individual cognitive emphasis in social psychology from its earlier focus on groups. Another influence was the rise of existential theories in both clinical and personality areas. The émigré members of the former Frankfurt School, a group of Marxist intellectuals previously based at the Institute for Social Research in Frankfurt-am-Main, Germany, continued their work in the United States during the '40s. Some members of the group, Theodor Adorno, the social critic, and Else Frenkel-Brunswik (wife of Egon Brunswik, whom Tolman befriended and supported in his escape from Europe), joined Daniel Levinson and Nevitt Sanford at Berkeley to produce, in 1950, what at the time was a quite influential book on the personality characteristics of authoritarian types, *The Authoritarian Personality*, of whom there was no shortage in world politics during the 1940s.

Another Frankfurt School associate was Erich Fromm, who, although he was an early émigré arrival, first came to wide notice in the United States with his book *Escape From Freedom* (Fromm, 1941). Fromm, like Wilhelm Reich, saw modern life as presenting a dilemma to persons who had become disassociated from their society through their participation in a mechanistic, profit- and war-dominated capitalist society. The end product of this, Fascism, resulted from humans not being strong enough to withstand the lure of authoritarian leaders: The goal of therapy or self-understanding would be to gain the autonomy and personal strength needed to be an individual in a deindividualizing world. *The Authoritarian Personality* sold well, yet it

Theodor Adorno (1903–1969, Germany–USA) German intellectual and social critic, mainstay of the interdisciplinary Frankfurt School: emigrated to the United States during World War II and returned to Europe afterward.

Else Frenkel-Brunswik (1908–1958, Poland–Austria–USA) Psychologist and personality theorist; married Egon Brunswik (1903–1955) in 1938 after emigrating to the United States.

Daniel Levinson (1920–1994, USA) at Berkeley and who went on to become well known in the field of adult development: known for his books on the "seasons of life" of women and men.

Nevitt Sanford (1909–1996, USA) Psychologist at Berkeley until dismissed for not signing the 1950 Loyalty Oath; reinstated in 1959, moved to Stanford and later, in 1968, founded the Wright Institute for the training of socially responsive clinical psychologists.

Erich Fromm (1900–1980, Germany–USA) Socialist humanist psychologist who was influential in the development of humanistic psychology; his personality theory, blending Marx and Freud, continues to be included in surveys of personality theories.

did not last as long in personality theory as the work of Fromm, another Frankfurt associate, who adjusted his Marxism to American liberalism and turned, in the 1950s, toward theorizing about love. Another important émigré contribution was that of Rudolf Arnheim (1904–2007), who was an early theorist of the relation of film and art. He had studied with Wertheimer, Koehler, and Lewin in Berlin, and after being forced to leave Germany for Italy, then England, he arrived at last in the United States. Here his patron was Max Wertheimer (1880–1943), who arranged for him to have an academic post at the New School of Social Research in New York City, a magnet for émigré intellectuals during the period. Arnheim is appreciated, at least among those psychologists sensitive to the arts but probably more so by artists, for his many works on the psychology of art, including his *Art and Visual Perception* (1954), a magnificent work of precise European scholarship and aesthetic sensibility produced in the free air of New York. While he was completing that book, though, the direct influence of Gestalt psychology, in its original form, on American psychology was declining due to the aging and deaths of its early proponents: Karl Duncker in 1940; Kurt Koffka in 1941; Max Wertheimer in 1943; and Wolfgang Koehler in 1959. Over the following decades its mentalism would survive and be transmuted into cognitive psychology.

The inclusion of Divisions 11 and 12 (they soon combined into one Division of Clinical Psychology—that is why there is no Division 11 today) was another step toward recognition of a quasimedical clinical psychology specialty in psychology, one with aspirations to be the equal of psychiatry. Some of the factors that combined to produce this result have already been seen: the long history of psychologists doing research and mental testing in hospital settings; the support of psychiatrists who incorporated psychological theory into their systems and welcomed psychologists as colleagues; the widespread acceptance of Freudian theory among both medical psychiatrists and nonmedical psychologists; and the good track record of psychologists serving as mental health specialists in frontline hospitals during the war. Add to this Carl Rogers's (1902–1987) reports, formalized in *Counseling and Psychotherapy* (Rogers, 1942), of good results for noninvasive, client-centered psychotherapy, which suggested a viable, efficient method for delivering counseling services. Dissatisfaction with the overcrowding of hospitals and the conditions in some of them, along with rapid disenchantment with invasive psychiatric techniques (although lobotomy, electroshock, and insulin shock would persist into the 1960s), were further incentives toward developing an alternative method of care. Above all, as with research and applied science, the availability of funds for training clinical psychologists increased immensely at the close of the war. Several reward payments for service were approved by Congress and in force, collectively termed the "G.I. Bill." Unemployment benefits, reduced-rate guaranteed loans, and—most importantly, for psychology—government support for college study swelled the ranks of new clinical psychologists. The expansion of hospitals mandated by the Hall Burton Act and the increases in the number and size of Veterans Administration (VA) hospitals, along with their rising patient populations of returning veterans, provided a nurturing growth medium.

The culminating event of the decade for clinical psychology was the conference arranged by a new assistant professor of psychology, Victor Raimy, at the University of Colorado, Boulder, in 1949. The "Boulder Conference," as it has been known since that time, brought together professionals from a cross-section of mental health sectors: psychologists with and without private practices, psychologists attached to hospitals, VA and otherwise; nurses; social workers; and psychiatrists (Raimy, 1950). The outcome was

Victor Raimy (1913–1987, USA) Professor of clinical psychology at the University of Colorado; was instrumental in bringing together the psychologists who met at Boulder in 1949 and who wrote the post-conference report.

the definition of the clinical psychologist as a "scientist–practitioner", a formulation known as the "Boulder Model of clinical psychology." This was based on the plan created by David Shakow (1900–1981), a psychologist who had his first experiences with psychology studying "Jungenfroid" in settlement house classrooms on New York's Lower East Side, and who had for years served as a researcher and proto-clinician at the Worcester State Hospital in Massachusetts, a seedbed for the training of clinical theorists for many years (Garmezy & Holzman, 1984). Based on this plan, a clinical psychologist would be expected to be trained to the doctoral level as a clinical psychological specialist and to be engaged both in providing professional clinical services, including psychotherapy, as well as conducting scientific research on methods of treatment and other aspects of mental health (Shakow, 1965).

The expansion of clinical psychology coincided with the introduction of several new therapies as well as updates to older ones, mostly by adding quantification. By 1949, group therapy had emerged from its occasional use by psychoanalytically oriented individuals on the east coast and had spread to the west coast, where it mixed with psychodrama (invented by Jacob Moreno in the 1910s in Vienna) and other expressive therapies, including Wilhelm Reich's and Fritz Perls's, to form a quintessentially Californian approach to psychotherapy as a passionate, interpersonal encounter. In 1949, the minister of the Berkeley Unitarian Universalist congregation, J. Raymond Cope (1905–1988), made his church available to a group of clinical psychology students—among them Timothy Leary, of whom more later—who began to formulate a way of measuring the interaction among group members to assess the degree of change in the encounter. In the same year, Wilhelm Reich published *Character Analysis* (Reich, 1949), his major theoretical work describing the technique of de-armoring character and revealing the tender individual within. Around him, America was changing: Already primed for attack on "subversive" elements in the U.S. population by the activities of Martin Dies and the U.S. House Un-American Activities Committee, a large part of America turned its aggression on its own citizens, accusing them of the sin of Communism and finding many ways to discredit and silence them. Waiting in the wings was Senator Joseph McCarthy, whose polemic style, termed "McCarthyism," came to define, for some time to come, the epitome of American character assassination. Alongside his analytically derived therapy, Reich began to emphasize more and more the

Jacob Moreno (born Levy, 1889–1974, Romania–USA) Pioneer in psychodrama and group therapy.

Fritz Perls (1893–1970, Germany–USA) MD and psychotherapist. Student of Kurt Goldstein and Wilhelm Reich; evolved a psychotherapy he termed "Gestalt Therapy," which was widely successful in the United States in the 1960s.

universal energetic basis of life, and gave a name to this energy: the "orgone." In specially constructed chambers (to the untrained eye they looked like large plywood crates) he claimed to be able to capture and focus this energy for healing purposes, mental and physical. In 1949, Reich was already a marked man. Targeted in an article in the magazine *New Republic* as a medical quack, he was now the focus of a Food and Drug Administration investigation into claims that he had made about the benefits of orgone energy, claims which he had printed in brochures and distributed by mail (Greenfield, 1974).

In 1949, Soviet Russia exploded its first atomic bomb: Americans felt themselves once more under threat of attack by a foreign enemy. In 1949, the discrimination conviction of the manager of Katz's Drug Store in Des Moines, Iowa, who had refused to serve a Black woman, Edna Griffin, at the lunch counter the year before, was upheld by the Iowa Supreme Court. It was the first of many similar protests to come. And in 1949, Donald Hebb (1904–1985) published *The Organization of Behavior* (Hebb, 1949). A student of Karl Lashley, Hebb proposed that learning leads to new connections being formed between neurons, which together form "cell assemblies." For this postulate, his name was suggested as a candidate for the Nobel Prize many years later, an honor that with characteristic modesty he turned away. But in what area would Hebb's Nobel Prize have been awarded? Hebb was always a psychologist, never a neurologist, biologist, physicist, medical specialist, or economist. There was then, and is not now, a Nobel Prize for the science of psychology. The cell assembly was not necessarily a new idea, but since that time, in psychology, it has never been out of view.

THE FAMILY STORY: WAR AND PEACE

The outcome for psychology was far different after the Second World War than it was after the First. Then, psychologists still had to scuffle to prove to industry and to psychiatry that they could be of use. Psychologists not only participated in more areas of activity during the Second World War, but there were many more of them by the war's end. A collection of external factors aligned to make conditions optimal for a vast expansion of psychology. The first peacetime year, 1946, saw an established pattern of federal support for research in science, technology, and the expansion of medicine at record rates. More importantly, the reorganization of the APA allowed clinical psychology equal status with the other branches of psychology, a status that allowed it to assert itself as a profession in its own right, as a competitor with medical psychiatry. This marked the start of a long, increasingly contentious relation among psychology, medicine, and health-related professions that also continues today. This also made it, at the time, an attractive career choice for people of a psychological bent like Harry. Most of the early clinical psychologists got their start in a seedbed provided by a confluence of military and medical forces, the VA hospitals, expansions of which sprang up overnight across America during the '40s. This ensured that they would have an arena in which to practice. Implicitly, it also ensured that another connection between making war and doing psychology would remain unbroken.

The main scientific psychological theories that came to maturity during the 1940s were contingent on and responsive to the events of their time, and yet they played little direct role in the lives of the Black family. For Harry, the confluence of the acceptance of clinical psychology as a profession and the further access to university education through the support provided by the 1944 G.I. Bill allowed him to develop his internal and individual approach to psychological problems, both those of society and those in his own sphere. No one at the universities that Harry attended, the University of North Carolina and the University of Tennessee, prescribed any particular psychological theory, and the range from which he could choose expanded yearly. There were even parapsychologists at Duke, but Harry was, as a veteran of combat, more realistic in his outlook. Under his teachers' direction, Harry was able to develop an early eclectic style influenced equally by the pessimism of Jung and Freud, the self-reliance embodied in Sullivan and Rogers, and the resilience embodied in the theorists of psychological adjustment. Looking at it from current perspectives, his approach would be characterized mostly as existential. Harry followed the career of Albert Ellis with interest, and over time adopted many of the techniques of ratio-

Albert Ellis (1913–2007, USA)
Creator of rational emotive
behavior therapy (REBT)

nal emotive behavior therapy (REBT). The "tough love" aspects of REBT (we would call them that today) appealed to a part of Harry that saw life in stark, survival-oriented ways. Harry had personal reasons for becoming a practitioner as well. He had embarked on the study of psychology in part to deal with his war experiences, which, like many returning veterans, he was unwilling to unlock fully, and in part to deal with his wife's cycles of depression. Because Harry had privileged, although not unlimited, access to hospitals and did his internship and early practice in a VA facility, he was able to assess the effects of the then-popular somatic treatments, electroshock and lobotomy, as well as to compare well- and ill-run hospitals. He became committed to extra-hospital care for all of his clients, a characteristic of clinical psychology that has continued since that time. There has never been a shortage of clients, and Harry embarked on his profession as an individual therapist in 1953 after obtaining his license to practice in Tennessee, one of the first states to enact a licensing statute for clinical psychology. Alongside this he had an official position as a consulting psychologist with the VA, with the view of a wide horizon of professional possibilities and a soon-full caseload.

For both Rosa and Helen, the relation between the official theory and practice of psychology was less direct than it was for Harry, but not less formative. Rosa's overt activism was tempered by several things. She perceived the fight of labor against capital as largely successfully decided in labor's favor. Also, like many individuals who had some connections with American versions of Communism during the 1930s, the realization of the horrors of war on all sides, including the Soviet side, removed any sense she had of the ideality of human relations in a socialist utopia. In 1945, favorably impressed by a book she received for review, *Human Nature and Enduring Peace,* a collection of essays by some of the same individuals that Harry had met in North Carolina in 1941, she determined that she would adopt a pacifist stance. Along with this, through the early part of the decade, she developed the sense that with advancing age, circumspection was preferable to visibility. She realized that her homosexuality, which she recognized as such and which was fully and mutually satisfied in her relationship with Francine, her partner, was something for which she would find little social support or theoretical explanation. She had already experienced other colleagues being denied employment for being indiscreet, and was anxious to remain at work, partly because she loved the work and partly because freelancing was touch-and-go even in a war economy. The neighborhood into which she and Francine moved in New York City in 1943 was complaisant, and they were able to blend anonymously into the great city. Psychology hardly admitted the existence of women at the time, let alone homosexual women: Evelyn Hooker at UCLA was only just starting to examine homosexuality. Alfred Kinsey's *Sexual Behavior in the Human Male* emerged to great public acclaim and misunderstanding in 1948: Its companion volume on the human female, which established the normative nature of homosexuality in women, would appear 5 years later. Far more troubling to Rosa was the sheer viciousness of the reaction of American conservatives to anyone who expressed views that did not extol corporate capitalism and military industrialism. The beginning of the "witch-hunt" phase of conservatism was already evident by 1947—it would eventually cost indigenous and émigré liberals their jobs and, in Wilhelm Reich's case, his freedom. That there appeared to be a permanent state of war did not help matters, and Rosa withdrew from public

Evelyn Hooker (1907–1996, USA) Psychologist whose studies in the 1950s showed that there were no differences in adjustment and mental health between heterosexuals and homosexuals.

Alfred Kinsey (1894–1956, USA) American biologist who became America's best-known scientific sexologist with his collaborative works Sexual Behavior in the Human Male *(1948) and* Sexual Behavior in the Human Female *(1953).*

activism entirely by 1948, although she maintained some ties to groups involved in promoting peace initiatives.

For Helen, Eddie's induction in 1943 shattered the shell of complacency that had surrounded her for her first 25 years of life. Alone and with a new daughter, and dependent not on her husband's engineering salary but instead his Army stipend, she was faced with maintaining a home far from support of her relatives, arranging for daycare (fortunately, in those times, people pulled together and it was available), and going to work in what had previously been an all-male domain, a bomber plant near Los Angeles. After an initial short bout of terror, she found that she not only liked, but relished the independence that employment conferred, and the confidence that doing what had been previously a "man's job" engendered. However, when Eddie returned in December 1945, and when her wartime job ended, it was not hard to return back to old patterns. The Cold War was heating up and the Korean War was on the horizon. Eddie was too old to be called back, and promotions and prosperity led to an idyllic suburban existence in southern California. The seeds of future connections to feminism had been planted, however, and would eventually bear fruit some years hence.

The 1950s

THE PSYCHOLOGICAL COALITION'S FIRST DECADE

The 1950s, in American society as well as psychology, were characterized by two pairs of opposites: liberty versus repression and conformity versus creativity. As mentioned in the preceding chapter, repression of suspected Communists and other left-leaning individuals was in full swing at the beginning of the decade, driven by long-standing partisan enmity as well as fresh anger over the loss of atomic superiority to Soviet Russia. In late 1949, China, an ally in the Second World War, became an enemy as well, because of its conversion to Communism, and a provocation in June 1950 resulted in the United States entering another war, this time in Korea, with China as the largest background adversary. This resulted in the drafting of another group of young men as well as remobilizing veterans of World War II. The sense that America was still under attack resulted in the creation of an aura of fear and suspicion that permeated American society. While the Second World

War involved everyone and promoted attitudes of shared sacrifice, collective offense, and a focus on common goals, the Korean War era promoted a defensive attitude in the country, and for a time a focus on the loyalty of citizens. In California, for example, legislators demanded that all state employees sign an oath pledging loyalty to the United States, its government, and Constitution, something that divided intellectuals employed at the universities in the state. Those who saw this demand as an infringement on freedom and a cancellation of what had been fought for during the previous war and who refused to sign had their contracts terminated. In their number was E. C. Tolman, pictured in *Life* magazine, a photographic substitute for television, cleaning out his office after his termination in August 1950. Another member of the faculty, Hubert Coffey, the graduate advisor of Timothy Leary, was similarly terminated. This was a reflection of the repression that spread gradually through America in the early 1950s, which resulted in the hounding of individuals whose past as social activists had led them to join radical groups in the 1930s. The election of Dwight Eisenhower as President in 1952, the first Republican to hold office in 24 years, was a signal that the fundamental tenor of society would be conservative, and the social action would need to be carried out in alternate, indirect ways. Ultimately, the internal purge of Communists came to an end when Senator Joseph McCarthy falsely accused the Army of harboring Communists, but this did not lessen the focus on defense. Public fear shifted to the possibility of nuclear attack. The fallout shelter was added to the American architectural vocabulary, and banks of guided missiles were installed at the perimeter of most major American cities and in underground silos on the Great Plains.

Hubert Coffey (1910–1988, USA) Berkeley professor of clinical psychology influenced by Kurt Lewin and his associates as well as by his relationship with his teacher Beth Wellman at the University of Iowa and her ideas about the effects of environment on the improvement of IQ scores.

Alongside this heightened awareness of potential conflict, collectively called the "Cold War," Americans received a sharp blow to national superiority on October 4, 1957, when the Soviet

Union was the first to launch a satellite into orbit. Immediately, massive amounts of money and personnel were directed to the "Space Race," building competing satellites, more advanced rockets, and capsules to be occupied by astronauts, who became iconic figures on all magazine covers when their identities were revealed in 1959. The astronauts were not only men, but military men: The competitiveness of the Space Race merged with the rest of the Cold War activities to keep military aims active and, as well, to create new areas of production devoted to those aims. Just before he left office, Dwight Eisenhower warned against what he termed the "military–industrial complex" and its potentially warping effects on the aims and values of America.

America, however, is nothing if not paradoxical, and at the same time that these threatening and anxiety-producing developments were occurring, the country was entering a hypertrophic state of development producing all the benefits of peace. President Eisenhower turned out to be politically moderate, an opponent of the McCarthy "witch hunt," and also a supporter of civil rights. Supported by cheap loans for education and housing, families formed and the population swelled rapidly. The "Baby Boom" brought with it vastly increased demands for housing, schools, hospitals, and especially for consumer goods. Experience gained by American occupying troops observing the efficiencies of the German *Autobahnen* combined with studies carried out at least in part by psychologists on highway safety in the United States led to the construction of an immense network of limited-access highways, allowing unprecedented mobility. President Eisenhower was instrumental in getting the 1956 Federal-Aid Highway Act passed to fund the building of these highways: in 1990, President George H. W. Bush signed a law changing the name of the interstate system to the Dwight D. Eisenhower National System of Interstate and Defense Highways. Manufacturing, because of increases in income and benefits resulting from successful negotiations by powerful unions, became the prime middle class occupation and led to generally rising expectations of an ever brighter future. Volkswagens, designed in Germany during the Nazi period, were one of the earliest products built in Germany after the war and were first imported to the United States in 1949; Toyota imported its first 287 cars 9 years later. Funding for housing was increased and suburbs of single-family homes began to spread out over the farmland surrounding cities. Funds for defense and support of veterans were augmented by exponential increases in the federal budgets for health and aerospace as well. By 1953, a substantial proportion of psychological research was funded by defense-related money. Universities, identified as the agencies by which science would produce both new workers and discoveries, also increased in size, and a college education became more and more the rule rather than the exception. For example, the University of California, between 1944 and 1960, added three campuses: Santa Barbara in 1944, Riverside in 1954, and Davis in 1959, to be followed in short order by San Diego in 1960, Irvine in 1965, and, also in 1965, Santa Cruz. Hospitals and medical research facilities likewise continued to expand, both to keep up with the population and to carry out congressional mandates for research and development. Mental hospitals continued to expand, reaching their all-time population high point of 560,000 patients in 1955, the same year that Disneyland opened for the first time in Anaheim, California.

For the newly established coalition of theoretical, applied, and clinical psychology, the 1950s were a time of expansion and opportunity. Not that psychology spoke then, or speaks now, with one voice: In fact, it was probably only in 1946, at the very beginning of the coalition, that something like unity in the field could be imagined. Although the American Psychological Association (APA) worked hard to establish commonality among psychologists, publishing its *Publication Manual* in 1952 and the first edition of its *Ethics Code* in 1953, but as the 1950s went on, the former tensions between the coalition partners resurfaced. By 1959, the first break between the "pure scientists" and their applied and clinical colleagues occurred with the formation of the Psychonomic Society. Even before this, psychologists began to identify with organizations outside of the APA that reflected their specific interests in neuroscience, aspects of social work, and styles of psychotherapy. A general trend toward fractionation had begun. Sigmund Koch, tasked with editing a six-volume work, *Psychology as a Science*, opined as it went to press in 1959 that even within its theoretical domains there was no "psychology," but only a collection of "psychological studies". Though he repeatedly articulated this position (Koch, 1993), the coalition continued on.

Sigmund Koch (1917–1996, USA) Experimental psychologist and editor of comprehensive studies of scientific psychology, who eventually became a humanist critic of scientific psychology.

Further cleavages were visible at the level of fundamental philosophical principles. The age-old question of free will came to a head in a debate at the 1955 APA convention, published in a 1956 issue of *Science* (Rogers & Skinner, 1956), where B. F. Skinner and Carl Rogers faced off over the question of whether humans were essentially determined or free in terms of choosing their direction of growth. Seen against the background of current events, one of the most significant of which, for Cold War America at that time, was the brave but ultimately unsuccessful uprising of anticommunist Hungarians against their Stalinist government, the battle went temporarily to Rogers. Even though Skinner was never in favor of a coercive, restrictive environment, his view that life was only a process of reacting to events convinced only about half of its intended audience of psychologists, and less of the general public. Intellectuals that could have sympathized with a monistic physicalism also had more richly colored fatalisms to choose from by 1956: It was, after all, the era of the Beat philosophers and the French existentialists.

Depending on one's intellectual and emotional needs, these philosophies and many others were translated into therapies that were available for all types of private clients of the now rapidly multiplying Boulder model clinicians. Individuals who prized their control and choice could choose Rogers; those who needed to connect their lives to the world at a religious level could choose from a spectrum of spiritually oriented therapies, from Jung to Zen Buddhism, to a variety of theologically based philosophies transmuted into clinical practice by pastoral counselors. Those who could benefit from confronting either their life's mistakes or their inner emptiness could challenge themselves with rational emotive behavior techniques, Adlerian analysis of their maladaptive responses to inferiority, or a variety of Existential therapies. Freudian psychoanalysis in tens of flavors was widely available: most therapists during the 1950s indulged in at least a little Freud. Those clients who did better with others than alone could choose group therapy. For those who couldn't decide at all, therapists obliged by developing eclectic, adaptable hybrids of all these and more. Public clients were another story. The main event of the 1950s in terms of managing major mental illness—schizophrenia and mania—came with the sudden introduction of psychoactive drugs: lithium in 1949 for mania, a variety of anxiolytics during the early 1950s, and the antipsychotic chlorpromazine (Thorazine) during the same period. These seemed, in comparison with the ineffective and often cruel therapies of the previous years, to provide cures, or at least good enough simulations of them that closure of the mental hospitals, unthinkable in 1950, was envisioned as a real possibility by mid-decade. The introduction, toward the end of the 1950s, of behavioristic methods based on classical conditioning and token reinforcement was another hopeful element that weighed as positive evidence on the behaviorist side of the determinism-freedom scale. By 1960, the full modern complement of therapies was available with supporting evidence for each: Rosenzweig's contention of the equality of effect of therapies, presented again by Eysenck in 1952 with a decidedly pessimistic spin (Eysenck, 1952), continued to hold true. As the general public became more aware of the existence of psychotherapy, an expanding number of private practices filled.

Hans Eysenck (1916–1997, Germany–Great Britain) Psychologist whose work focused on intelligence and personality; an often acerbic and contrarian critic of the field, especially its clinical parts.

Though these seemed like boom times for clinical psychologists, there were signs of impending danger ahead. For one thing, the tacit agreement between medicine and psychological psychotherapy was straining. Many of those who had been instrumental in the creation of the bonds between them had died or retired to other interests, and a new generation of psychiatrists emerged to question the qualifications of what they saw as psychiatrists practicing without medical licenses. One reaction was the drive toward licensure of clinical psychologists, which began in 1950 and picked up speed through the decade. By 1967, only three states had not put licensure laws into effect: Indiana, North Carolina, and Hawaii, all of which did so soon afterward. Licensure put the Boulder definition into practice: Clinicians had to have achieved a doctorate or had to show that they were practicing psychotherapy as a primary occupation for several years before licensing went into effect. For some years afterward, "grandfathered" clinicians, some with a Master's of Arts (MA) or even less academic training, were not uncommon. Another strain, though not perceived as strongly until the next decade, was the beginning of the struggle between psychiatrists and MD physicians over control of the prescription of psychoactive drugs in connection with therapy. Other battles began to be joined over practice privileges in hospitals and permissible titles. Should a PhD clinician be able to represent her- or himself as a "doctor" in advertising, and, as with law, what services were acceptable to advertise? Most of these conflicts were settled, at least in the short run, with compromises that gave physicians the upper hand but which allowed psychologists to fit into the niches they were carving out. State and governmental agencies imposed fewer constraints on practice. Depending on the state, clinical psychologists were assured of the value of their services in the military; in educational settings, especially in remedial education; and in prisons and other correctional facilities. Federal law regulating nursing homes led to the building of new facilities for the aging population, one of the first to be discharged from the overpopulated state hospitals, and two new APA divisions, Division 20 for Adult Development and Aging and Division 22 for Rehabilitation Psychology, formed toward the end of the 1950s to represent the growing number of psychologists concerned with gerontological issues. Various sources of support, too, were available for doctoral training, making graduate study in psychology an attractive proposition.

From the perspective of theoretical psychology, one way of summarizing the decade is to see it as the decade in which the question of cognitive versus behavioral explanations of behavior was decided emphatically for cognition. Theories without self or agency lost, and have not regained, their ability to convince psychologists of their validity or usefulness. Theories, derived from Gestalt, Tolman, Lewin, or biological sources, continued to develop and proliferate. This turn toward cognition, rather than behavior, as the focus of psychology had several consequences. One of these was a shift inward in social psychology from the outward-focused, activist psychologies of the previous decade. Kurt Lewin, newly moved to the Massachusetts Institute of Technology with his colleagues and students, had ambitious plans to realize change by implementing strategies based on person–environment functionalism. For example, among these were plans to study the process of integrating housing, part of the social agenda of racial acceptance that had gained some traction during the 1940s. Lewin, by now associated with the phrase "nothing is as practical as a good theory," proposed a system that he called *action research* (Lewin, 1946), in which interventions in existing social systems would be monitored and modified to produce an upward spiral of positive change. He and others in his circle committed to several racial integration projects, and were at work on these when Lewin died suddenly in February 1947. In retrospect, it may have been fortunate that he lived only as long as he did, as his Socialist tendencies could have had chilling repercussions. After Lewin's death, the Lewin group pulled back somewhat from its social activism. Most of its members moved to Michigan, and as they became ensconced in the university became more laboratory rather than field oriented. Work that involved integration diminished as the number of activist social psychologists who had access to racially or culturally integrated student populations in universities diminished. Work on racial integration in housing proceeded, but as the '50s went on, urban renewal and the creation of suburbs and broad highways to access them led to dissolution of whatever fragile integrative bridges had been built. "White flight" to the new suburbs accelerated, even as the Supreme Court acted on the question of the legality of "separate but equal" educational facilities and decided unanimously in *Brown v. Board of Education* in 1954 that segregation was contrary to the Constitution.

The social science and psychology research that influenced the Court then was already nearly 15 years old. At the time the Brown decision was reached, social psychological research had, by and large, shifted to the examination of the effects of grouping on the individual's internal attitudes, thoughts, and behaviors. Emblematic of this shift was the fate of the fieldwork of members of the Lewin group at the Harwood plant in Virginia during the Second World War. There, action research had been put to the test, and the results, published by Coch and French (Coch & French, 1948) and cited many years thereafter, were quite promising for the proposition that the availability of democratic procedures for setting work goals and other functions of work management would lead both to increased morale and increased production. Eventually, though, only its results, summarized in textbooks, were available: The 1953 publication of *Group Dynamics* represented more of a retrospective of successful past work than a template for future advances. Instead, the main paradigms of 1950s social psychology—Asch's conformity studies; Festinger's studies of cognitive dissonance—emphasized the individual within and against, rather than integrated into, the group. This trend continued into the next decade,

Solomon Asch (1907–1996, Poland–USA) Gestalt-oriented social psychologist who conducted famous studies of conformity.

Leon Festinger (1919–1989, USA) Polymath psychologist who originated the idea of cognitive dissonance; later in his career he gravitated toward anthropology.

when society, seen through the lens of social psychology, was increasingly seen as influencing individuals in malevolent ways.

In 1946, E. G. Boring addressed the psychologists gathered for the annual meeting of the Eastern Psychological Association (Boring, 1946). Planting his tongue firmly in his cheek, he asked his audience, "What qualities would a potato need to be conscious?" Boring, then 60 years old and already known as "Mr. Psychology" by his peers, knew very well the old saying attributed to many earlier psychologists that psychology, by 1940, had lost first its soul, then its mind, and then its consciousness. "It still has behavior of a sort," continued Boring, but rather than dismiss the last resort of psychological science, he instead interposed the idea of a robot, to which functions could be added. Into his hypothetical potato–robot (Boring was 6 years ahead of the appearance of Mr. Potato Head), he introduced memory, motivation, purpose, selection, attention, and other "mentalistic" terms that he knew would distress many—though not all—of his behaviorist-era hearers.

Boring, at the time, was trying to lure to Harvard, where he headed the department of Psychology, either B. F. Skinner or D. O. Hebb, and his talk was designed to articulate his position, and sound out theirs, on the role of internal mechanisms in behavior. Hebb turned him down flat, remained in Montreal, and advanced a sophisticated neural theory 3 years later; Skinner accepted, and commenced to flatly state that even if there were a brain in the head, it wasn't worth knowing about, so long as one knew the history of reinforcement. In fact, it was Boring's robot, a metaphorical extension of mechanized minds that had been sketched and sometimes even built in miniature by psychologists for 30 years previously, that came closest to the way that cognitive science was conceived—born, according to George A. Miller (1920–2012), on September 11, 1956, at the First Dartmouth Conference on Artificial Intelligence. It was in that year that Miller published a famous paper, "The Magical Number Seven (Plus or Minus Two)," in the *Psychological Review* (Miller, 1956), in which he presented the cumulative evidence for a mathematical regularity on the quanta of information accessible to attention and memory across all cognitive operations. Miller, who got his start along with Timothy Leary at the

University of Alabama working with Donald Ramsdell, a student of Boring's (and of Stanley Smith Stevens and Lashley as well) who had studied the psychoacoustic effects of frequency modulation (FM) during the 1930s, spent World War II as a graduate student at Harvard working on problems of electronic communication, and moved afterward to Bell Labs and Rockefeller University. There and at many other sites across the United

Donald Ramsdell (1904–1965, USA) Mentor of both George Miller and Timothy Leary at the University of Alabama; trained as a psychophysicist at Harvard and eventually became head of a VA psychology service near Boston.

States, physicists, mathematicians, logicians, communications theorists, and electronics specialists combined their talents to perfect the modern digital computer. The first mass-produced computer, the IBM 650, was offered for sale in 1954: 450 were sold. By 1963, a survey of cartoons showed that cartoonists—and by extension, the general public—perceived psychologists as 60% couch-bound therapists, to be sure, but also over 20% as "mad scientists" programming electronic brains (Ehrle & Johnson, 1963). In 1959, psychologist Carl Hovland (1912–1961), a communications and persuasion specialist at Yale, could summarize an exact analogy between computing and thinking, using the terminology of computer science: programming, algorithms, and decision structures (Hovland, 1960). Howard Kendler, astute historical observer of psychology during the modern age, characterized this as the 1950s psychologist's dream: the ability to put a cap on the head, wire

Howard Kendler (1919–2011, USA) Student of Abraham Maslow and Solomon Asch who became a historian of the field and a critic of its blending of science and activism.

it to a television set, and watch the mind at work on the screen. A few years later, Paul Meehl posited the 'autocerebroscope' as a thought experiment (Meehl, 1966).

The 1950s were defined musically by jazz: the flights of Charlie Parker's sax; the cool probes and questions of Miles Davis's trumpet; the drive of Oscar Peterson's piano. Jazz of one sort or another had overtaken all of popular music during the previous 30 years; there was little that could be heard on the radio or danced to that didn't have its influences. Even the orchestral composers of the time were attracted to the new possibilities of tone and rhythm that emerged from jazz. The essence of jazz is improvisation in all its forms; creative leaps into the unknown, reconfiguration of existing melodies, unplanned conversational dialogues. About this phenomenon, psychology had been largely silent. Much of what it said about music was bound up with 19th-century German experimental psychology and acoustics. Psychologists like Carl Seashore and Max Meyer pursued the basics of tonal recognition and combination: Seashore's student, Milton Metfessel, devised, in the 1920s, an ingenious photographic technique to analyze vibrato. But interest in composition of any kind, classical or improvisational, was an unknown continent.

Milton Metfessel (1901–1969, USA) PhD student of Carl Seashore at the University of Iowa. Wrote on both the psychology of thinking and on music in both its psychological and cultural aspects, and developed "spelled speech" as a method for developing automatic readers for the blind. Died in a California flood.

One of the few psychologists to address this question was B. F. Skinner. Skinner's ideas took years to gestate. His 1970 paper, "Creating the Creative Artist" (Skinner, 1970) is as good a statement of the problem of starting a composition, whether it be painting, drawing, or musical, as exists. However, it says little more than that, in artistic composition, one step follows another, and that the most important step is the first one, upon which all of the others depend.

But this does not say very much about exactly which steps will be chosen after the first one.

The emergence of a new sequence of sounds that make sense in their configuration (their Gestalt: configuration, or "whole shape," is the nearest translation to Gestalt that has been found) seems mysterious.

But for Skinner it was no problem to explain this. All behavior, Skinner asserted, is lawful and is determined by the reinforcement history of the individual. Extrapolating from the predictable patterns of response of the pigeons and rats in his and his colleagues' laboratories, Skinner asserted in his theoretical books, *The Behavior of Organisms* (1938) and *Science and Human Behavior* (1953), that this dependence on prior reinforcement was the common feature that linked all of the disparate forms of behavior together. Between 1934 and 1957, Skinner gave much attention to language, and evolved a complicated description of the ways that individual utterances in a language could be predicted from their prior reinforcements. The term "improvisation" does not appear in the 458 pages of *Science and Human Behavior*, and the term "improvise" appears exactly once. In discussing imitation, Skinner wrote that

> "imitative" repertoires cannot approach continuous fields from which new instances will automatically emerge. To some extent, skilled dancers may improvise a dance in which one introduces a series of steps and the other follows, just as a tennis player is to some extent automatically in possession of the proper reply to a new offensive maneuver, but the corresponding fields which provide for the duplication of behavior in true imitation are lacking. (Skinner, 1953, pp. 121–122)

Consistent with his conception of behavior in which any seemingly unplanned sequence of actions, an improvisation by definition, is really controlled by both its reinforcing consequences as well as shaped by its prior reinforcements, the improvised dance or the tennis volley is a special and apparently exceptional instance of formal imitation, which is apparently the standard for skilled performance. That amateur jazz trumpeters had been buying transcribed Louis Armstrong solos and Bix Beiderbecke recordings for years to imitate them without becoming them was lost on Skinner. Yet he persisted in insisting that the most complicated episodes of language behavior were traceable to some prior reinforcing events.

In his William James lectures on language in 1948, Skinner described an episode in which a new, unplanned sequence of behavior emerged in the context of imitation. He described a

9-year-old girl's practice session at the piano, and transcribed the course of both her actions and the sequence of her verbal expressions. After a mistake is made, Skinner charts the interchange between keyboard and linguistic behavior:

> *No, wait! (plays correctly and reaches the end of piece.) Hah! (Plays a few bars of a new piece.) Let's see. Is that right? I'll do it once more. (Finishes the piece.) Ah, now I can study something else.... (Makes another mistake.) I'll have to start all over again. (Difficult piece. Emits a few Gosh's. Works on difficult passage.) Oh, my finger, it hurts so much! But I'm going to MAKE it work! ... Aw! (Looks at clock.) Come ON! (Adjusts clock. Calls out to father in next room.) Daddy, I'm making this clock go slowly— I don't have time to practice. I turned it around an hour. I've got so much time to practice.* (Skinner, 1948/2009, pp. 155–156)

In 1957, Skinner published *Verbal Behavior*, replete with examples like the one above, which today we would call a form of "self talk." Its publication was a most significant event in the history of cognitive science, since it called forth a review by a young linguist from the University of Pennsylvania, Noam Chomsky (Chomsky, 1959). In that review, Chomsky methodically addressed

Noam Chomsky (1928–, USA) Linguist, philosopher, and political activist and critic.

Skinner's claims to be able to predict verbal productions from prior reinforcing events. The essence of Chomsky's criticism was this: A science of behavior such as Skinner's should be able to establish the prior stimuli, the reinforcing consequences, and the stability and reproducibility of the behavior emerging from the reinforcing situation. Chomsky allowed for the possibility that language could be reinforcing; he allowed for the role of self-motivation and self-control mediated by language, but he insisted—correctly—that the exact form of the expressions and their integration into the context in which they were produced is rarely, if ever, traceable back to observable and measurable prior conditions. The primary piece of psychological evidence Chomsky invoked to show that a complicated sequence like the one in the example above is a problem to be solved, and not the description of a set of stimuli and responses that explain it, was delivered

by Karl Lashley in 1950 at a symposium on problems of the relation of the brain to behavior (Lashley, 1951). Lashley, who 20
years earlier revealed the immensity of the problem of explaining
the representation of learning in the brain, now tackled the question of exactly what sequences of neural activity would be chosen
to produce a behavioral result if several possible solutions were
available. This is in fact the problem of composition: How, out
of the infinite possibilities of recombination of musical notes,
does Mahler's Ninth result, or, in the example above, how does
the mildly creative solution to the problem of practice time—
resetting the clock—result from the foregoing pattern of motor
behavior and self-talk? Why do the actions and the accompany-
ing motivational phrases emerge in just the order that they do?
Put in musical terms, how is a flight of improvisation possible,
and, most importantly, why does it seem error free? Chomsky
observed that children imitate and improvise with language all
of the time, and learn the grammatical rules and structure of their
languages with minimal observable reinforcement. He posited
a brain-based computational system that rapidly autocorrected
language as it was being learned, essentially speeding up and
automating the process of learning interconnected with language
that Skinner attempted to describe. Language learning, like perception, is too fast to be captured by an analysis into observable sequences of interaction with environment, and much of
language is internal and unob-
servable. Chomsky's review
marked the end of the idea that
behaviorism could account for
thought, at least. Between 1940
and 1960, all psychological
thinking converged on the idea
of the brain as a mediator. The

*Sir F(rederic). C(harles). Bartlett
(1886–1969, Great Britain)
Psychologist best known for his
contribution to the theory of recon-
structive memory in his 1932 book
Remembering: A Study in Experimental and Social Psychology.*

eminent English memory researcher Sir Frederic Charles Bartlett
published his book *Thinking: An Experimental and Social Study* in
1958, toward the very end of his career. In it he compared thinking to tennis in the rapidity and perfection of its adjustments to
conditions. Even earlier, William James had compared thought

to the flight of a bird, appearing here and there at rest, but always with motion between. The improvisational jazz of the 1950s is the accompaniment of psychology's continuing search, since that time, for the neural paths of improvisation, in both thought and language.

Cognition and internal states also emerged in the 1950s versions of theories of motivation. Formerly, during the 1920 to 1940 period, motivation was conceived in very simple physiological terms. People moved because of internal "drives" (exact mechanisms unspecified) of hunger, thirst, sex, and other physiological or biological needs. In the late 1940s, Harry Harlow, Abraham Maslow's graduate mentor at the University of Wisconsin began to publish observations of exploratory behavior motivated seemingly without any of these physiological goads, but rather solely on the basis of satisfaction of curiosity. In 1953, James Olds (1925–1976), working in Hebb's and Milner's lab at McGill University, serendipitously discovered a region in rat brains, which, when stimulated with electric current, produced incessant bar pressing in a operant behavior chamber (Olds & Milner, 1954). While Olds and his colleagues were careful to speak of the phenomenon in terms of reinforcement rather than specific emotional states, virtually everyone else was more than ready to say that Olds had discovered "pleasure centers." During the 1930s, at the Harvard Psychological Clinic, Henry Murray postulated, on the basis of the analysis of responses to the pictorial Thematic Apperception Test (TAT), which he and Christiana Morgan designed together, a complicated system of perceptible human needs, each prefaced by the letter "N." In the mid-1950s, David McClelland, also at Harvard, isolated one of these needs, the need for achievement (N ach), through TAT analysis, and soon afterward went to India to teach novice entrepreneurs,

Harry Harlow (1905–1981, USA) Comparative psychologist/ primatologist who conducted experimental investigations of the biological bases of love.

David McClelland (1917–1998, USA) Harvard psychologist: proponent of achievement motivation.

based on his findings, ways to increase N ach and economic improvement as well—an early example of the successful use of a cognitive strategy to change behavior (McClelland, 1961). In 1953 Nathaniel Kleitman identified the stages of sleep, and in 1956 Hans Selye defined the stages of the stress response, both of which expanded not only the vocabulary of motivation but also of consciousness and emotion as well.

Applied psychologists of all sorts continued their activities without letup: testers tested, counselors counseled, and consultants consulted. The focus on defense and later in the decade on aerospace created a new class of psychologically trained designers, who soon formed another division in the APA, the division of engineering psychology, Division 21.

Nathaniel Kleitman (1895–1999, Russia–USA) Physiologist who published groundbreaking studies on sleep; discoverer of REM sleep.

Hans Selye (1907–1982, Hungary–Canada) Endocrinologist best known for proposing a theory of the response to stress, the General Adaptation Syndrome.

Over 500 new psychological tests were added to the *Buros Mental Measurements Yearbook* between 1950 and 1959. On the border of clinical psychology and applied psychometrics, in 1954 Paul Meehl (1920–2003), who, along with being a practicing clinical psychologist also was a leading figure in the philosophy of science, published what in retrospect seems a most prescient book, *Statistical vs Clinical Prediction in Psychology* (Meehl, 1954). In it, he summarized what was known to that date about the comparison of clinicians' judgments compared to the predictions of psychological tests. In 19 out of 20 studies where clinical judgment could be compared with predictions from tests, tests proved superior. This finding resulted in decades of denial, but ultimately resurfaced 50 years later, as valid as ever.

In 1955 and 1957, psychologists convened two major conferences on creativity that have now been forgotten. More permanent in memory is the characterization of the 1950s as a time of intense pressure to conform: the best-sellers of the time with social science connections were *The Organization Man*, *The Man in the Grey Flannel Suit*, and *The Lonely Crowd*. In

1957, Wilhelm Reich, after his conviction on mail fraud charges and after having been compelled to burn many of his books, entered the federal prison at Lewisburg, Pennsylvania. Reich, although he said he had no religion, had fortitude and faith. He prayed his version of the Lord's Prayer "Our Love/Life, who art from heaven ...." Reich, proselytizer of the liberating orgasm, beloved by Beat poets and literary figures, who, like Otto Rank and Carl Jung wished to get beyond the rationality imposed by culture and by psychology as well, died in Lewisburg of a heart attack at 60 on November 3, 1957. The circumstances of his death are a reminder of the social and cultural limits of psychology that can be crossed only at great personal peril. One year earlier, Robert Lindner (1914–1956) died in Baltimore at 41, also suddenly of a heart attack. Lindner became well known as one of the most popularly accessible writers on the analytic process. His book *The Fifty Minute Hour* (Lindner, 1954) was one of the ways in which the U.S. public was awakened to the potential of therapy. Lindner had gotten his academic start at Lewisburg, not at the prison, but at Bucknell University, and came to psychiatry directly from experimental psychology. He earned his doctorate at Cornell in 1939. He is best known for his book about the results of his "hypnoanalysis," a technique he invented while he was working at Lewisburg Federal Penitentiary after finishing his graduate work and while obtaining his MD. He was most interested in the ways in which prisoners' experiences in childhood and youth had led them to their prison sentences. In 1955, James Dean and Sal Mineo starred in a film about adolescent confusion and tragedy, which, though it took nothing else from Lindner's 1944 book summarizing his Lewisburg studies, took its title—*Rebel Without a Cause*. In the America of the 1950s, with its superficial calm and its seething discontents underneath, those on the verge of coming of age in 1960 may have necessarily, being adolescent, had to rebel. Soon they would have sufficient cause. Meanwhile, the economic indicators rose, along with the tensions of the Cold War. In 1960, a new division of the APA emerged—Division 23: Consumer Psychology.

THE FAMILY STORY: A HOLDING PATTERN IN THE JET AGE

The 1950s found the Black siblings and their families in various degrees of disconnection from both psychology and the events that surrounded them. Applied cognitive psychology, in its 1950s incarnation, interested Eddie, Helen's husband, and he occasionally read articles by aviation psychologists working on contract for the Office of Naval Research. Rosa, Harry, and Helen all experienced stress—the stress of middle age, though that was hardly in view as a psychological construct at that time. Harry had to deal with his wife's continuing depression and, toward the end of the decade, her first affair. His son was coming of age in much the same way as Harry himself had done, though without as much criminal involvement. Donald, the 1950s teenager, was the full embodiment of the wayward youth that psychology had defined 30 years before, and though there was ample theory about adolescence by this time, it was of little help in Donald's and Harry's relationship. Harry was prone to overbook and to work late, and wove a cocoon of work around his distress. Nor were the new theories based on social perception and self-deception anything more than interesting diversions from the daily round of clients with problems a lot like Harry's own. Harry had evolved his own version of dissonance reduction and recognized himself in Festinger's descriptions of the process when he encountered them late in the decade. But by that time Harry had turned more inward and pessimistic.

If Harry was disconnected—as a later generation of psychologists would name it, "burned out" by the grind of a daily medical practice in all but name—Rosa and Helen were completely in a holding pattern. Francine and Rosa had each other, their jobs, their many diversions in the city, and their small circle of friends who shared the secret of their clandestine relationship, and days slipped into other days and became years. Helen devoted herself to Carolyn, who grew up obedient, principled, and virtually trouble-free. Los Angeles in the 1950s was, for the affluent middle class such as Helen and Eddie were, an air-conditioned island into which little bad news entered. Carolyn was the only Black in her high school in Van Nuys: Pacoima, a Black community a few miles away, was a world apart. To the north, in San Francisco coffeehouses, there were rumors of revolution, but the "Beat Generation" held little fear for the complacent in California. Beat Culture was good copy for Rosa to edit for the newsweeklies but reached no farther, and when Carolyn chose and was accepted in the entering Class of 1963 at the University of California, Berkeley, her parents were satisfied and proud.

It was against this backdrop of middle-aged, middle class fatigue, withdrawal, and insouciance that the most momentous events of the 20th century in America began to stir. *Brown v. Board of Education* along with research by Gordon Allport on prejudice rumbled within psychology.

It took far more than the results of psychological and sociological investigations, important as they were, to bring racial justice to America. It took thousands of courageous individual acts (Rosa Parks's refusal to follow a race-based seating restriction on a Montgomery, Alabama, city bus in 1955) and military compulsion (the deployment of the National Guard to desegregate the Little Rock schools in 1957) and ultimately a grass roots movement operating at a spiritual as well as an intellectual level that assembled hundreds of thousands of people in Washington, DC, in 1963 to hear Dr. Martin Luther King Jr.'s galvanizing speech for the movement toward racial equality. Among King's many influences was the philosopher and theologian Henry Nelson Wieman, whose work King examined for his doctoral dissertation at Boston University. Wieman had deep roots in psychology. In his own doctoral studies, he pursued the fundamental issue that William James engaged, the nature of interest, and the rest of his career was devoted to understanding how separate human interests could be united for a common good.

Psychologists did not notice this deep connection to the religious roots of psychology in King. By the 1950s much of psychology had lost touch with its religious origins. "A science without a soul" was the preferred ideal for the profession. It was understandable that Harry interpreted Carl Rogers, another psychologist from a religious tradition, as secular. Harry's irreligion went deep. His father insisted that the children be brought up without reference to their grandparents' traditional Judaism, and his cousin who took the children in was indifferently observant. Neither Rosa nor Helen had any particular connection with religion. Rosa, Harry, and Helen were mostly deaf to the religious overtones of the greatest social struggle of their times. Rosa and Harry were also hampered by the prejudices, occasionally openly expressed, that they brought with them from their New York upbringing.

However, Harry and Helen's children, Donald and Carolyn, perceived the world differently than their parents. The struggle for equality was central to defining each of their lives, as well as psychology, in the decades to come.

The 1960s

THE PSYCHOLOGICAL COALITION IN THE 1960s

The 1960s were brought to the United States on television. A rickety and infrequent curiosity only 15 years before, TV was, by 1960, in virtually every home, every bar, every motel, every mental hospital, every prison—the flickering screen was everywhere. Newton Minow, then the chairperson of the Federal Communications Commission, described TV in 1961 as "a vast wasteland" (Minow, 1964). Full of game

Newton Minow (1926–, USA) Attorney and chair of the Federal Communications Commission, 1961–1963.

and quiz shows, insipid situation comedies, soap operas, and hectoring commercials, it demonstrated seemingly little social value. In ensuing decades, psychologists would engage in inconclusive debates about whether violence on TV had social effects. Yet TV had evolved to the point where it was obviously transmitting the messages of current political and social events rapidly through the whole culture. "The medium," said communications theorist Marshall McLuhan in 1964, "is the message" (McLuhan, 1964, p. 7). Television, by its nature, would structure the images

Marshall McLuhan (1911–1980, Canada) Widely read and cited communications and media theorist during the 1960s and 1970s.

it presented to render them pictorial, disconnected from each other and from ongoing reality. TV brought a presidential convention, distant and blurry, into selected living rooms in 1952. In 1960 it brought, to almost every living room in the United States, the two candidates, face to face, debating.

In 1970, Gil Scott-Heron (1949–2011), the Black jazz poetry artist, said that "the revolution will not be televised," playing on the disconnect between the surreality of the screened image and the actuality playing out on the street. Bad, biased, and hateful journalism existed then, as now, on radio, in newspapers, and on television, but the news commentators on the three major U.S. broadcast networks, Frank Reynolds, Eric Sevareid, Chet Huntley, David Brinkley, and Walter Cronkite were respected figures that represented, for the most part accurately, an objective view of current events. Of course the news is selective and complete impartiality is impossible. Yet, even via this imperfect screen, images leaked through that seared the consciousness of Americans and let them know that the seeds of reconceptualization of international relations, planted in the postwar reaction against Communism, and the revolution in conceptions of racial injustice, planted 65 years before with the *Plessy v. Ferguson* Supreme Court decision mandating "separate but equal" as social policy, had taken root and were rapidly growing.

Among these images were the aerial photographs of Russian ships with missiles and nuclear warheads lashed to their decks, trailing long wakes as they sailed toward Cuba in October 1962. For several days tense negotiations were carried out. Nationwide relief was felt as the ships reversed their course. Later, in the 1970s and 1980s, this event would be analyzed by psychologists for clues to its successful resolution. At the time, however, it was just another indicator of the uncertain and fearful status of life in the world.

During the next year, in June 1963, President John Fitzgerald Kennedy stood by the Berlin Wall, a symbol of the divide between Soviet Communism and American individualism, and pledged solidarity to the cause of a free Berlin in a reunited Germany, declaring "Ich bin ein Berliner!" In August of 1963, the cameras panned hundreds of thousands of people massed in the Washington, DC, Mall, assembled to hear one of the most famous speeches ever delivered in America, Martin Luther King Jr.'s "I Have a Dream" speech. Later, during the mid- and late 1960s, cameras caught the lurid halflight of burning stores and houses in the Black ghettos of Los Angeles, Detroit, Cleveland, Newark, and other American cities where frustration had passed the point where aggression could be retained. This part of the revolution, at least, was televised.

On November 24, 1963, the day before the cameras captured the long, slow funeral procession of John Fitzgerald Kennedy, 35th President of the United States, gunned down by an anomic psychopath, millions of Americans witnessed a murder in real time on their screens as Jack Ruby shot Kennedy's assassin in the basement garage of the Dallas Police Department. Camera crews arrived to capture the angry expressions of the members of Martin Luther King Jr.'s associates standing on the balcony of the Lorraine Motel in Memphis after his assassination on April 4, 1968. Cameras caught the confusion and panic as John F. Kennedy's brother, Robert, fresh from a primary election victory in California on June 5, 1968, was shot in the kitchen of the Ambassador Hotel in Los Angeles.

Every evening starting in 1965, all the networks showed new footage taken on the ground with the troops in Vietnam. Columns of soldiers threaded their way along pathways through high reeds by rice paddies, troops waved as they passed cameras while cruising upriver on patrol craft, and explosions and balls of smoke and fire rose over besieged troops at airfields under Viet Cong attack. What television didn't thrust into the living room, however, print journalism did: photographs of a Buddhist monk's self-immolation in protest of the South Vietnamese government; a girl running naked from her village during a bombing; a South Vietnamese army officer in the act of shooting an enemy caught on the wrong side of the lines. Possibly the only image that wasn't captured was that of Norman Morrison, a Quaker from Baltimore, who burned himself to death beneath the office of the Defense Secretary at the Pentagon to protest the war. It remained for a poet, George Starbuck (1931–1996), to immortalize him (Starbuck, 1971).

Officially, the psychological coalition proceeded, for most of the 1960s, as if it were not tuned into national television regarding Civil Rights and Vietnam. There were many reasons why psychology lagged behind events in civil rights. For one thing, though psychology had contributed to lighting the fuse of the struggles of the 1960s, by 1960 many Whites had moved to the sidelines. Kenneth Clark, whose study with his wife Mamie Phipps Clark was one of the major elements of the social science argument that helped overturn segregation in *Brown v. Board of Education*, was invited to the White House in 1963 with several of the highest-ranking representatives of Black culture in the United States to talk with Attorney General Robert Kennedy, John F. Kennedy's brother. Interviewed in *Pageant* magazine, Clark recalled that he had predicted in 1955 or 1956 that demonstrations and violence would occur, because, he said, "I thought they were the only way to counteract evasiveness" (Clark, 1963, p. 726). "What I didn't predict," he continued, "was the fact that the moderate Whites would settle for so little as they were able to settle for, for instance, in Little Rock, in New York, in Boston, in Oklahoma" (Clark 1963, p. 726). He commented further that, taking the responses of labor unions, churches, and educational institutions together, "I didn't recognize how inept, how morally empty they were" (Clark, 1963, p. 726.) Although individual Whites would go to the South to march, sit in, and even die for the cause, the burden of organizing and demonstrating fell on the Blacks themselves. Psychologists, overwhelmingly White and male, no doubt were among those who were active in or sympathetic to the cause of civil rights. Also, psychology had no large accumulation of research findings that could support the mobilization of either nonviolent demonstrations or aggressive public protest to gain social goals. In fact, much psychological research and thinking had, over the past 50 years, emphasized and reinforced individual and group differences rather than integration. Beyond this implicit reinforcement of discrimination via method, there were psychologists who were frankly segregationist and racist. Ultimately, psychologists' isolation in the academy, their cultural backgrounds, and their focus on integrating individuals by adjustment and assimilation—carried over from the 1930s—rather than on managing immediate mass social change pushed psychology, as a field, to the periphery of civil rights, at least as they pertained to color. It was individuals, young—and some not so young— idealistic psychologists, graduate and undergraduate students, professors, and practitioners who participated, along with thousands of other Americans in the marches, demonstrations, and conflicts that changed the racial dialogue in the United States.

The pages of psychology's journal of record, the *American Psychologist*, recorded few traces of the Vietnam conflict, a central feature of American life in the second half of the 1960s. Reasons for this are not difficult to find in the way that Vietnam impacted American culture. People in America did not see Vietnam coming in the way that they had anticipated earlier wars. Although the U.S. government tried to convince the public that it was a strategic necessity, citing the "domino effect" of surrounding countries in Southeast Asia becoming Communist that theoretically would occur if South Vietnam fell to the Communist North, Americans were not convinced. The war, like an unplanned pregnancy, came at an inconvenient time. It was perceived by some, of course, as a call to duty. There was a draft, and young men at that time answered draft calls as a matter of course, since the draft had been in effect since the truce ending the Korean War in 1953. There were also volunteers. For some, as in all wars, it was seen as a personal challenge to be met. For others, going to Vietnam reflected payment of a debt of loyalty and service to their country that their fathers had incurred in World War II. For some, it was even an extension of the general idealism that suffused the United States during the early 1960s and the beginnings of the Civil Rights era. Still, most young men didn't choose to go, and waited instead for the draft. Over the preceding 10 years the draft had meant a couple of years of service on an American, German, or Asian base, with no life to be laid on the line. From the beginning, the Vietnam War was a bloody hell, fought in an ambush-prone country against a determined, resourceful, and often hidden opponent. It soon became clear that Vietnam was not a ticket to glamorous heroism, and young, draft-age people, following well-established psychological principles (though they didn't look them up in their psychology textbooks), developed a variety of avoidance responses to this unpleasant, unwanted event. One way to avoid Vietnam was to change the channel. There were many opportunities to do this in hyperprosperous America in the 1960s, both on the TV and in life. Much that was interesting and entertaining was going on. You could switch from Vietnam to the Beatles leaving their plane for a New York concert or for a pan shot of the Woodstock Festival in 1969; one could switch to glamorous Las Vegas or to Johnny Carson's comedy patter. You could get rich, if you were outside of draft age (over 26). One could avoid the draft by getting married, and before that loophole was closed in August, 1965, many did. One could avoid the draft by going to school, and until the upper age boundary for that deferment was changed in 1967 to 24 years, school could be a long-term solution. This, of course, played into the burgeoning academic side of psychology. An 18-year-old student entering a psychology program as an undergraduate in 1966 was legally protected from being drafted—as long as he was a student in good standing—until 1972, unless he had the "bad luck" of doing well in his 4-year program and finishing it before that time. Graduate students in medicine, or in their fifth year of work toward a doctoral degree, were also exempt. This allowed many of the students who entered psychology in the early '60s to continue their graduate work unimpeded by service. One could work in an essential employment job, for instance, designing or building control systems for weapons or working on defense-related experimental psychology contracts might qualify. Unfairness resulted. Those who were unable to afford college or trade school—usually poor, many Black—were disproportionately represented in the ground troops. Statistics aren't available for the number of psychologists of later decades who served in combat, but the proportion is probably small relative to the number of psychologists who saw combat during the 1940s. Unlike in World Wars I and II, upper-echelon psychologists of national stature and their graduate students did not flock to the colors. Beginning in 1965, with more restrictions on deferments and with the ugly reality of the war flung onto the living room rug every evening, a vast national sentiment against the war arose among both those who would be directly affected by it as potential combatants and by disgusted civilians. Violent clashes began to occur between civilians on the two sides of the war issue. Bumper stickers reading "War Is Not Healthy for Children and Other Living Things" competed with the ubiquitous flag sticker, which adhered to the rear windows of "hawkish" sedans. Some opponents of the war followed their consciences and left for Canada, Sweden, or other countries. The U.S. Secretary of Health, Education, and Welfare resigned in 1968 because he could no longer support the Johnson Administration's prosecution of the war. The war became the central issue in the political campaign for president in 1968, and police attacks on protesters outside the Democratic Party Convention in Chicago further inflamed national tensions. The conflict between pro- and anti-war civilians moved into the universities, where, aided by radical student groups that linked several other liberationist issues to the war, students demonstrated, struck, and even in some cases performed violent acts against property and individuals. Similar radicalized revolutions occurred in Europe in 1968, which led, for a time, to the impression that a general revolution was developing. However, this was short-lived. On May 4, 1970, at Kent State University in Ohio, four students at a demonstration against the presence of the National Guard on the campus were fired on and killed, and nine more were wounded, by National Guard troops that were called out to maintain order. It is not clear whether this was intentional or unintentional, or whether the students who were killed and wounded were all taking part in the demonstration (Lewis &

Hensley, 1998). At this point the high waters of revolution were reached and the flood subsided. A lottery draft went into effect in 1971, and by 1973 no further combat troops were sent to Vietnam. Meanwhile, all through this time, veterans were returning home after their combat tours. They were met by indifference and sometimes outright hostility, but like all veterans of wars, most returned to their lives and succeeded in them.

There were lots of reasons for troops in Vietnam to be hopeless. While the Army provided ample psychological assistance in selection, training, and to a limited extent, counseling to recruits, the troops that reached Vietnam often were sent to areas that were understaffed and were thrust immediately into combat with few, if any, psychological support personnel available in the rear (Huffman, 1970). No war's methods of killing are humane, but those of Vietnam had a particularly gruesome character. Soldiers were asked, occasionally outside of the rules of war by sadistic commanders, to inflict casualties on civilians. Chemical warfare and destruction by sheets of gasoline-fed fire were common. Narcotics and alcohol were freely available. An existentially dark outlook characterized the Vietnam experience, captured in some of the most popular film depictions that appeared after the conflict had ended: *Full Metal Jacket; Apocalypse Now; Coming Home.* A Vietnam veteran, perhaps more than the veterans of wars where combatants were selected from all social and economic levels of the population, was amply at risk for psychological problems on his return. There appears to have been little preparation by psychologists for this during the 1960s. Counseling psychologists concentrated on civilian problems. Hospital clinicians worked to develop ways to implement the new community mental health system. Military psychologists, based on their conference presentations at the American Psychological Association (APA) conventions during that period, focused on issues relating to training and selection, not on combat, retention, or the return to civilian life. In fact, during that time, a resolution was advanced by another APA division to abolish Division 19, the Division of Military Psychology, one of the original coalition members (Gade & Drucker, 2000).

Back home, psychology was exploding in terms of numbers and activities. Within clinical psychology, the 1960s' experience was shaped by federal laws and initiatives, as it had been for the previous two decades. Nicholas Hobbs, an educational and developmental psychologist who became known during the next decade as "the children's advocate" for his work in developing programs for special education and for children with disabilities, was selected as the official in charge of selection of volunteers for the newly created Peace Corps, one of the first actions of the incoming Kennedy Administration in 1961 (Hobbs, 1963). "Ask not what your country can do for you; ask what you can do for your country" was the memorable phrase from his inaugural address that January. By mid-

Nicholas Hobbs (1915–1983, USA) Developmental psychologist who focused specifically on children with disabilities.

year, the first recruits were in the field, beginning a program that had been envisioned by William James in *The Moral Equivalent of War* many years before: an army, he said, enlisted to fight against the evils and challenges that nature poses for humans. Two years later, the Community Mental Health Act of 1963 was passed, hastening the closure of the incarcerative mass mental hospitals that only a decade before had been the standard of care for the severely mentally ill, as well as the developmentally disabled, epileptic, and especially the aged demented. In 1964 and 1965, programs that had been started in the Kennedy Administration were aggressively enacted as part of President Lyndon Johnson's Great Society initiative. Voting rights and other civil rights protections were coupled with educational reforms, including intervention in early childhood education (Project Head Start), antipoverty programs, and, most notably in terms of the number of Americans they would affect, Medicare, which guaranteed medical care for the aged, and Medicaid, which guaranteed a basic level of health care services for the poor. Added to these, over the next 2 years, were the National Endowment for the Arts and the Corporation for Public Broadcasting.

One of the architects of this collection of programs, and their chief administrator for the 3 years of his term, between 1965 and

1968, as Secretary of Health, Education, and Welfare, was John W. Gardner (1912–2002), a protean figure in American intellectual life who prior to his service in the Johnson cabinet was the head of the Carnegie Corporation, a primary source of funding for progressive projects in the social sciences (McFadden, 2002). Like Frances Perkins, the Labor Secretary of the 1930s who had advanced the New Deal social legislation, Gardner came from an intellectual background in social science. He held undergraduate and graduate degrees in psychology from Stanford and completed his PhD at the University of California at Berkeley in 1938. Taken together, over the next several years these programs gave wide scope for the advancement of both clinical and applied psychology, with increases in funds for test development and for new educational materials, for psychologists to be employed in consumer product testing and review, and even for psychologists with interests in the arts.

The combined effect of the Community Mental Health Act and the Great Society's medical programs was a further infusion of energy and resources into rapidly developing clinical psychology. Paul Meehl's Presidential Address to the APA in 1962 addressed a specifically psychiatric subject, schizophrenia (Meehl, 1962), and while disputes went on over boundaries between medicine and psychology as well as over insurance coverage for psychological services, clinical psychology had evolved into a viable alternative to traditional psychiatry. Psychologists who followed Menninger's lead in identifying social problems as the root of psychiatric ones were gratified by the possibility of providing innovative mental health service delivery in community settings: Optimism was in the air. Family systems therapy was added to the still expanding mix of treatments, and in California especially, programs combining group therapy with intense residential treatment experiences— sometimes in stunningly beautiful natural surroundings complete with modern individual cottages and pools—began operations: Esalen for emotional disorders and Synanon for drug addictions. In 1955, E. C. Tolman, architect of the modern synthesis between cognition and behavior, addressed the APA convention on the role of Freudian mechanisms in a cognitive system. Freud combined with cognition. Based on the discovery of Dr. Aaron Beck's private journals, we now know that the principles behind the 1960s development of the therapeutic treatment that would have the most lasting impact on clinical psychology, cognitive behavioral therapy, were Freudian (Rosner, 2012). In 1969, Ivar Lovaas (1927–2010) reported success with intensive behavioral intervention with severely autistic children. The publication of the *Diagnostic and Statistical Manual of Mental Disorders*, 2nd edition (*DSM-II*) in 1968 provided psychologists and psychiatrists with the first modern version of the now familiar clinical diagnostic manual, and added levels of systematization and standardization to the diverse range of treatment approaches.

David Hubel (1926–2013, Canada–USA) Neurophysiologist and codiscoverer, with Torsten Wiesel (1924–, Sweden), of feature detectors in the retina. Shared the 1981 Nobel Prize for Physiology or Medicine with Torsten Wiesel and Roger Sperry.

In academic psychology, the 1960s was the era of the brain: the time when neurophysiology replaced comparative psychology as the foundation of biopsychology. David Hubel and Torsten Wiesel's work on the columnar organization of the cerebral cortex; Roger Sperry's publication, in the October 1968 *American Psychologist*, of his findings on the two consciousnesses of the split brain (Sperry, 1968); and the beginning of the work of Patricia Goldman-Rakic on the circuitry of the frontal lobes were central events.

Roger Sperry (1913–1994, USA) Neuroscientist who conducted groundbreaking work on the organization of the brain for perception. Shared the 1981 Nobel Prize for Physiology or Medicine with David Hubel and Torsten Wiesel for his work on the split brain.

Patricia Goldman-Rakic (1937–2003, USA) Neuroscientist who made significant advances in knowledge of the structure and function of the brain's frontal lobes.

The 1960s were also the era in which cognitive psychology matured and linguistics, cognitive psychology, and developmental psychology began to fuse, for example with the work of

Lila Gleitman, who began to study the structural and functional properties of child language. The formal representation of models of the mind in the "boxologies," computer science-inspired boxed flowcharts of hypothetical mental processes, abounded: The Atkinson-Shiffrin three-box model of memory (sensory, short- and long-term) appeared in 1968, augmented 6 years later with Alan Baddeley's postulation of "working memory." Ulric Neisser's book *Cognitive Psychology* appeared in 1967 and led to the publication of many subsequent textbooks in the field.

Lila Gleitman (1929–, USA) Developmental psycholinguist long affiliated with the University of Pennsylvania.

Richard Atkinson (1929–, USA) Psychologist and past president of the University of California system. Creator, with his student Richard Shiffrin (1942–, USA) of the influential memory theory described in the text.

Alan Baddeley (1934–, Great Britain) Memory theorist most often cited in connection with working memory.

Ulric Neisser (1928–2012, Germany–USA) The first modern cognitive psychological generalist: his 1967 book Cognitive Psychology *was the canonical text in the field in its time.*

Personality came into its own as a focus of psychological study during the 1960s. Formerly the province of theorists of abnormality and diagnosis like Frederic Lyman Wells or of synthesizers like Gardner Murphy or Gordon Allport, enough theories of personality development had emerged that separate textbooks of personality theories could be assembled. A separate *Journal of Personality* had already been publishing for years: The further progress toward growth and expansion of the personality subfield was symbolized by the change in title of the *Journal of Abnormal and Social Psychology* to the *Journal of Social and Personality Psychology* in 1965. New texts in personality included the concepts of locus of control, originated by Julian Rotter (1916–) in 1954 and published in its complete form as a personality theory in 1966, and social learning as a determinant of the development of personality characteristics. Albert Bandura's (1925–) iconic "Bobo Doll" studies date from 1961 and his comprehensive statement *Social Behavior and Personality* was published in 1963

(Bandura & Walters, 1963). Toward the end of the decade, situational determinants of personality, expectations of reinforcement, and principles of self-control were synthesized by Walter Mischel (1930–) in his 1968 *Personality and Assessment*. Even today, most comprehensive multi-theory personality textbooks are museums of the explanatory theories available to the psychologists of the 1960s. It is interesting to note what they often exclude: Wilhelm Reich's energetics; the authoritarian personality; and Timothy Leary's extension of Harry Stack Sullivan's system, published in 1957 as *The Interpersonal Diagnosis of Personality: A Functional Theory and Methodology for Personality Evaluation* (Leary, 1957). These exclusions suggest, in the way that Reich's fate in the 1950s also suggests, a circumscription of psychology by its surrounding society's collective self-perception, as well as that society's perception of what the boundaries of psychology ought to be. Whatever psychology shall be, it shall not be cosmic, but rather realistic; it shall not challenge authority; it shall be individualistic, not collectivistic.

The question of how psychology is perceived by its surrounding society attracted a fair amount of attention during the 1950s and 1960s. Three examples from of the 1960s shed light on how psychology, which during this decade experienced exponential growth and extended its theoretical and practical activities to virtually their current dimensions, ran up against limits to its growth and took the form it now holds. These are: the first publication, in 1963, of Stanley Milgram's (1933–1984) study on obedience to authority (and its later elaborations, summed up in the popular short supplementary social psychology textbook, *Obedience to Authority*, in 1974); Abraham Maslow's (1908–1970) theorizing during the 1960s about peak experiences and the optimization of human experience; and Timothy Leary's (1920–1996) experiments with mind-altering drugs.

Milgram, because of his Jewish heritage, grew up in full consciousness of the Holocaust and its aftermath. He elected to study how people in a totalitarian society could unleash cataclysmic aggression against others. He did this by focusing not on the aggression expressed by in-groups to out-groups (although that was a tactic readily available at the time), but by studying the actions of individuals placed in a situation where they were required, by lawful instruction, to individually inflict pain on another individual. He utilized a paradigm for studying aggression that had been designed by Arnold Buss at the University of Pittsburgh (Buss, 1961), a device that appeared to be an element of conventional laboratory electronics and that delivered, from the subject's point of view, hurtful and ultimately dangerous shock to another individual isolated from view. The results of Milgram's studies are well known. Then, and now in replications, individuals instructed to deliver painful consequences to another will, if the authority of the command is perceived as legitimate, do so, mostly without much compunction. Milgram's study fit in with other studies of the periods that tended to show humans as less than compassionate to others: for example, bystander studies that showed how easy it was for people to ignore others in distress in public situations, or studies of vandalism taking place when individuals were led to think they were not observed. The studies fit also into the tenor of the times in social psychological experimentation, which had moved further from studies of dissonance to the adoption of game theory, for example the prisoner's dilemma situation and other situations in which it was possible to inflict harm on another for personal gain.

Arnold Buss (1924–, USA)
Experimental psychologist who did
important early work on aggression
and whose "aggression machine"
was adapted by Stanley Milgram
for his obedience experiments.

Maslow, though a generation older, came from a background similar to Milgram's. During the 1930s he established himself as a researcher working with Harry Harlow at the University of Wisconsin on the aggressive and competitive drives of monkeys, ultimately becoming known for his work on social dominance. But he shifted his interests from interpersonal dominance to personal excellence. During the 1940s and 1950s, he studied the lives and characterological dimensions of individuals superior in their abilities to transcend their human limitations and achieve full expression of their potential. The concluding chapter of his *Motivation and Personality* (Maslow, 1954) asked the question of why psychology had undergone coarctation—a physiological term that means "narrowing," like narrowing of the arteries. In its concluding chapter, "Toward a Positive Psychology," he asked why psychologists put humans in 4-foot high rooms and then say that no human could stand more than 4 feet tall. (Was this an allusion to the then-new studies by Adalbert Ames, Jr., of the perceptual illusions of the Ames Room [Behrens, 1994]? Perhaps, but more likely, it is a paraphrase of a similar expression of Alfred Adler's.) Through the 1960s, Maslow's idea that humans could live in very different and more liberating circumstances than their status quo allowed aligned well with the growth of the humanistic movement in psychology, which collected many of the impulses for personal and social liberation in one nexus. A general sense of utopianism began to spread across psychology and began to take concrete form in, for one example, communal living organizations. Skinnerians, theoretically relegated to the antihumanist camp by the exchange between Skinner and Rogers in 1956, established communities during the 1960s based on the communal and utopian ideas contained in B. F. Skinner's 1948 prospectus for a benign community, *Walden II.* Maslow became a management consultant, among other things, suggesting a "Eupsychian" dimension to the organization of work that would allow all the positive energies of humans at work to be liberated. He became the patron of Paul Bindrim (1920–1997), who had begun to practice nude psychotherapy in California. Maslow had written extensively on nudism and saw it as another frontier of human nature to be exceeded, and while serving as APA president in 1967 to 1968 he defended Bindrim against ethical issues that were raised against nude psychotherapy by clinicians (Nicholson, 2007).

Leary came from an Irish Catholic background and so was at least the equal of Milgram and Maslow in guilt. A West Pointer who washed out in 1941 during his first year there, he had

Adalbert Ames, Jr. (1880–1955, USA) Scientist who contributed to psychology in many areas, most famously by constructing an illusion embodied in a constructed room that appears in normal perspective only from one restricted vantage point.

narrowly escaped being sent into combat in 1943 through the intercession of his and George Miller's undergraduate instructor at The University of Alabama, Donald Ramsdell, who got Leary a post at a military hospital in Pennsylvania instead. Afterward, as has already been traced in this history, he became one of the leading theoretical clinicians of the 1950s. The publication of his *Interpersonal Diagnosis of Personality* in 1957 should have marked the high point of his early professional success and should have been the platform on which a successful academic theoretical career—the aim of most theoretical psychologists of his time— would be built. However, grief over his wife's suicide in 1955 led him to leave his career and his academic ties, and to descend, traveling in Europe, to despairing depths, from which he was rescued and restored to an academic association with Harvard University by David McClelland, who saw potential eminence in him. In 1960, Leary was introduced (by Frank Barron, a researcher of creativity and a Berkeley classmate) to psilocybin, and he experienced a life-

Frank Barron (1922–2002, USA) Psychologist important in the study of creativity; good friend of Timothy Leary.

changing epiphany. Already having rejected "grey flannel suit" conformity, Leary set out to examine, experimentally, the dimensions of the experience that had confirmed, for him, the expansibility of mind and the limitlessness of creative power locked in every individual's brain. One of his graduate students, Walter Pahnke, conducting a controlled study on Good Friday 1962 with undergraduate and graduate students of the Harvard Divinity School, demonstrated that the ingestion of psychedelics indeed interacted with the religiously toned environment to produce a transcendent experience. Powerful enemies at Harvard saw to it that he was soon dismissed, and Leary then went on a personal crusade to bring his discovery of individual mental liberation to everyone, which fit well with the developing drug culture, which, like the Army 10 years earlier, had discovered lysergic acid diethylamide (LSD). Leary changed from Harvard professor to LSD guru overnight, and because he was careless, he eventually ended up in a California prison, from which he escaped in 1970, to be captured 2 years later in Afghanistan(!) and remanded again to prison (where one of his fellow inmates was Charles Manson, the celebrated psychotic mass murderer of the time). Richard Nixon, who won the U.S. presidency in 1969 campaigning on the promise to restore law and order to what seemed to be a developing anarchy, pronounced Leary "the most dangerous man in America" (Devonis, 2012b).

The fates of these three individuals reflect some of the limits that society places on psychology, limits that were clarified during the 1960s. Maslow's celebration of human potential—and the Humanistic psychology movement, which obtained APA divisional status in 1972—have fallen on hard times. Maslow's complexity has since been reduced to a formula, the motivational pyramid, which stands like a forlorn monument presiding over the reduction of his rich characterization of multiple human potentials into the managerial imperatives to excellence that dominate corporate culture today. Few if any traces of the communalism of the 1960s remain. Historically, America has been hospitable to the founding of communes, but not to their continued existence. Nude psychotherapy, or anything like it, is hard to imagine now in the context of current interpretations of the APA Ethics Code. Even Maslow himself, in his letters and diaries of the 1960s, was disappointed in the way that people focused on the benefits of self-actualization while expecting to achieve them at no cost. One of the ideals embodied in the programs of what was termed at the time "The Great Society" was that poverty and want—the elemental "d" levels of Maslow's systematic analysis of the challenges to be faced in achieving liberation—would be removed from the American landscape. An official "War on Poverty" was declared, and under its banners of the Great Society marched forward. However, as of now, psychology doesn't seem likely to lead the movement for the restructuring or transcending of current economic views.

After his pardon in 1976, Leary continued to be, as he termed himself, a "cheerleader for change," touring the country in the 1980s to promote the coming benefits of digital interconnection, and of course unrepentant about his drug use. (Though, why should he have been, having paid the social penalty for it?) It took 44 years until a similar experiment to Pahnke's Good Friday was again performed, producing similar results (Devonis, 2012b): This reticence in psychology to address important phenomenological and ethical questions connected to drugs and consciousness suggests that the research transmitted several implicit messages. One such message is that individual transcendence needs to be divorced from drug experience: religion is good, but artificial religion is not. Or, perhaps more accurately in terms of what has transpired over the past 40 years regarding the position of religion in U.S. society, religion that allows transcendence while punishing drug use and other forms of social excess—however that religion defines them—is what is socially acceptable. Any violation of sinful taboos is suspect. A further message, that social mores and legislation will set boundaries on what can and cannot be examined experimentally, is also bright and clear. Leary's experience brought to light the unintended consequences of psychological discoveries in America, when these conflict with current laws. Leary may have done more, unintentionally, than anyone in psychology to change the focus of the U.S. government's legislative and health services from the War on Poverty to the War on Drugs, which began immediately after the 1960s and has had continuous and baleful social effects.

Milgram's discoveries are perhaps the longest-lasting effect of the 1960s, within and outside of psychology. Not only the obedience studies but also his later studies on social closeness (think of all the variations on the theme of "six degrees of separation") are among the first to come to mind when psychology is the subject. The subject of how far one should go in obeying authority was broached during the 1960s in fundamental ways in American society. Even within psychology, Milgram encountered resistance to the conclusions that could be drawn from his studies. One of the keenest ones came from the developmental clinical psychologist Diana Baumrind (PhD Berkeley, 1955):

Diana Baumrind (1927–, USA)
Developmental psychologist known
for her theory of parenting styles.

I do regard the emotional disturbance described by Milgram as potentially harmful because it could easily effect an alteration in the subject's self-image or ability to trust adult authorities in the future. (Baumrind, 1964, p. 422)

Serious critiques offered by colleagues, not by external force of law, led Milgram to deflect his aim toward less socially confrontational research. Outside of psychology, the persistence of the Milgram study in countless variations may seem counterintuitive. Why should a society that is ever more invested in obedience and surveillance be interested in a psychologist whose essential message is to resist laws that conflict with compassion and common sense? Probably, in the context of a society that since 1970 has become hyperpunitive, the idea of resistance to authority has been driven underground and what remains is the Milgram study interpreted as positive proof that a, if not *the*, fundamental rule of social behavior is in fact obedience. One of the ways the Milgram study can be read is as supportive of a definition of society as consisting of rulers and ruled, commanders and commanded, and inevitable falling into line. Taken together, these three challenges to the social order mounted by psychologists in the 1960s may ultimately have unintentionally reinforced future tendencies toward reaction and repression in American society.

But in the 1960s, such bleak consequences were not envisioned. As the decade came to a close, George Miller addressed the APA as its president (Miller, 1969) and offered a challenge to the assembled membership: Give psychology away! He observed that psychology, during the previous decades, had done well by itself and its members. It had multiplied its official organized membership by many thousands; it had become a profession that developed expertise in intervening in all aspects of human life. A quarter century of coexistence among the clinical, theoretical, and applied areas of psychology had produced, in Miller's view, a vast fund of knowledge and expertise. But according to the charter of the APA, which was founded in 1892 and incorporated in 1925, was not one of the organization's goals to advance human welfare? Psychologists had certainly advanced psychologists' own welfare, but what of that of the surrounding society? These questions were particularly pointed in the context of the late 1960s: a society in ferment, with young people seeking "change" in amorphous ways, and severe challenges to the existing social order. What psychologists must do, Miller said, was find the ways in which psychology could be relevant to social change, and offer its services and findings to those who could best use them: community activists, teachers, medical personnel, elected officials, and all the other members of society who would benefit from knowing the relations between cause and effect in human behavior that had been amassed to date.

The year 1970 is the halfway point in this account of psychology's recent activity. The challenge to give psychology away was continually echoed in the coming years. How well psychology understood and responded to it, and how well the surrounding society received psychology's gifts, are subjects for the next three chapters.

THE FAMILY STORY: A TIME OF GREAT CHANGES

The 1960s were the most eventful decade in the 20th century in terms of shaping the direction of society. It was during this period that the lag between events and theory was shortened, and psychology became part of the running dialogue of ideas and actions that make up social and political life. For the most part, however, Rosa, Harry, and Helen did not feel consciously political. Instead, it was as if events were moving them along, that they were being lived by the times.

Although operant behaviorism had been around in some form since B. F. Skinner published *The Behavior of Organisms* in 1938, frontline clinicians in individual practice like Harry by and large ignored it or incorporated it only sparingly into their practices. Harry's reaction to the idea that clients' behavior should be charted, scheduled, and managed was to growl "fascist" at the idea and press on. Harry was now fully licensed in North Carolina and was working his usual 10- to 12-hour days. Though the violent phase of the Civil Rights Movement was heating up farther south, it was not as evident in his part of North Carolina, although sporadic incidents occurred. Economic and social boundaries ensured that, from the beginning of his practice, he did not see African American clients, and thus was blind to a whole area of life. His son, Donald, on the other hand, was aware of the civil rights movement from the beginning. He quit the University of North Carolina in 1961 during his senior year and moved out, eventually joining a student group that participated in sit-ins and protests in the deep South between 1962 and 1964. Father and son grew further apart, and at the same time Harry's marriage finally collapsed and dissolved in 1963. At 52, Harry was alone with his clients.

Had he been of an Eriksonian turn of mind he might have been able to frame his state of mind in terms of the later stages of Erikson's theory, which was near the height of its popularity at that time. If he could have seen himself objectively, he would have seen a man going through the motions, dispensing little except weary patience and occasional insight to his depressed and anxious patients. But Harry was not much for theory. In this time before the ethics code was fully developed, there was no official requirement that a therapist in Harry's position—today we would call him "impaired"—seek therapy himself. In 1964, for the first time, Harry deduced that he was experiencing a level of distress that called for expert assistance. His choice was a young therapist who had just finished a course in the then new discipline of family therapy. The language of interpersonal dynamics connected well, for Harry, with his background in analytic psychology and systems theory, the legacy of his training in the late '40s and early '50s. More than that, the weekly sessions over the next 2 years gave him a necessary respite and an opportunity to take perspective not only on his immediate family situation but on the course he had so far run in his life. It was during this time, in 1965, that Donald had joined the Marines and was heading for Vietnam.

Helen and Eddie, in Los Angeles, slipped unconsciously into middle age, while Carolyn, their daughter, did well at Berkeley. In those years Berkeley was a center for all sorts of political and social ideas, both in the classroom and on the street, and Carolyn decided, upon graduation in 1963, to join the newly created Peace Corps and work in Ecuador, where she stayed for almost 2 years. On her return to the Bay area in March 1965, where she moved in with a group of friends—a "commune" typical of the times—she was 5 months pregnant by an Ecuadorian man who did not follow her to America. Helen and Eddie followed her pregnancy's progress with trepidation. On May 31, 1965, Carolyn's daughter Juana was born prematurely. On December 7, 1965, Eddie died.

At this point both Carolyn and Helen were on their own as women in a society that for years had not created places for them. Once again, Helen's luck held: Eddie was adequately insured and also left a small pension, enough for her to relocate to the San Francisco Bay area to be near her daughter and granddaughter. Carolyn was lucky, too, to be living in that place at that time, for California, and the Bay Area in particular, were especially well connected to the roots of activist feminism. Theoretical feminism had been around for a while—Carolyn and most of her friends had read *The Second Sex* and *The Feminine Mystique*—but what she, her baby, and her mother needed now were support and advocacy, and both of which were available. Helen talked herself into a job with a manufacturer of electrical equipment in Richmond. The Vietnam War was in full swing and there were government contracts and war prosperity much like 25 years before. This allowed her to provide an apartment for Carolyn, Juana, and herself, and she began to take courses in social work at night at the University of California in San Francisco. She graduated with an master's in social work in 1967 and was hired by the State of California as a caseworker. She stayed in the Bay Area for 6 more years, until Carolyn got a steady job as a printer and Juana was near the age when she could be "latchkey." Carolyn lived for a time with a Chicano

Rights activist but soon found she preferred to be on her own with her smart, inquisitive daughter and her friends in the women's community.

At this time, Helen reached out to her siblings by letter. Harry's response was friendly but cool, and she understood that he preferred his solitude. Rosa, by contrast, seemed happy to hear from her younger sister, whom she had not seen for 30 years. In her reply to Helen in August 1969, Rosa sent a copy of a column she composed for a gay newspaper in New York in July, the first column she had written in over 20 years. It was about the events that happened in June at the Stonewall Inn in New York City, the first spontaneous violent resistance to oppression by the gay community. "Vindicated?" it read. "No, not vindicated. I feel liberated."

At this point it becomes plain that there are two parallel and mostly non-interactive histories in action in the recent history of psychology in America. On the one hand is the gradual development of cognitive neuroscience. On the other is once again the phenomenon of the force of events driving the evolution of psychology. The momentum for civil rights that began building in the 1950s increased during the 1960s and activated movements for equality, all of which were primed for action in previous decades. The rapid-fire events of the 1960s that changed so many things at once—perceptions of race, the role of women in society, gender roles, the definition of family—presented psychology with a series of *faits accomplis*, for which theory and practice would need to be developed over the coming decades.

The 1970s

THE PSYCHOLOGICAL COALITION IN THE 1970s

By any measure, the 1970s and 1980s were marked, for psychology, by a continual upward change in professional self-designations as indicated by membership in the APA, a marker of the increase in the number of practicing psychologists now well distributed in all areas of U.S. culture.

In 1970, the APA listed 37,000 paid divisional members. Of these, 3,544 were members of Division 12, Clinical Psychology, and 1,944 were members of Division 17, Counseling Psychology. A Division of Psychotherapy, Division 29, had just been formed and contained 2,040 members. In comparison, the division of Educational Psychology, Division 15, the most populated applied division, had 3,094 members. By 1997, the total divisional membership stood at 87,437—6,662 clinical; 3,040 counseling; 5,679 psychotherapy; 3,520 psychoanalysis (this division, Division 39, was newly formed in 1980). Meanwhile, Educational

Psychology's membership had fallen by nearly a thousand, to 2,257. To give some further context to these numbers, the U.S. population in 1970 was about 203 million; in 2006, it hit 300 million (NBC News said that this would be "good for the economy"); in 2014 it reached 317 million. There are complaints that it is growing too slowly.

In 1970, there were about 15,000 members in the "other" APA, the American Psychiatric Association. Supposing that the combination of clinical, counseling, and psychotherapy represented, with little overlap, the number of American Psychological Association members also so engaged, then psychiatrists outnumbered psychologists by about 2 to 1. Membership in professional organizations does not completely count the number of individuals engaged in practice. The number of psychologists is always difficult to count, especially with the number of competing psychotherapeutic and counseling professions that continued to emerge during the 1970s. On the whole, it was a much larger workforce—the word the APA began to use to describe its membership at this time and later—than was available in 1948, the first year that paid divisional membership statistics were recorded. Then, there were 5,391 total members in the APA, with 787 clinical and 466 counseling members. Interestingly, the complaint was repeatedly voiced from almost the beginning of the coalition's formation that the clinicians' concerns drowned out those of the other practitioners, to say nothing of those who saw themselves engaged strictly in scientific research. The 1959 split of the Psychonomic Society from the APA drew off some of the "pure scientists," but by 1970 the percentage of clinical, counseling, and allied psychotherapeutic divisional members had actually declined from a quarter of the Association in 1948 to around a sixth in 1970. Other associations and nonaffiliation were also options.

Psychology entered the 1970s as a well-established, lucrative coalition of professions. While some of its activity over the rest of the decade could be understood as directed toward meeting the challenge of selfless public service, for the most part psychologists were interested in career advancement. This workforce had been exhorted, by the outgoing APA President George Miller in 1969, to seize the "revolutionary" potential of "giving psychology away": In the 1970s and thereafter the idea of giving psychology away was and still is a constant rhetorical feature in official APA documentation. The idea, however, came into immediate conflict with the way that psychology had developed up to this time, and with the inertia characteristic of large bureaucracies. By 1970, psychologists were well integrated into all levels of social and educational administration. They were being inducted into the developing health care system, which was showing the first signs of the consolidations and corporatization that have now come to be its hallmarks. The two APAs—the American Psychological Association and the American Psychiatric Association—themselves became more corporatized in structure, progressing from professional societies with presidents and a small cabinet and board to organizations with a member president and semi-permanent CEOs. In the case of the American Psychological Association, the position of Chief Executive Officer had existed since at least 1962, when it was held by Arthur Brayfield, Jr. Neither organization had evolved a plan for officially mandating pro bono psychiatric or psychotherapeutic services, although the evolution of the APA ethics code suggests that pro bono work and even therapy was becoming common as part of the service component

Arthur Brayfield, Jr. (1915–2002, USA) Personnel and counseling specialist, PhD student of Donald Paterson at Minnesota. An award for the best dissertation at the Claremont Colleges in California is named after him.

of that clinical psychology had developed, especially among those clinicians who also held teaching positions in which service counted toward tenure. But tradition was against anything less than fee-for-service, and the main activities of the APA over the previous 2 decades in connection with clinical psychology were aimed at defining the dimensions of professional activity, carving out a space next to psychiatry for psychological private practice, and gaining a toehold in the insurance system.

The other parts of the coalition were similarly unequipped to donate psychological services. University-based teachers and researchers were more than ever competing for federal and foundation grants: Big science—or at least larger-scale research—was replacing little science. Though the universities continued to expand, there was, by the middle of the 1970s, less heat in the economy and "retrenchment" became a reality to work around, usually by being more aggressive in obtaining resources. Psychologists, armed with good negotiating skills and generally well versed in social interaction, moved into university administrative positions with some regularity. There, influence and control over funding decisions and resource allocations worked to the benefit of a growing presence of psychology in the academy, but at the same time against an altruistic attitude. Applied psychologists had spent decades installing themselves in the machinery of business, education, the military, and media and advertising, and were, even more than the academicians and clinicians, attuned to the need to compete in these profit-driven sectors.

To some extent this gradient of resistance to the idea of giving psychology away was countered by the fact that psychology, for most of its life, was not proprietary. Patents were not taken out on findings about the responsiveness of the retina or therapy techniques or on systems of training negotiators or salespeople, although the days of assertion of control over copyrights and distribution of psychotherapeutic services were soon to arrive. In the case of testing, copyright was already a well-established principle. Ideas, of course, were and are free, and anyone willing to adapt them could find many resources in the behavioral and group dynamics literature to assist in designing in-house psychological interventions. However, the number of private, nonpsychologist individuals who turned first to psychology to help manage their businesses, children, or classrooms was probably smaller than most psychologists would like to think. Miller suggested making interventions in classrooms and in communities more visible and available for general application, but commentators at the time noted that there was a good deal of imprecision in the transmittal of knowledge from the laboratory to the education school, to the ultimate end user, the classroom teacher.

Complicating this was the sudden change in the economy from the booming quasiwartime era of the late 1960s to a period of economic malaise. For the first time, Americans experienced being shut off from essential energy needs. The 1973 Organization of Petroleum Exporting Countries (OPEC) embargo on crude oil from the Middle East hit Americans where it pinched most—in their wallets and gas tanks. Their immense cars with aircraft-carrier-like flat hoods had fuel economies of around 11 miles a gallon and were suddenly a liability: Retail gasoline prices increased 300% and an era of resource scarcity and uncertainty began. Internal American politics were likewise unstable. From the summer of 1973 through August 1974, the news was full of investigations of illegal activity connected to spying on political rivals that the U.S. President, Richard Nixon, might have abetted. Ultimately, Nixon resigned to avoid impeachment and was succeeded by Gerald Ford, who pardoned him in 1976 for anything that he might have done. The combination of the blow to American perceptions of invincibility caused by the withdrawal, between 1973 and 1975, from Vietnam along with the revelation of America's vulnerability in energy resources, added to the shame brought on American conservatism by the Nixon episode as well as to the feelings of anger at what, to conservatives, was perceived as the imposition of civil rights laws. This combination of forces led to a strengthening of conservative, antiliberal tendencies in American politics, signified by a shift in the South of the Whites opposed to civil rights from the Democratic to the Republican party, a shift that had begun with the aggressive states' rights politics of Strom Thurmond of North Carolina in 1948. This turn to conservatism began to set agendas for the following decades, and ensured continual unsettled racial relations as well as a continual search for redress for military defeat.

Further sources of frustration for conservatives resulted from the persistence of liberal majorities in the Senate and the Supreme Court, leading to legislation and decisions that realized further egalitarian goals beyond those already achieved in 1965. One of these took the form of the Equal Rights Amendment, by which it was intended that "equality of rights under law shall not be denied or abridged by the United States or any state on account of sex." A permanent offering in every congressional session since 1923, it was finally passed on March 22, 1972, and ratified within a year by 30 states. The Supreme Court's decision, in *Roe v. Wade* in January 1973, that abortion was legal until viability, exacerbated conservative frustrations. Abortion, over the next several decades, became protective coloration, replete with images of babies, for resistance to gender equality and, especially, women's independence. The death penalty, another core tenet of conservative social philosophy, was declared unconstitutional in 1972. (It was reinstated in 1976.)

In June 1969, the Cuyahoga River in Cleveland, as it was wont to do occasionally, caught fire. Though it was rapidly put out, in the context of several other warnings issued by biologists, population specialists, and resource analysts, it served to catalyze an environmental movement, for which symbolic birth occurred on the first Earth Day, April 22, 1970.

The response of officially organized psychology in the 1970s to these political and social events was the same as it had been during the preceding two decades—the creation of further interest groups reflected as new divisions in the APA. For example, there were several groups of psychologists that had interests in subjects that coalesced around the idea of environmentalism. Some psychologists in the area of aesthetics and art were interested in the appearance and beauty of landscapes, the architecture of cities, and other characteristics of the natural and built environment. Others in various areas had had their curiosity piqued by the publication of warnings of impending environmental catastrophe, such as Rachel Carson's *Silent Spring* in 1962, a chilling depiction of the effect of pesticides on the current American biota, or by Garrett Hardin's 1968 article in *Science*, "The Tragedy of the Commons" (Hardin, 1968), which

Rachel Carson (1907–1964, USA) Biologist and ecologist, well known as a writer on scientific subjects.

Garrett Hardin (1915–2003, USA) Ecologist and population theorist.

presented a neo-Malthusian scenario of the effects of unregulated consumption of resources by an exponentially increasing population. They combined to form Division 34, Population and Environmental Psychology, in 1973. Earlier, in 1970, a diverse group of psychologists with a collective expansive vision of human potential and a commitment to a phenomenological approach to psychology emphasizing human freedom of choice formed Division 32, Humanistic Psychology. Both of these were examples of psychologists forming collectives about 10 years after the ideas had appeared in culture: a typical pattern that also held for the formation of the Division of the Psychology of Women, APA Division 35, in 1974.

The proximal internal cause for Division 35's formation was the report of the task force convened for the purpose by the APA leadership to examine the role of women in the Association and which reported its findings in January 1973. But the momentum had been building in culture since the 1960s. In 1955, the Dodge division of Chrysler Motors offered a car specifically dedicated to "Her Majesty, the American Woman." Rose, lavender, and white throughout, with vanity mirrors, a makeup kit, and a matched set of luggage with a hatbox, the Dodge La Femme symbolized the return, after the Second World War, of women to the role of ornamenting the men in society. But even then, many philosophical and ethical forces were combining with the realism of increased number of divorces and the perceived need for two incomes to manage the new consumption-driven lifestyle of the middle class. The early 1960s saw the publication of *The Feminine Mystique* by Betty Friedan (1921–2006), which was soon followed by several other books detailing the inequities inherent in gender inequality. By 1969, a women's liberation movement had emerged (along with movements for gay liberation, Chicano and Latino/Latina liberation, and others), complete with newspapers, magazines, popular songs, and visible public demonstrations.

The formation of Division 35 also ratified changes that had been developing in psychology for some time. For 50 years, no woman had been APA president. In both 1972 and 1973 women were elected (Anne Anastasi and Leona Tyler, respectively), and since then 10 women have been APA presidents. In a way, it was belated recognition of the roles that women had played in the development of psychology since its beginning. In the time span of this history, women were a large part of the staffs of industrial consulting organizations and were also very frequently employed in educational and guidance settings as mental testers. The more prestigious academic positions, however, were often out of reach. Sometimes women were able to gain academic employment because their husbands were also eminent psychologists. Catharine Cox, who as a graduate student had worked closely with Lewis Terman at Stanford and coauthored, with Terman, a well-cited study on genius (which included, famously, estimates of the IQs of Beethoven, Washington, and other historical figures) married Walter Miles and, as Catharine Cox Miles (1890–1984), had a distinguished career at Yale beginning in the 1930s (Ball, 2010). Yet, in the same era, Florence Richardson Robinson (1885–1936) was denied an academic position alongside her husband, Edward S. Robinson, because of antinepotism rules that effectively excluded women (Froese & Devonis, 2000). Nevitt Sanford, commenting in 1976 on the differences between graduate studies at Berkeley in the 1970s compared with the late 1930s, observed that women who did get accepted to graduate programs were accepted by their male peers (Sanford, 1976). The question was, though, how many women PhDs entering university employment were similarly accepted? This depended on local conditions. At UC Berkeley, for example, sympathetic male faculty had made it possible for women to gain a prominent place in the academic environment since the time that George Malcolm Stratton promoted women's graduate careers in the

Anne Anastasi (1908–2001, USA) Psychometric specialist and author of a well-respected textbook on the theory and practice of mental testing. President of APA in 1972.

George Malcolm Stratton (1865–1957, USA) Early American experimentalist whose study on vision with inverted lenses earned him a permanent place in the history of perceptual studies; later he wrote extensively on conflict resolution and pacifism.

early years of the 20th century. Another of Timothy Leary's mentors, Jean Macfarlane, was the second woman to gain a PhD at Berkeley and was, in the 1940s, director of the clinical training program there. However, this was not universally the case. At Harvard at that time, the male hierarchy was dead set against women's participation. As late as 1951, E. G. Boring wrote that

Jean Walker Macfarlane (1894–1989, USA) The holder of the second PhD conferred by the University of California to women, she was the head of the clinical psychology program at Berkeley and conductor of a significant longitudinal study of development, the Guidance Study.

women could not compete with men because they could not manage the hours and the workload of men (Boring, 1951).

Along with this form of internal redress of past injustices, the formal recognition of women as a distinct group within the psychological coalition reflected another instance of the conjunction of science and politics in psychology. For example, the 1977 citation recognizing the early career contributions of Sandra Lipsitz Bem, who with her husband Daryl Bem was already well known for her creation of a scale to measure psycho-

Sandra Lipsitz Bem (1944–, USA) Theorist of egalitarian development and constructor of the Bem Sex Role Inventory, a measure of androgyny.

logical androgyny, noted explicitly that her shift to investigating androgyny reflected a combination of politics and research interests (APA, 1977). The incorporation of a representative division of women also reflected the tacit recognition that gender parity both in undergraduate and graduate study in psychology was increasing. Over the next 15 years, psychology would be the first scientific or medical field to reach full gender parity, if not equity.

Clinical psychology continued to contend with medical psychiatry for authority in treating mental illness. Neither David

David Rosenhan (1926–2012, USA) Forensic psychologist with a dual appointment in law and psychology at Stanford University.

Rosenhan's study "On Being Sane in Insane Places" (Rosenhan, 1973) nor Paul Meehl's "Why I Do Not Attend Case Conferences" (Meehl, 1973) from his 1973 collection, *Psychodiagnosis*, lent much confidence to the enterprise. Rosenhan sent normal graduate students to mental hospitals with the instructions to say that they were hearing voices saying "empty," "hollow," and "thud." All were admitted and diagnosed: One stayed for 49 days. Meehl sent up the slovenly logical and statistical reasoning of his colleagues in memorable style. The newest additions to the mix were the first PsyD programs at the University of Illinois and at Hahnemann University in Philadelphia. The PsyD was conceived soon after the Boulder model began operating. Starke Hathaway at Minnesota, mentor to Paul Meehl and developer of the Minnesota Multiphasic Personality Inventory, pointed out in a 1958 article that the psychologist would always be a "second-class citizen" in comparison to psychiatric colleagues, able to be "turned on and off" at will by medical personnel when they need diagnostic or testing assistance, but dismissed when therapy begins (Hathaway, 1958). Part of the reason for this, said Hathaway and others, is that the Boulder scientist–practitioner clinician spent too much graduate study time doing the empirical PhD work, which didn't allow for enough time to build therapeutic fluency. (Harry, for example, worked for over a year and a half on his doctoral thesis at the University of Tennessee in the '50s, a comparison of Rorschach test scores with selected aspects of the MMPI profile in mania. He thought it was a good piece of work, but his advisors thought that it might need more data and analysis before publication, so he dropped it after obtaining the PhD and never did any more empirical work other than what was necessary to interpret clients' test scores.) In place of this, suggested Hathaway and others, a course of study that included the essentials of psychotherapy practice, similar to the intense practicum experiences of an MD rotation, would lend credibility to the new practitioner, who would enter the competition with psychiatry with well-honed skills. A conference at Vail in 1973 ratified this idea, and the PsyD began to proliferate. Meanwhile, across established clinical psychology, the trends of the 1960s continued. Humanistic therapies became more frequently encountered; group and family therapy also prospered; and, as mass hospitalization continued its change to community-based treatment, psychologists continued to find employment in eldercare and rehabilitation as well as in a variety of addiction-related units that sprang up to replace the services previously provided in state hospitals. The private "rehab farm" became a feature of the therapeutic landscape.

Higher education continued its expansion through the 1970s, though not as rapidly as in the previous decade. Universities and colleges built extensively and added faculty regularly, while across the United States the community colleges underwent tremendous growth, providing employment for many more academic psychologists as teachers of basic psychology and, by somewhat relieving the load of introductory course delivery from the state universities, providing a relief valve that allowed research to expand in the larger universities. Scholarship and publication became more compulsory during this time, and journal space expanded to receive the results. Even in 1940 it was impossible to avoid specialization. By 1970, multiple subspecialties within psychology departments and the texture of the research output became more fine grained. Again, as with the preceding decade, only the barest contours of the richness and complexity of the research output can be indicated by sampling. In all of psychology, the "cognitive turn" was ascendant, and this was evident in developmental psychology by an intense research focus on language acquisition in infants and children. Researchers in those fields were already becoming aware of demographic changes in the United States and concentrated some attention on early bilingual experiences, which they found were generally beneficial for linguistic as well as reasoning development. Within neuropsychology, the result of the previous 2 decades' isolation of neurotransmitters and the empirical study of drug effects led in two directions: first, to a series of refined theories about the anatomical distribution and functional role of neurotransmitter systems, and, second, to discoveries of new neurotransmitter systems. Most prominent among these was the discovery of the endorphins by Candace Pert and Solomon Snyder in 1973. Historical closure was added

Candace Pert (1946–2013, USA) Neuropharmacologist and codiscoverer, with Solomon Snyder (1938–, USA), of the opiate receptors in the brain. Later a proponent of many approaches to holistic medicine.

toward the end of the decade by Kandel's multiple publications of his and colleagues' findings showing conclusively that nerve structure and function were physically modified during associative learning, as theorists of brain representations of learning—Pavlov to Hebb— had postulated (Walters, Carew, & Kandel, 1979). Incidentally, research collectives of upward of five authors in the biosciences became common at this time, a reflection of the growth of the large laboratory concept and its expansion throughout the universities. In cognitive psychology, as in developmental psychology, linguistics led the way in directing research, with studies in story grammar and scripts for understanding behavior becoming common. Perception studies took a cognitive turn as well, and there was, as there was in the late 1940s, substantial crosstalk between those two fields during the 1970s. Roger Shepard at Stanford University published his work on mental rotation of images (Shepard & Metzler, 1971), and Irving Biederman at SUNY Buffalo began work on image recognition in complex natural scenes (Biederman, Glass, & Stacy, 1973). This work would lead to his theories of recognition of objects by geometric shape analysis, a naturalistic and Gestalt-like complement to the expanding work in perception on mechanisms at the receptor and cortical levels, such as feature analysis, and phenomena such as centrally determined color illusions. Gunnar Johannsen (1973) demonstrated biological motion, the ability of the perceptual system to resolve species-significant patterns from limited information (patterns of luminous dots on joints). A sign of the times was James Cutting's extension of this work

Eric Kandel (1929–, Austria–USA) Eminent neuropsychologist, theorist, and lately historian of psychology and its relations to art. Awarded the Nobel Prize for Physiology or Medicine in 2000.

Roger Shepard (1929–, USA) PhD student of Carl Hovland at Yale (1955), prolific cognitive psychologist particularly identified with theories of mental representation of spatial relations.

Gunnar Johannsen (1911–1998, Sweden) Psychologist and perceptual specialist whose research interests included event perception and biological motion.

by programming a computer to generate point-light displays in 1978. By this time, computers had become accessible and indispensable to cognition and perception laboratories (Cutting, 1978). The interfacing between cognitive science and computer science continued apace: The first practical personal computers appeared during the latter part of the decade and became rapidly integrated into psychology labs. Almost overnight, skill in wiring and electrical circuitry became less desirable than programming expertise. Whole rooms full of discarded analog timers, button press boards with 10-watt indicator bulbs, and war surplus electronics cabinets from the 1940s could be found in any psychology department by 1980.

James Cutting (1947–, USA) Perceptual psychologist with wide interests both in the perception of motion and in the relation of art and psychology.

Behavior analysis using Skinner chambers and pigeons continued on its previous trajectory, but held little attraction for most research psychologists, who had gotten comfortable with the way that the cognitive-behavioral synthesis had developed since Tolman's time. Among the Skinnerian behaviorists, in fact, there were factional splits, with some even accusing Skinner, the founder, of illicitly allowing species-typical behavior to contaminate a purely reinforcement-based enterprise. Skinner, for his part, replied by saying that he had never denied the role of genetic and neurological substrates in behavior and that species-typical behavior was an old story for those who studied behavior in laboratories. For a time, some of the orthodox Skinnerians devoted effort to simulating "insight" in pigeon chambers to demonstrate that the so-called "mental" acts of animals could be accounted for by complex reinforcement schedules (Epstein, Kirshnit, Lanza, & Rubin, 1984). But in the 1970s, parsimony of explanation was not in fashion. Undergraduates were more often attracted to films of ducklings imprinting on Konrad Lorenz, who,

Konrad Lorenz (1903–1989, Austria) Comparative psychologist and ethologist specializing in the study of species-typical behavior. Corecipient, with Niko Tinbergen and Karl von Frisch, of the 1973 Nobel Prize in Physiology or Medicine.

sufficiently rehabilitated from his wartime past, had, along with other comparative psychologists, a 1970s vogue. Harry Harlow's studies of the role of comfort in motivation (the cloth/wire mother studies of the late '50s), Frank Beach's 1960s accounts of interindividual animal sexuality, and a number of ape language studies all formed an anthropomorphic counterpoint to the operant cage. Those behaviorists that had not already become respected economists (like Herbert Simon) migrated toward social criticism: Barry Schwartz began his analysis of complex social and political behavior in the '70s, and Skinner's turn to explaining culture as a function of differential reinforcement date from this time (Skinner, 1970, 1978). One of the most influential programs of behavioral research in the 1980s and beyond had its origins in the late '60s and early '70s. Richard Solomon's graduate student, Martin Seligman, conducted, between the time of his PhD thesis at the University of Pennsylvania in 1967 and the mid-'70s, the studies that led to the popularly accepted view that "helplessness"—the disinclination to act to relieve unpleasant circumstances—was itself learned. Briefly, he trained dogs to perform an action to avoid shock in a two-chambered box, and then rendered the shock unavoidable through action. Faced with this situation, his dogs, like other organisms had in the past when placed in similar situations intended to induce an experimental form of

Harry Harlow (1905–1981, USA) Psychologist and primatologist who studied motivation and attachment in nonhuman primates. He also mentored Abraham Maslow.

Barry Schwartz (1946–, USA) Psychologist working in a behavioristic tradition who has written widely on the economic and social consequences of human behavior.

Frank Beach (1911–1988, USA) American comparative psychologist who studied sexual behavior across species.

Herbert Simon (1916–2001, USA) Political scientist, economist, and psychologist who pioneered cognitive economic models. He won the Nobel Prize for Economics in 1978.

Richard Solomon (1918–1985, USA) Physiological psychologist whose shock-avoidance paradigm was adopted by Martin Seligman in his studies of learned helplessness.

neurosis, became passive recipients of the punishment. Studies of the effects of punishment had been undertaken for a long time in psychology and tended to show that punishment was usually ignored, avoided, or attacked. Seligman's conclusions that punishment might have lasting and even fatal emotional effects (Seligman, 1975) injected a note of hopelessness into the otherwise optimistic behavior modification literature.

In the social and personality sphere, by far the most remembered study of the period is that of Philip Zimbardo (1933–), who, though he had been active and largely unremarked for some years before, achieved worldwide notice with his Stanford Prison Study carried out in 1971 (Haney, Banks, & Zimbardo, 1973). This study, a staple of introductory psychology still today, involved setting up two equivalent groups of pathology-free undergraduate male students, one of which would be assigned prisoner roles while the other would take on the roles of guards. As far as possible, in keeping with the ethos of field research in social psychology, which was still active at the time, conditions were structured to provide convincing physical simulations of the booking, jail, and prison counseling situations. Student prisoners, after being collected in real police cars by the Palo Alto police, were stripped and assigned numbers and demeaning clothing. Student guards received mirrored sunglasses, khaki uniforms, and badges. The outcome is well known: Zimbardo and his associates had to terminate the 2-week experiment after 6 days because the interactions became more actual rather than simulated prison events. This study added to the perception engendered over the preceding 2 decades by social psychology that, similar to the obedience forces unleashed by Milgram, there were tendencies toward cruelty inherent in individuals that were only kept at bay by inhibitive forces. That this implicitly reinforced a Freudian view may have been a reason that Freudian psychology kept its vigor through this otherwise cognitive, behavioral, and largely consciousness-focused time. The Zimbardo study is an example of some of the ways in which psychological research intersects with public policy and the tides of history. It was ironic that immediately after the study concluded, a prison riot took place at Attica State Penitentiary in New York, which was nationally televised as it was brutally repressed. Within a few years, the War on Drugs and punitive long-term sentencing for drug offenses, which impacted Blacks and other ethnic minorities disproportionately, began to result in increases in prison populations, which led to the explosion of prison construction and the incarceration industry that characterized America in the 1990s and beyond. The closure of mental hospitals further exacerbated the trend toward mass imprisonment by making the prison the ultimate destination for schizophrenics and other mentally ill individuals who escaped the porous community network of mental health care. One further consequence of the prison buildup was the creation of more job opportunities for psychologists, especially in states where psychologists and psychiatrists had formed adequate working relationships, such as California. No division of correctional psychology formed in the APA; however, the membership of Division 18, Psychologists in Public Service, increased to accommodate a wider range of incarceration options (Baker, 1996). The interpretation of the Zimbardo study as a depiction of the inevitable cruelties of prison life did very little, if anything, to stem the rising tide of incarceration.

Further in applied psychology, new federal laws provided opportunities for expansion: the creation of the Occupational Safety and Health Administration in 1970 and the passage of the first Federal Clean Air Act in 1970, as well as PL 94-142 in 1975, mandating equality in accommodations for all learners, which led to many new job opportunities for persons with psychological backgrounds: compliance specialist, environmental designer, and special educator. Psychologists had been involved in education from the very beginning, and P.L. 94-142 further increased the focus on psychological services demanded in education since the 1965 Education Act was passed. Special education and compensatory early education intersected with a controversy that emerged in psychology in the early to mid-1970s and continues, with variations, today. That controversy started with the publication of an article in the *Harvard Educational Review* in 1969 by Arthur Jensen, an educational and psychometric specialist at the University of California, Berkeley, titled "How Much Can We Boost IQ and Scholastic Attainment?" (Jensen, 1969). Briefly, Jensen collated the available data, including the early data on Head Start, a federally mandated early education program intended to counteract the effects of poverty and discrimination on the educational opportunities and attainments of the poor. He reported indifferent to negative results for such programs, but it was his incidental mention that the persistent differences in educational attainment observed might be due to underlying genetic factors that set off, in the context of the post-Civil Rights Era in psychology, overtly hostile criticism, some of which was directed at Jensen himself. (He was, for example, burned in effigy on some campuses.)

Arthur Jensen (1923–2012, USA) Educational psychologist at Berkeley who was a significant contributor to the study of intelligence, especially in connection with the question of how it might be inherited.

This event linked back to a long tradition of ambiguity about race and intelligence in the United States, which had its roots in early compensatory education and connects to the foundations of applied psychology in the United States, its testing function. The original Binet–Simon tests were designed to support French programs at the turn of the 20th century and were intended to provide support for intellectually challenged learners in an inclusive educational program. The tests, when they crossed the Atlantic and were translated physically into English and metaphorically into American culture, partly served their original purpose of identifying students for whom either remedial, or in fewer cases, like Rosa's in the 1920s, augmented educational intervention was appropriate. However, they also quickly became taken up by individuals in psychology with vested interests in excluding immigrants, and also among those who were overtly racist. In 1976, Robert V. Guthrie's (1930–2005) book *Even the Rat Was White* (Guthrie, 1976/2003) detailed the depth of animosity toward Blacks and other minorities emanated from psychology as it made its way into American society in the early 20th century, a history that had lain entirely hidden until that time.

White psychologists and biologists of the 1920s and 1930s with a commitment to racial theories and underlying convictions about the inferiority of races other than their own quickly turned IQ and other test results that showed differential performance or achievement between groups into absolute statements of essential racial differences. It was only with difficulty that these theories were countered, but by the end of the 1930s a substantial literature had grown up to show that much of the difference that was observed was due to environmental influences. Among those who were involved in the effort to counteract the overtly racist or, if not intentionally so, conceptually hereditarian interpretations of IQ, and the resultant failure of education, compensatory or otherwise, to modify these differences, were the psychologists who were also active in other areas of cross-racial studies and who contributed to the social science evidence that repealed segregation in education. But after the 1954 *Brown* decision, there were still psychologists who held at least some version of an unchangeable cross-racial intellectual difference hypothesis.

Henry Garrett (1894–1973, USA) Author of a popular book on experimentation in psychology, Great Experiments in Psychology *(1930), and president of APA in 1946.*

Very few, like Henry Garrett of Virginia, ex-president (in 1946) of the APA, were vociferous and unrepentant racists who admitted the fact. Others, however, based either on covert social attitudes or on their neutral stance toward reported scientific data, were distressed that the immediate response to Jensen was not a scientific dialogue of facts but instead a caustic war of accusatory words. In July 1972, the *American Psychologist* contained a letter signed by 50 individuals deploring the "physical dangers into which scientists had been put" by the protests against Jensen, and underlining the signers' commitment to the possibility that genetic explanations of differential performance were not only statistically reliable but reflected underlying physical differences as well (Page, 1972). The signers included the Nobel laureates F. H. C. Crick (one of the codiscoverers of DNA in 1953) and Jacques Monod (the leading microbiologist of the time); and also Paul Meehl, the clinician–philosopher so often encountered so far in this narrative. Acrimony over this issue developed among psychologists at the time, and opponents of hereditarian views marshaled evidence for interactions between environment and genetics as well as counterfactual evidence for group achievement. Some also damned the other side for its insensitivity to moral and ethical issues, which, in their collective view, were not separable from practicing social science (Kamin, 1974). This explosive issue, which resonated far outside of the parties immediately involved in the controversy, was a large fissure in what had been to this time an at least superficially cohesive coalition.

In 1973, two eminent psychologists addressed the APA at its convention in Montreal. Leona Tyler (1906–1993), who had been active in the field of testing and applied vocational guidance for over 30 years, and whose roots in psychology went back to her undergraduate studies in 1925, delivered her Presidential Address, while D. O. Hebb, whose cell assembly theory and its associated "conceptual neurology" set the direction of neuropsychological research since he proposed it 25 years before, both delivered calls intended to direct and inspire psychologists. Tyler (1973) addressed the potential of creating a "hopeful" psychology that would, in her words, "increase our individual and collective understanding of our own nature, and to join with others in building a structure of human relationships richer than any the world has heretofore known" (Tyler, 1973, p. 1029). The context for her remarks was the recent publication of B. F. Skinner's widely circulated book in 1971, *Beyond Freedom and Dignity*. In it, Skinner advanced the view that stable and good cultures were not the result of the sum of individual unconstrained choices, which could only result in chaos or unpredictable foci of behavior, but rather resulted by design. Sources of reinforcement, properly arranged, rather than illusory autonomous inner selves, determine the course of behavior. Cultures that wanted better music, for instance, should reinforce not only those who create it but those who participate in playing it and listening to it. Skinner saw cultures that emphasized freedom, another name for escape from aversive control, over rational systems of control, as ultimately in danger of destruction from mismanaged systems of reinforcement. He was no friend of lotteries, which disconnected reinforcements from behavior (coincidentally or not, multiple state lotteries began operating in 1971 and 1972). Nor did his emphasis on the necessity of aversive control play well in feel-good America. And in suggesting that, perhaps, humans have too many choices, and make too many poor ones because of this, he put himself at odds with the rapacious consumerism that had come to define modern America.

Skinner's implication that the ideal economy would be planned went counter to all aspects of American culture as it had been shaped to that time. Skinner was damned as a fascist, or worse, and for a time one of the permanent unanswerable questions of psychology came into sharp and public focus: How free are we, and how free should we be? Tyler, in the tradition of William James, who argued that even if free will were an illusion, only a belief, it was still a useful one, exhorted psychologists to freely choose several things that also went against the developed psychological and social culture. Psychologists, she said, should design their research in collaboration with those that will participate in and benefit from it. In saying this she alluded to recent changes in the APA Ethics Code following on the Milgram and Zimbardo studies, which mandated much heavier scrutiny of research by ethics panels. Clinical psychologists should abandon what had become a common phrase in psychology, the "medical model," where psychologists intervened to restore troubled individuals back to a standard of normality. They should instead, she suggested, facilitate recovery by meeting individuals where they are in their lives, and take their cue from healers within culture—persons, for example, who helped alcoholics from a base of their own experiences in overcoming the addiction. Psychologists, she said, should be actively searching for opportunities to collaborate with individuals at all levels of society to improve social conditions. This echoed Miller's 1969 challenge to "give psychology away" and outlined at least the landscape of potential interventions for psychologists who choose with hope for a better society in mind.

Hebb (1974), by contrast, agreed with Skinner that human behavior was determinate: small a fact, he said, that had been acknowledged by everyone important in psychology to that date, including "Mr. Psychology" E. G. Boring and William James. "I may choose to goof off," said Hebb, "but that's not indeterminism." In his remarks, Hebb chose a term redolent of both Gestalt and systems thinking about psychology. Psychology, he said, was biopsychosocial, an interconnected network of scientific relationships determining behavior, and he made a plea that all psychologists—"the rat brain plumber" as well as the social activist and the cognitive specialist—recognize the fundamental unity of their endeavor. But, asked Hebb, what is the purpose of psychology? Returning to a much older position than the modern one, which states that psychology is the science of mind and behavior, Hebb said that psychology is ultimately about the mind.

The oldest conceptualizations of psychology are tripartite, and Ernest Hilgard, one of the architects of the coalition from 1945, summed them up in 1980 as the "trilogy of mind": cognition, affection, and conation (Hilgard, 1980). Both "cognitive" and "behavioral" (a more streamlined, modern conception of "conation") had become equally acceptable adjectives to describe psychological activities. Yet the third term, "affection," was, as emotion-related terminology always is, still unsettled in the 1970s. Affection refers to an emotional dimension: Which emotion-provoking aspect of life would psychology choose in the newest iteration of its old trilogy? The combination of these ideas from 1974—social action for the common good, the determinate nature of behavior, and the preeminence of mind—set a conceptual problem for psychology. Practically speaking, it would be solved by selecting a direction to follow that incorporated all the major dimensions of psychological activity that had developed over the past 50 years. Solving the equation of mind plus medicine plus the public good resulted in a strengthening of the alliance with medicine. Visible evidence for this was the formation, in 1978, of Division 38, Health Psychology. Psychology revised its trilogy to read cognition, behavior, and health, which brought centrifugal forces into the coalition's official body, the APA, to a peak over the next decade.

THE FAMILY STORY 1970s: AN END, THE MIDDLE, AND A BEGINNING

Long lines of cars streamed up Interstate 95 in North Carolina with their headlights on in the early afternoon of October 15, 1969 (unusual, because daytime headlight use was not automatic as it is on many cars now.) Their drivers had turned on their lights to support a nationwide protest against the Vietnam War, the Moratorium, but the war still had several years to go, although the role of ground troops was winding down and the activity was shifting to air bombardment. Harry would remember that date not because of the Moratorium, but because that was the day that he had to sign the first involuntary commitment order for Donald to get him into emergency mental health treatment in Charlotte. This was relatively easy to accomplish then, but within 3 years the U.S. Supreme Court took up the issue of whether committed mental patients' rights to due process were violated under existing commitment laws, North Carolina's included. Later, in 1975, it became even harder, after *O'Connor v. Donaldson*, to get a commitment order (Vrana, 1991).

Harry was not unfamiliar with postcombat reactions such as those of his son, who had returned to the United States from his second tour in Vietnam in June 1969. He returned with drug and alcohol addictions and a set of persistent behavioral and emotional symptoms that we now recognize and diagnose via the *Diagnostic and Statistical Manual of Mental Disorders*, 5th edition (*DSM-5*), as posttraumatic stress disorder. Then, though, there was no *DSM* diagnosis for the condition, although there was a *DSM-II*. Vietnam was hardly the popularly accepted and well-supported war that was Harry's war, and Harry never wanted to talk about his experiences in that one. Some said that the Vietnam veterans were more likely to suffer a reaction to their experience because of the lack of support at home, or the realization that they were coming back to a place that never noticed that they had left. Harry knew that what Donald was experiencing was not unusual for anyone who had experienced combat, and Donald had experienced a lot.

Fifteen or 20 years before, when Harry was just starting in practice, commitment might have meant a quite lengthy stay in a state hospital, but it was now the 1970s and mental health care had changed decisively. It was 10 years after the Community Mental Health Act of 1963 was enacted, the most visible evidence of which was the sharp decrease in mental health beds and the closure of facility after facility nationwide. Laws limiting the ability of relatives and law enforcement authorities to detain individuals indefinitely without consent were beginning to appear on the books. North Carolina began to mandate a maximum brief holding period, after which a court order would be necessary for an extension of the time. Donald began to bounce in and out of the VA hospitals, public hospitals, and private hospitals. He oscillated between periods of employment and dereliction.

Harry realized that he was not equipped, professionally or personally, to manage Donald's multiple problems. They had become less and less close as Donald had grown older, and neither Donald nor Harry thought, when both could comprehend each other, that a 35-year-old living under his father's roof was a good idea. Donald's periods on public assistance or in jail became more frequent, and times when he was employed became fewer and fewer. Harry studied what was available in the literature on Vietnam veterans, which was not extensive (Brady & Rapoport, 1973), and searched for substance-abuse treatment. Harry's expertise was in helping otherwise stable individuals to cope with intra- or interpersonal problems from a logical, rational position. Since his divorce and his own experience with therapy, he had adopted more and more the viewpoint of rational emotive behavior therapy, which enabled him to distance himself to an extent from his son's problems. Yet Donald was not rational, nor did he adapt to therapy, nor after several years was he able maintain any economic or social stability. Harry arranged for Donald's two periods in residential alcohol and drug treatment, which had experienced new growth since the 1950s, but each ended quickly: the first because of adverse reactions to an alcohol antagonist drug, which produced unbearable nausea, the second because, after a course of implosion therapy, he became violent to the staff and eloped. By 1980 Donald was homeless, surfacing from time to time in large cities in the South and Southwest. Harry had become inured to the fate of his son and pushed it back into that large reservoir of stoic acceptance of grief that had become a large, mostly unconscious presence in his thinking.

For Rosa, the 1970s brought age that she finally had to acknowledge: she turned 65 in 1974; her partner Francine was already 3 years older. For neither Rosa nor Francine was any medical intervention necessary, as each was reasonably healthy. Both Rosa and Francine were able to take advantage of Social Security and Medicare, programs that were the legacy of the New Deal and the Great Society and reflected that influence of that part of the social sciences that emphasized the common developmental needs of everyone. They also benefited, well into the future, by a program to cap rent increases and control their payments on their apartment in lower Manhattan. Corrosive and rapacious individualism was always a possibility in the United States and it was their good fortune that this aspect of it was blocked in this instance. Rosa took a small pleasure in the payback for the McCarthy years, when President Nixon was threatened with impeachment and resigned from office in 1974. Neither she nor most others in those years foresaw the inexorable political reaction to the Civil Rights Acts and other changes wrought in the 1960s, which would begin in the 1970s and continue remorselessly to the present, needing to be fought at every turn. Rosa had unofficially "come out" in 1969 with the publication of her column on Stonewall, and was in demand as a kind of celebrity writer and speaker at gay liberation events, which during the early '70s were becoming more numerous and visible. Although she and Francine were never discriminated against because of their relationship, and although neither had ever seen their own behavior or their union as pathological in any way, they were gratified when an 81-word statement removed homosexuality from the *DSM-II*'s list of mental disorders (Glass, 2002). This occurred almost concurrently, in January 1973, with the publication of the *Roe v. Wade* decision guaranteeing a right to individual choice in reproductive decisions concerning abortion, a foreshadowing of many future political battles to come. The most important effect of psychology on Rosa's life was, like the effects of many beneficial psychological interventions, unnoticed as such. In 1968, at the height of protests worldwide against war and corporate domination of human affairs, Rosa was invited by a friend to attend, and eventually to join, a liberal religious congregation that allowed her to form friendships with other individuals who shared her pacifist views in a nonpolitical setting. In the early 1970s this congregation hired a director of religious community activities who had recently completed advanced coursework in psychology and had specifically read the growing literature on social engagement and positive attitudes in the elderly, as well as the literature that suggested that younger individuals could form more positive conceptions of aging if they were brought into proximity of older individuals in a shared, mutually satisfying activity (Botwinick, 1970). The director made a plan to engage senior and younger members of the congregation in discussion groups about important social events of the times, and developed a group formation plan that unobtrusively used a "jigsaw" approach to bring together those individuals, regardless of age, who had complementary interests and who were likely to synergistically learn from each other. These groups were quite satisfying to their participants, Rosa among them, and she volunteered for more of these sessions than she had expected. This new access to social contacts, along with her continued supportive relations with Francine and her other friends, helped Rosa transition successfully into retirement, which she officially did in 1976.

Jack Botwinick (1923–2006, USA) Psychologist and psycho-gerontologist; held a joint appointment in psychology and neurology at Washington University in St. Louis.

For Helen, the '70s were quite different from the two decades that preceded them. She was, after she finished her degree work in 1968, perpetually busy and always, it seemed, on the way to somewhere on a freeway in a car. While Juana was growing up, she also was a regular presence in Carolyn's life, but after 1974, with Carolyn well-established in a regular job and Juana nearly 8 years old and involved in school and many other activities, it seemed a good time for Helen to move back to the Los Angeles area. A job had opened up as a coordinator of mental health care promotion in the Los Angeles Public Schools, working as a liaison person between psychiatric and psychological services and guidance and placement programs in the schools to provide timely support for distressed students. Helen's experiences with Carolyn and Juana, whose biculturality Carolyn encouraged, including making sure that Juana had many opportunities to interact in both Spanish and English with many diverse individuals, led her to be promoted to a post in which she would be involved with managing multicultural mental health for the Los Angeles School System. This proved to be a point where developing psychological theory directly impacted her activity, since this was the time at which comprehensive visions of health and resiliency promotion were taking hold in academic circles and percolating outward into practical initiatives. Helen had day-to-day contact with the expanding multicultural population of Los Angeles in a much more intimate way than did most residents, and she was energized by it. She did not notice that she was nearing 60; she felt more fulfilled than she had in years; she saw only challenges and opportunities, shortcomings in service delivery to be remedied, injustices to be corrected, and underrepresented populations to be inducted into the larger community.

For Carolyn, the early part of the decade was a happy, fulfilling time. She was part of the coalition that brought Harvey Milk to the San Francisco Board of Supervisors in 1977, an exciting and uplifting experience. Most of all she enjoyed interacting with her bright, inquisitive daughter Juana. Possibly the greatest direct and positive effect of psychology was Juana's early experience watching *Sesame Street* on television, which she did regularly between the time she was 3 years old until she was in second grade. *Sesame Street* was conceived as a response to less-than-optimal media experiences for children. One of its originators was a psychologist, Lloyd Morrissett, who had studied communications theory in the 1950s

Lloyd Morrisett (1929–, USA) PhD student of Carl Hovland at Yale; student of the effects of mind on performance.

and experimental psychology with Carl Hovland at Yale (Hovland & Morrisett, 1959), and who was intimately acquainted with the power of media and the processes by which communication could be best aimed at its intended recipients. It may have been a small contribution to Juana's environment, but *Sesame Street*'s emphasis on diversity, inclusion, and multilinguality was a steady one that reinforced her mother's and her mother's friends' efforts to build a multicultural environment in which Juana would feel at home. The assassination in 1978 of Harvey Milk by a mentally unbalanced political opponent left both Carolyn, at 35, and Juana, at 13, with feelings of loss and vulnerability.

The 1980s

THE 1980s: THE INCLUSIVE COALITION

In 1981, Ronald Reagan, dubbed by many "The Great Communicator," took the oath of office as President of the United States. In some ways he was a caretaker president; however, when he did act, his actions represented a fundamental shift in electoral politics and the undercurrents that translated popular opinion into public policy. In the period between 1927 and 1969, administrations sympathetic to liberal social policy—Governmental intervention in and regulation of social affairs—were in office for 28 of those 42 years, and the other third of the time the more conservative parties did not try hard to dismantle the structures put in place by their predecessors, at least those that served psychology's purposes. It was during the relatively conservative Eisenhower years that government first stepped in, for example, to enforce desegregation. Between 1970 and 1980, power resided mostly in Congress: President Nixon was hamstrung by scandals. His successor for a brief time, President Ford, as well as the Democratic winner of the 1976 election, Jimmy Carter, a humanitarian though not particularly a social visionary, were both hampered in their efforts by a succession of energy crises and relatively poor economic conditions. Rules, laws, and policies enacted during the 1960s continued under their own power. But Reagan's election was the beginning of a period in which primarily conservative forces held sway over law and policy. Since 1980, Republicans have held the presidency for 20 of 33 years, and their opposition has had to contend and compromise with vastly more conservative Congresses antagonistic to liberal social principles.

Two years before Reagan's inauguration, an Islamic revolution in Iran ousted the autocratic government of Mohammed Reza Shah Pahlavi. There, the politics of oil and the internal politics of national self-determination fastened on religion as a vehicle by which national power could be consolidated. One outcome of the installation of the Islamic Republican government in Iran was the taking of several American citizens hostage, a situation that could not be solved by the American military forces during President Carter's remaining tenure of office. On the day that Reagan took over, the hostages were released. This was exemplary of the way that he was the beneficiary of events, which conferred on him the stature of a problem solver. He survived an assassination attempt during his first 2 months in office, which gave him an aura of invincibility. (His would-be assassin has remained in a mental hospital since that time: As of 2013, at age 57, he was allowed home visits of 10 days' length.) During his presidency, the Soviet Union, weakened by extensive bloodletting in Afghanistan, imploded, eventually taking with it the rest of the "Soviet Bloc" countries in Central Europe. Reagan, on a trip to Europe in 1987, stood by the Berlin Wall and exhorted the new, relatively liberal Russian President Mikhail Gorbachev to tear it down, an event that eventually occurred in November 1989 during the presidency of George H. W. Bush. By the efforts during the previous decade by a master diplomat, Henry Kissinger, to orchestrate alternating peace overtures with threats of nuclear holocaust delivered by U.S. missiles based in Germany, some aspects of the breakup of Communism were no doubt hastened.

The perception of Reagan as successful on the larger front of winning the long-standing Cold War with the Soviet Union hid some of the other dealings of his administration. During the 1980s, volatility remained high in the eastern Mediterranean, where the United States had maintained forces stationed in Lebanon in support of Israel, a U.S. ally continually in conflict with its neighbors. The destruction of U.S. Marine barracks in Lebanon in 1983 by a radical anti-Israeli faction augmented tension in the area, which further increased with continuing hostage-taking there. The Reagan Administration, committed as well to supporting repressive regimes in Central America that were favorable to American economic interests, organized an illegal swap of arms to Iran brokered by Israel—forbidden by a Congressional mandate—for Irani funds that would be channeled to support Nicaraguan allies.

This lengthy précis of American foreign relations may seem unrelated to psychology, but in fact it underscores the degree to which the United States had become enmeshed again in world affairs as a military force. These foreign intrigues served to divert attention from many of the changes, slow and subtle, that happened domestically during the period. One result of Reagan's aggressive stance toward the outside world was a buildup of the U.S. military, which helped, as always, to stoke the sluggish economy of the early 1980s. One of the most significant films of the era was a TV movie that depicted the ways in which a nuclear war between the Soviet Union and the United States would affect people in everyday America, *The Day After*, which aired in November 1983. Graphic and gripping, it is said to have moved Ronald Reagan deeply when he saw it. Yet the film did not result in mass protests about U.S. military activities. Far from that, the U.S. mood shifted toward more trust and less questioning of the President and government, and a sense, vicarious to be sure, of an actual victory of U.S. arms achieved with no cost. This psychic relief allowed fuller concentration on what was the most salient activity fostered by the laissez-faire free-market policies of the Reagan years, individual wealth accumulation.

"Greed is good," pronounced Gordon Gekko, the fictional trader in the 1987 film *Wall Street*, who stood for a cast of real figures in business that were the symbolic representation of a major social shift in America from the ideals of common purpose and shared responsibility for the sick and the poor embodied in the social legislation of the preceding 40 years. Americans in the '80s still celebrated inventors, the most prominent of which at the time were the creators of the personal computer, but the adulation rested mostly on the fact that their inventions made them rich. It was in the 1980s that the business school expanded to the level, in funding and in square footage, of institutes of social and behavioral science; in fact, well beyond them, in terms of attracting students and leverage in universities. The master's of business administration (MBA) began to be the graduate degree of choice, heading to the current 50:1 ratio of MBAs to PhD psychology students (Maital, 2013). The U.S. economy itself changed radically. In 1987, Richard Nixon joined the small ranks of U.S. presidents about whom operas were written, John Adams's *Nixon in China*. President Nixon and his wife visited China officially during the Vietnam War, in 1972. The visit had the effect of driving a wedge between the Soviet Union and China, a major step in the process of negotiating a way out of Vietnam, but even more importantly, it opened for the first time in modern history the whole country of China as a potential economic market, an act comparable to the entry of United States ships under the command of Commodore Perry into Tokyo Bay over a century before. The radical nature of this historic visit became clear after the 1980s, when American economic policy changed from a focus on support of home production, with wages and working conditions negotiated between government, management, and workers' unions, to a policy favoring profit by any means necessary. This marked the beginning of the replacement of the American manufacturing economy with a "service economy." Dangerous, dirty, or even well-compensated, clean, routine factory work, when it was not assigned to the growing corps of artificially intelligent robots that began to populate factories, began to be sent to countries with human populations that would do it for comparatively low wages. This resulted in the gradual closing of historic American industries. Among the first to go were textile and clothing manufacturers in the South, where 40 years before, at the Harwood Manufacturing Company in Marion, Virginia, the Lewinian experiment in democratic work processes took place. On August 31, 1992, after years of tax and economic policies favorable to moving production to lower-cost environments, the Harwood Manufacturing Company finally closed its doors (Barlett & Steele, 1996). Radio and television manufacturing, steel making, and other technical industries were built up in Japan and Western Europe. Favorable exchange policies resulted in large increases in imported electronic goods and even automobiles, historically a foundation of American prosperity. Factories that had been the main support of cities decamped, and vast tracts of U.S. cities became desolate. Jobs that emerged to replace the lost manufacturing industries were in clean, business-suited environments: sales, "management" of all sorts, information systems, and finance and banking, bringing along with it the usual coteries of lawyers. The ideal American worker evolved to be a management professional who could navigate the economic system to her or his best advantage, rather than the historic figures of the farmer (farm employment dropped below 3% in the decade) and the factory worker. In 1981, in response to a strike by unionized air traffic controllers, Ronald Reagan replaced them overnight with replacement controllers and effectively defied the union, signaling the start of a rapid decline in the effectiveness of labor unions. Unions that had previously been essential to the negotiation of educational and health benefits incidentally favorable to psychology were increasingly cut out of the political process. Participation in the real estate market, which vastly increased its presence in American economic life during the 1980s, became aligned with class and race: "White flight" to the suburbs did not slow its pace (Wilson, 1987). The Reagan campaign of 1980 consolidated the conversion of the White southern blocs that had previously voted for Democratic candidates into solid Republican supporters, reorganizing the resistance against racial and cultural equality along party lines, a strategy that eventually divided communities across America based on their degree of resistance—based on religion, culture, or history—to the ideal of an egalitarian America. Predictably, in this new environment, the Equal Rights Amendment, the women's equality amendment that had been ratified by 30 states within a year of its approval in 1972, failed in 1982 because of the resistance to it in all the states of the Confederacy, along with Nevada, Arizona, Utah, and—somewhat surprisingly—Illinois. During the decade, immigration to the United States, which was officially illegal but remarkably well tolerated, rose steadily. The country that had imagined itself as integrated in housing, education, and all other aspects of common life became, by the end of the 1980s, a shiny set of new center-city financial towers ringed with seven-lane expressways that passed over a patchwork of ghettos on their way to the mall and its ring of "big box" stores. In 1988, Wal-Mart opened its first supercenter in Washington, Missouri, a community with a population that was 97% white. Meanwhile, retailers and food stores receded from poor neighborhoods. The "food desert" emerged.

Against this background American psychology sailed on, adaptable and flexible, increasing in numbers of practitioners as well as students. Industrial psychologists developed new skills in counseling those workers cut during downsizing or offshoring. The general state of American intellectual life was well insulated from outside reality. Much attention was given to postmodernism, a collection of theories that intertwined power, gender, sex, and consciousness in an attempt to reconcile Freudian and Marxist ideas mostly with feminism. Some theorists—the most prominent among them was Michel Foucault—went beyond attempts to theoretically deconstruct (loosely: analyze the various subtexts within and behind official reality) patriarchal capitalism and took a more aggressive position regarding the hegemony of state power over the individual's self-expression, and the ultimate sources of the need for confinement and repression of various unwanted elements in society (Foucault, 1977). It was couched in an arcane language that wasn't really necessary. By this time the full documentary reality of the history of the Holocaust was available for anyone who wanted to read it, and the actual process of creating a new set of incarceration structures was well underway for those who could turn their eyes momentarily from the freeway to the new, almost lightweight-appearing prisons surrounded by laser detectors and razor wire that cropped up in Illinois, New York, Ohio, California, and everywhere. Psychologists in public service, as noted in the previous chapter, adapted to this new prison reality by becoming involved in all phases of their operation and design.

Craig Haney, a participant in Zimbardo's 1971 study, became, during the decade, a prison psychologist and ultimately one of the few psychologists at the intersection of theory and appli-

Craig Haney (1947–) Participant in Philip Zimbardo's prison simulation, and now a professor of psychology at University of California Santa Cruz and an advocate for prisoners' rights and against capital punishment.

cation in prison science (Haney & Zimbardo, 1998). Another reflection of the rise of postmodernism in the American Psychological Association (APA) was the inclusion, for the first time, of psychoanalysts as official members of its coalition in Division 39 (a reflection of the gradual decoupling of psychoanalysis from medicine). The APA added a division of clinical neuropsychology, another specialty area where the advances in both cognitive and brain studies translated into an acceptable medical support occupation for psychologists. It added a division of law and psychology, reflecting the long history of psychologists' interest in their abilities to contribute to the judicial system, short of becoming lawyers and judges themselves. In this area also, Paul Meehl had pioneered practice and analysis of the relation between clinical psychology and legal practice. His article, "Law and the Fireside Inductions" (Meehl, 1971), offered a typically mordant comment on the extent to which psychologists' findings could penetrate established legal culture. From the empirical side, cognitive psychologists during the 1970s forged an applied psychology of testimony that called into question one of the basic and unquestioned principles of criminal law: the veracity of eyewitnesses. Psychologists increasingly found employment, during the '80s, advising clients, for a fee, of the best way to present themselves to juries, recommending with indifferent success changes in legal language in the direction of more accessibility and understandability, and offering expert testimony on clients' mental states, as psychiatrists had been doing for at least a century. Psychologists interested in law could also find employment with the APA itself, since it continued to develop, during the decade, into a prominent lobbying and consulting organization with government, offering, on the one hand, amicus curiae opinions on social issues (APA, 2013), and on the other, negotiating with legislative power in Congress for psychology-friendly laws. A division of private practice emerged, reflecting the anxiety about the state of private psychological practice in an era of corporate medicine and increasingly competitive alternative providers of therapy. By the mid-1980s the practicing clinical social worker, nurse practitioner, and pastoral counselor were all well established and competing in the search for yet untreated elements of the population. Further subdivision and specialization of clinical applications continued: A new division of family psychology was formed, and interest was shifted to previously marginal areas of potential treatment. For a time in the mid-1980s, anorexia and bulimia were a focus of public attention, and, tied to a new interest in adolescent psychiatry, led to increases in clinics specifically devoted to problems of this type.

In its search for a unifying paradigm or set of principles, progress has been made in psychology over the years by consolidations or new arrangements of the separate individual productions of new research findings. One such persistent productive consolidation was Tolman's synthesis of behavior and cognition in the 1940s. Another was Hebb's conceptual neurology of the 1950s. The 1980s presented a range of consolidations of this sort, some of which failed to thrive and some of which persisted. In the 1980s, Albert Bandura's *Social Foundations of Thought and Action* (Bandura, 1986) bid to capture the whole spectrum of human behavior via the basic principles of social learning theory: vicarious reinforcement, observational learning, predictive knowledge, enactive learning, incentive motivation, self-regulatory behavior, self-efficacy, and cognitive regulators. Any human's behavior at any point in the life cycle could be described by a combination of these factors, and, by generation of potential paths determined by different degrees of action of each of these factors on prospective behavior, predictions could be generated. Under the last section, "cognitive regulators," were included the laws or moral standards that a human internalized as heuristic or prescriptive guides for behavior. Another consolidation that first appeared in the 1980s was Robert Cialdini's *Influence: The New Psychology of Modern Persuasion*, published in 1984 (Cialdini, 1984). Cialdini, aiming to show how individuals' behavior is shaped by others, organized the evidence from more than 25 years of accumulated social psychological study into a set of principles: similarity, automaticity, social proof, attractiveness and liking, authority, reciprocity, conformity, and contrast. Taken individually, these could be seen as stages in the turn inward among social psychologists to focus on the mind of the individual perceiver of others. However, in Cialdini's presentation, they were overtly intended and marketed as the principles underlying successful influence. (They were very marketed successfully, too, as proved by six further editions of the text over the following 25 years.) Cialdini has a broad readership base: He became better known in the marketing community than in psychology, and his text has been praised by marketing specialists. Hardly anyone has managed to read through all of Bandura. Neither Cialdini nor Bandura offered any specific predictions derived from their assemblages of theories. In fact, Cialdini did not present any articulation between the theories at all. Why Cialdini has survived almost intact from that era is due to several factors. First, it has a specific end goal—the achievement of success in persuasion. Second, in contrast to Bandura, who offered a series of examples of "cognitive regulators" that appeared to be recommendations against genocide, racial prejudice, and antisocial human behavior, Cialdini avoided directive recommendations or projections for use of his multifunctional tool. That the marketers who took it up saw it as immediately useful in a sales and management environment was an unintended but

Robert Cialdini (1945–, USA) Social psychologist and Regents' Professor Emeritus of Psychology and Marketing at Arizona State University.

not unwelcome to them. Finally, Cialdini is simple: one third the length of Bandura and written in a cogent style, replete with accurate and specific examples of the principles in action.

The theoretical models of health psychology that began to emerge about this time share characteristics with both Bandura and Cialdini. Health psychology got its start with environmental psychology, and one of its earliest and most thorough theoretical presentations was presented by Andrew Baum, a leading environmental psychologist, and his colleagues David Krantz and Neil Grundberg under the aegis of the National Institutes of Health and the Uniformed Services University of the Health Sciences, in the *Annual Review of Psychology* in 1985 (Krantz, Grunberg, & Baum, 1985). It was an example of the kind of systems-based modeling that had evolved in psychology over the previous 30 years. Different factors, including beliefs in personal efficacy in adopting health behaviors; expectations based on experience of past behavior; and presence or absence of social support, models, and opportunities to learn from others regarding health behaviors, were combined in an integrative model to predict health outcomes. Models of this sort persist today: For instance, Regan Gurung, a leading health psychologist as well as a leading theorist of teaching, overtly calls his model a "biopsychosocial" one that includes genetics and reinforcement histories, expectations, and social support in the production of healthy behaviors (Gurung, 2013). Health psychology models are similar to Bandura's approach in emphasizing the cognitive and social learning factors that determine behavior direction as well as the effectiveness of models and the value of personal beliefs in control and self-determination of outcome (called "efficacy" by Bandura). They also follow the Cialdini model in having a specific goal, and moreover one that is generally acknowledged as an absolute good, regardless of political or social beliefs. "Health psychology" appears to have emerged as a way of answering the challenge posed in the previous decade to combine responsible and properly prioritized

Andrew Baum (1948–2010, USA)
Prolific generalist environmental
psychologist.

choice with respect for both determinism and the role of the mind. Its inclusion of both behavioral and cognitive elements satisfies the last two elements. Its focus on "health" avoided, at least superficially, inclusion of a specific statement regarding race and class and substituted a safer, less controversial, and possibly more socially inclusive goal. The inclusion, in 2001, of "health" in the APA mission statement, alongside the promotion of human welfare, was the endpoint of a long drift healthward in the coalition.

Much of early health psychology was research based, focused on assisting in epidemiological or community treatment studies or on investigating which methods of managing treatment compliance worked best. Here and there bits and pieces of a general model of biopsychosocial regulation of health behavior were implemented in geronotological environments, by bereavement counselors, or in addiction-related settings. While health psychology did not receive wholesale practical application outside, perhaps, of a few predecessors of the wellness management programs that came to be attached to health insurance plans in the next decade, nevertheless the overt connection of "health" plus "psychology" metaphorically defined psychology as a player in the social arena named "health care." And this has defined the battleground on which most of the struggles of the last few decades have been fought for the definition, purpose, and even the existence of the coalition of theoretical, applied, and psychotherapeutic psychology. During the 1980s, the American health care system expanded and became the focus of corporate mergers and consolidations, and changed from a physician-centered profession to the largest industry in the United States. Constant competition for insurance benefits among clinical psychologists, psychiatrists, and now other types of therapists qualified to receive third-party insurance payments became a focus of discussion among practicing psychotherapists, who were, like physicians everywhere, beginning to feel the effects of the increasing amount of state regulation of practices as well as the pressure of the expanding insurance combines called health maintenance organizations (HMOs) to minimize costs. Previously, in the 1950s and 1960s, when most psychotherapy had a psychodynamic orientation of some sort, psychiatrists and psychologists would see patients regularly over a period of months or even years, usually on a weekly basis. Introduction of cognitive-behavioral therapy for depression as well as focused behavioral therapies for anxiety disorders cut treatment times, a fact not lost on insurance accountants. The continual rise in the use of prescription drugs for treatment of psychiatric problems led to expectations that treatment that would have previously taken a year might be reduced to a few months, with brief maintenance visits afterward to check medications. As MD psychiatrists always had the legal right to prescribe controlled drugs, the lack of prescription privileges became evermore a stigma of subordinate status and major focus of clinicians' concerns. As "wellness" and preventive medicine became publicized as ways to avoid therapy altogether, insurance companies and HMOs found that the few new health psychologists who actually fit the model and were not involved in research settings could play a role in managing wellness and screening programs, shifting some billing away from clinicians. All of this, along with the introduction in 1987 of selective serotonin reuptake inhibitors for depression—Prozac—accelerated movements in the profession, demanding prescription privileges for psychiatrically effective drugs and hospital-admitting privileges for the diminishing number of public and private psychiatric beds, movements that would continue well into the next decade and result in some limited gains in each area. Those clients who could still afford to pay privately did so, and in the late-'80s boom there were clients available. While conservative politicians worked assiduously to reverse other social legislation of the previous 2 decades, funding for health care as well as health-related research remained constant or increased. By and large, psychotherapy was turning, like many professions in an intensely profit-dominated environment, into less of a relationship to be developed between therapist and client and more a struggle for survival on the part of the therapist. The change was gradual and the negative effects were adapted to with time. Meanwhile, the very severely mentally ill continued to be forced into homeless shelters, to the streets, and into jails and prisons. After 1973, forced commitment to a mental health facility was coupled with the necessity for the provision of treatment, and individuals retained the right to have legal representation and contest their detainment. Many were released back into the community to rotate again and again in and out of short-term detainment. In the long run, the only way that a severely schizophrenic person could get any form of long-term care was to commit a crime and then rely on the prison medical systems, which like the mental hospitals of old were always there for anyone in the system. This usually consisted of maintenance on medication and rarely on personal therapeutic contacts (Pfeiffer, 2007).

In the middle of the decade the coalition seemed superficially strong. Divisional membership numbers continued to climb and students continued to flock to psychology courses in universities and community colleges, resulting in regular replacement of retiring faculty and additions to psychology teaching staffs. Textbooks proliferated in introductory psychology, attaining their current form and including the usual accompaniments of study guides, professionally designed instruction manuals, and test banks, some even formatted in the huge floppy disk format for the new personal computers that were popping up on faculty desks. In the theoretical area, consciousness experienced a continuing resurgence of interest. Philosophers such as Thomas Nagel, who had in 1974 authored a provocative essay, "What Is It Like to Be a Bat?" (Nagel, 1974), in which he argued for an irreducibility of subjective experience to objective explanation, agreed with psychologists such as George Miller, who claimed, in a 1985 essay, that the "constitutive problem" of psychology is consciousness. Neuroscience expanded its repertoire of brain imaging, which had seen the beginnings of positron emission tomography (PET) and MRI scans in the mid- to late-1970s, and

Thomas Nagel (1937–, USA) American philosopher of science and of mind.

began to develop far more precise mappings of pathways based on neurotransmitter types than had been available up to that time. In cognitive psychology, it was the decade of the cognitive illusions. Daniel Kahneman and Amos Tversky demonstrated the pervasiveness of human misestimation of risk and misperception of logical relationships, stimulating, among other things, an upsurge of interest in training critical thinking techniques (Tversky & Kahneman, 1986). Donald Norman continued to write entertainingly about human-machine interfaces and their foibles (Norman, 1988). Theoretical models of learning by adaptation of simulated neural networks to changing environmental inputs were offered as a general theory of connectionism, integrating theories of memory, linguistics, and neural integration by McClelland and Rumelhart (1988). Several models for computing optic flow were constructed, and both connectionism and optic flow found immediate practical applications in the design of intelligent systems; for instance, the modules that began to appear in all vehicles at the time that "learned" their functions through experience, and the design and construction of aircraft head-up displays. These ideas were also informed by and found use in the production of computer-based animation. At the APA convention in 1986, participants could choose to attend sessions featuring Jennifer Freyd, a graduate student of Roger Shepard, who took his ideas of mental imagery a step further with elegant demonstrations of "representational momentum," where the presence of mental pathways for projected future motion could be revealed based on the comparison of reaction times to images representing degrees of expected versus unexpected motion-related change

Daniel Kahneman (1934–, Israel–USA) and Amos Tversky (1937–1996, Israel–USA) Psychologists who made seminal contributions to cognitive psychology; identified most often with cognitive biases.

Donald Norman (1935–, USA) Psychologist who has written extensively and entertainingly on issues at the interface of design and cognition.

James McClelland (1948–, USA) and David Rumelhart (1942–2011, USA) Pioneers in the theory of neural networks and "connectionism."

relative to the image's resting position (Freyd & Finke, 1985). They could hear Mihalyi Csikszentmihalyi (1934–), already well respected for earlier work on creativity and on the meaning of mundane existence (Csikszentmihalyi & Rochberg-Halton, 1981), who published *Being Adolescent* with Reed Larson in 1984, summing up the results of experience sampling with adolescents and positing a new concept, "flow," a mental state of concentrated attention driven by absorption in a task, a state relating cognition and emotion in a new way: in his terms, an "optimal" experience (Csikszentmihalyi & Larson, 1984). Or they could attend a special session, announced on a separate card, where Martin Seligman would speak on

Reed Larson (1950–, USA) Collaborator with Mihalyi Csikszentmihalyi on Being Adolescent *in 1984; theorist of positive adolescent development and of the influence of extracurricular and community activities on adolescent development.*

explanatory style and its effects on the persistence of life insurance salespersons, an outgrowth of his earlier work on animal models of learned helplessness and a step toward his formulation of a theory of optimism (Seligman & Schulman, 1986). The focus of his work at that time echoed the work of Edward Kellogg Strong (1994–1963), designer of the Strong Vocational Interest Inventory, who 60 years earlier had also found the selling of life insurance a fascinating study, combining many of the issues that still animated psychology in 1986: persuasion, cognitions, and emotions (Strong, 1922). Research funding was available: Reagan was a pragmatic conservative and was not averse to raising taxes (his revision of the tax code in 1986 would tax graduate stipends for the first time). Although another Senator from Wisconsin, William Proxmire, a Democrat, had sparred a decade earlier with Ellen Berscheid of the University of Minnesota over $84,000 dollars in grant

Ellen Berscheid (1936–, USA) American social psychologist specializing in the study of interpersonal relationships.

money to study love, this was now a cherished anecdote rather than an indication of a pattern of fiscal starvation.

So it was with some surprise that readers of several psychology and science-related publications read that a large number of nonclinical research scientists had withdrawn en masse from the APA 2 days before the beginning of its 1988 convention and had formed their own association, the American Psychological Society (APS), later to become the Association for Psychological Science. Ostensibly the reason was that the scientists had become discouraged by the increase in the amount of attention being given to the interests of clinical practitioners, especially as these related to relations with psychiatry or health insurance corporations. They, and the applied psychologists allied with them in a transitional subset of the APA in 1987, the Association of Scientific and Applied Psychologists negotiated a revised, independent status within the APA, but their proposal was rejected. Like any divorce, there were multiple reasons, not all of which could be articulated. Some of the discontent, it was said at the time, had to do with the relative amount of advocacy for theoretical psychological study versus clinical and practice issues.

At the 1986 APA convention, 44 divisions were represented. The newest was Division 44, the Society for the Psychological Study of Lesbian, Gay, Bisexual, and Transgender Issues. Nothing defined the 1980s as much as AIDS, which first appeared in 1981. By the end of the decade, few people in the United States did not know of someone, or know someone personally, who had succumbed to it. It cut a wide swath across the arts. AIDS took a central theorist of postmodernism, Michel Foucault (1927–1984). It claimed one of the members of my doctoral committee, the historian Donald Wilcox (1938–1991), and eventually the valedictorian of my high school class, Jeffrey Schmalz (1954–1993), at the time Deputy National Editor of the *New York Times*. It was the occasion of a black cover, instead of the then-typical dark blue one, on the special issue of the *American Psychologist* on AIDS, October 1988. AIDS thrust homosexuality into psychological discourse and official recognition by the coalition, something over 30 years of research had failed to do until that time. Another belated recognition was the official vote at the convention in August 1986 that confirmed the existence of Division 45, the Society for the Psychological Study of Ethnic Minority Issues, representing members of Black, Hispanic, Asian, and Native American psychologists. This represented the culmination of 23 years of official petitioning of the Association, which was started in 1963 by a committee of the SPSSI and in 1968 by the Association of Black Psychologists. Only in retrospect can it now be seen how momentous the change was in the 50 years since Gordon Allport addressed a few hundred members, virtually all males of Northern European descent, of the APA at Berkeley in 1939. By 1989, psychology had come to reflect the decades of collective social effort, in which it had a hand, in the inclusion—at least in principle—of people of all sorts, both in society as a whole and the creation of "a psychology of people" (Bronstein & Quina, 1988).

THE FAMILY STORY: SELF-DISCOVERIES

For Harry, Donald's inevitable suicide in 1981 was a turning point. At the age of 70, he was experiencing health problems that had become more insistent. Even though he had essentially no contact with him over the past several years, he still felt that while Donald was alive he had at least one connection to his family and past, but now there were none at all. His isolated immersion in his work wore on him, and he began to lose focus and interest in it for the first time in decades. Realizing this, he closed his practice in 1982. At first he was completely disoriented and could hardly think, but after a time he was able to start to disengage from the harness in which he had been strapped for 32 years and stretch himself. He had always been a reader, from his days in the bookbindery, and while this was not something he talked much about, he revered books. He had accumulated many of the other trappings of a successful professional—modern furniture, audio and video equipment, and a house custom-built in 1961 in a rural suburb—but he was indifferent to them and to other sensory pleasures for many years, except reading. Now, with time stretching out all around him into the lush countryside, he began to reflect on what had happened to him, in his life as a psychologist, because that was what most of his life was, his profession.

Thinking back over his experiences one evening, Harry considered all the ways in which psychology had intersected with his life, how the choice of a profession had shaped him. He remembered his start, and how lucky he was to have gotten a second chance as a youth. He remembered all of the experiences in work and travel that had structured his mind: He remembered the first days of his love with Joan, and the exaltation with which he realized that psychology as it was being worked out in the Harwood factory might become a curative path to fulfillment, for himself, for everyone. He thought back over his career. What had he done in the world? Was it any more than what any dentist or doctor provided, a way to help individuals in pain and crisis, acute and chronic, move beyond the things in their immediate circumstances that were impeding their growth or action? Probably not: Harry was a realist and smiled when he saw that he had, for the most part, sold friendship, a rare commodity, as William Schofield had put it (Schofield, 1964). He read the collection of essays about clinical practice, *Psychodiagnosis*, by the great philosopher of science/clinician from Minnesota, Paul Meehl, and found himself in agreement with all of it—he saw what he did in his career as not too much more than following recipes in a cookbook (Meehl, 1956), but he had used good cookbooks, and had done competent work and had called things as they realistically were. Of all the things that he learned to do as a clinician, he felt that he had succeeded best at helping clients understand death, their own and others'. Harry, from the start, knew that life was bounded on all sides by death, that death crouched everywhere, always familiar. It was from Freud, from the *Ego and the Id*, that he learned, and knew in his heart that the goal of all life is death,

William Schofield (1925–2006, USA) Psychotherapist and professor of clinical psychology at the University of Minnesota for 40 years.

and that the great task was to endure in the face of it. He thought of his son, and his unreachable and incurable pain, realizing though that this was fate, and that he had caused part of it, while other parts of it were far beyond his ability to predict or control. He thought about the world from which he was now detaching. Was it a good world? Yes. It had been challenged by human evil at Auschwitz, at My Lai, at Siem Reap; it had been blasted by nuclear weapons at Hiroshima, Nagasaki, and the Nevada and Siberian deserts; he had lived to see human compassion and the ideal of equality embodied in laws, and those laws continually attacked by the forces of hate and punishment—the way of the world, as far as humans could now see and understand it. And yet the world's population was more than twice what it was when he was born, an unimaginable number of lives, most of which were striving for and achieving some kind of completeness, wholeness, realization. He had done his part to help that. He remembered his favorite poems: William Butler Yeats' *Under Ben Bulben*; Rilke's *Idiot's Song*, and its refrain—How good. At the end of his reflections he looked up. A thunderstorm had passed, and the world around him was suffused with golden light. How beautiful the world had been! How beautiful it was, and how beautiful it would continue to be. Harry was content. He wrote down his reflections as an essay about clinical life, which ultimately came to Helen after Harry died and his possessions were dispersed. Then things moved quickly. His health declined rapidly and he sold his house: Fortunately, by 1983, social and psychological gerontology had advanced to make milieu communities for assisted living possible, and Harry moved into one, releasing himself from his long solitude, making friends (even one very close one with a widowed teacher), and dying peacefully in May 1986.

For a brief time in the 1980s, along with her work in the Los Angeles schools, Helen was an appointed consultant to the task force convened in California to foster self-esteem in the state (California Task Force, 1990). On the face of it, this seems like a Utopian and unrealizable idea, maybe due to our current cynicisms. That such a project of perceptual modification could be imagined, and planned for, speaks strongly in favor of the idea that by 1980 psychology and its allied fields were considered to be significant contributors to discussions of public policy. That had of course been the case for a long time in education and judicial areas, as the story so far shows. But what was new about the California self-esteem initiative is that it was intended to raise consciousness, stimulate emotions, and activate thoughts and behavior across a whole population: a specifically psychological intervention on a large scale. The roots of self-esteem stretched back to the beginnings of psychology at the turn of the 20th century: Many early psychologists starting with William James took the self as the centerpiece of psychology, and the development of widely used self-esteem scales in the 1950s and 1960s added credibility to the concept. Now, in 1980s California, a visionary state senator, John Vasconcellos, who, he said, found his way out of personal pain and confusion through his discovery of humanistic psychology (Vasconcellos, 2001) and who, after his heart attack earlier in the decade, asked his constituents to project the idea that they were scrubbing his arteries clean (it didn't work, so he switched to modifying his diet and exercise plans), joined an eminent sociologist at Berkeley, Neil Smelser, and Andrew Mecca, former director of the U.S. Army's drug treatment program in Vietnam and soon to be California's state director of alcohol and drug programs, to promote the idea that increasing Californians'

John Vasconcellos (1932–, USA) Visionary politician who represented Silicon Valley in the California legislature for 38 years until his retirement in 2004.

Neil Smelser (1930–, USA) Professor Emeritus of Sociology at the University of California, Berkeley; interdisciplinary sociologist.

Andrew Mecca (1947–, USA) Director of the U.S. Army Medical Corps' Drug Treatment Services during the Vietnam War, head of the California Self-Esteem Commission (1986–1989), and Director of the Department for Alcohol and Drug Programs for the State of California (1991–1998).

overall level of self-esteem would lead to improvements in all areas of society. It might even lead people to be more productive and to pay more taxes (Mecca, Smelser, & Vasconcellos, 1989).

(However, California conservatives had already voted in tax caps by referendum and the gradual nationwide strangulation of public revenues over the next 20 years had begun.)

As Juana grew up, she became intrigued by her own history, and when she was in high school she was able to spend a year in Ecuador as an exchange student sponsored by a U.S. international student exchange program. When she arrived there she felt as if she had lived there before. The wealthy Ecuadorean family with whom she stayed circulated among their relatives and friends in their large city, but even so, Juana could sense the vast difference between being poor and rich in a country that had just undergone an oil boom. She also had the advantage of bilinguality, which allowed her to read everything and speak with everyone. On her return, she entered college in Los Angeles in 1982, at age 17, the result of her being approved to start first grade in 1970 rather than in 1971 based on the observations of the psychologist in her Bay Area school district. Eventually, Juana decided to become a psychologist, so it is interesting to look at some of the experiences that led her to that decision. She had heard about her grandmother's brother, who was a psychologist in North Carolina, but there was no contact or interchange, so she could only imagine what he did—and he was not much on her mind. She entered college with an open mind and took a psychology course during her first semester there. The professor was using the first edition of a textbook (Houston, Bee, Hatfield, & Rimm, 1979) with an instructor's manual, written by Victor Benassi, then just at the beginning of his long career as a trainer of psychology teachers, that was frequently consulted because it was his first time teaching full time. One of the authors of the text, Elaine Hatfield, had been an associate of Ellen

Victor Benassi (1947–, USA) Faculty member and chair (1989–1998) of the University of New Hampshire Psychology Department; awarded the APA Distinguished Teaching of Psychology Award in 2003.

Elaine Hatfield (1937–, USA) Social psychologist (PhD Stanford, 1963) with a primary focus on love, sex, and attraction. Collaborator with her husband Richard Rapson on both scholarly works and novels.

Berscheid and was already well established as an authority on the role of attractiveness in the formation of social relationships and love. Juana found the text and the course interesting enough, but there were many other things that interested her more. Her language and especially her sociology courses led her to think more deeply about her cultural background. In 1985, in the spring of her junior year, she got a recommendation from her advisor in Sociology for a course to be offered in the fall. The instructor was an associate of the psychologists who, 6 years earlier, had founded the *Hispanic Journal of Behavioral Sciences* (Padilla, 2003). It was during that course that Juana had the experience that connected everything that she had been thinking for the past few years. The instructor had visited his colleagues in Central America and had come back with a copy of a paper written and delivered at a mental health conference in El Salvador by Ignacio Martín-Baró. Born in 1942 to a conservative Spanish family, he became a Jesuit priest and was posted to El Salvador, where he realized his mission to speak for the poor and oppressed (Portillo, 2012). He received a PhD in psychology from the University of Chicago in the 1970s, but it was in El Salvador that he stayed and wrote. The paper that her instructor gave her to read, titled *War and Mental Health*, was written in the midst of a civil war: on one side were the poor peasants and laborers whose lot in life Martín-Baró and his colleagues were working to better; on the other were the forces of counterrevolution, heavily supported by the United States. Atrocities happened daily: Terror suffused the country. The paper was in Spanish: Here can be found an English translation by Anne Wallace from the first collected English edition of Martín-Baro's writings (Martín-Baró, 1984/1994, p. 120). It was those words, Juana would say later, that made her realize what she would do with her life and her privileges.

It was against this background that Juana and her grandmother Helen had a conversation in the summer of 1988. Juana had started her graduate studies in an interdisciplinary program in South American Studies, a hybrid program that spanned psychology, cultural anthropology, and public policy, as she was interested in the question of cultural integration and especially in

immigration. Her mother's and grandmother's experiences in deal-
ing with the changing cultural mix in California and her own fas-
cination with her own multicultural essence had already led her to
take part, since beginning her graduate studies in 1986, in several
long-term residencies and internships in Ecuador and in Mexico.

Juana's conversation with her grandmother made a strong
impression on her and she noted it in her journal, which she was
keeping for a cultural psychology course:

*August 23, 1988: I talked with my grandmother today. She was exas-
perated with the meetings of the Self-Esteem Task Force. (I guess she
had to be part of it due to her position in the schools.) She can't understand why anyone would need to increase self-esteem in Californians—
they are already at the top of the cultural heap! She says that anyone
who thinks that making a person feel good will make them act is crazy.
I have to agree: It's like William James said—people feel good after they
act, not before. It's what they do that changes their mood. What we've
been reading about in this course fits in with that. Martín-Baró says
that people will only be psychologically well after they have conquered
injustice, and to do that takes education and action. Paolo Friere says
that the oppressed have to become conscious and then take action. Consciousness isn't feeling! Or at least, not feeling good about yourself.*

It's like with Angie [Angie was Juana's friend who had con-
tracted AIDS the previous year from unprotected sex with an
HIV-positive bisexual man]—*when that dentist wouldn't give her
the free treatment she was entitled to because of her disability, her therapist told her to march down there with a couple of other HIV positives
and raise hell in the office. What were they going to do, arrest AIDS
sufferers? Although they didn't seem like sufferers that day, and Angie
said it made her feel real[ly] good to do it…. I know that I have never
had a problem with not feeling good. I've never had to notice whether
I'm good or not. What I need to do is to understand others not feeling
good and find out why. Are they depressed? Is it because of their environment, because of the injustice and barriers in their way?*

*August 27: When my grandmother says that her biggest challenge is get-
ting people to understand that mental health interventions are necessary,*

I believe her. You can't just paint problems with self-esteem and make them go away. You can't come into the community with a solution and force it on people. People have to want it themselves; you have to make them understand that they will be better off with it. I can't believe the state of California thinks that doing self-esteem seminars is going to change our lives.

The 1990s and Beyond

THE PSYCHOLOGICAL COALITION IN THE 1990s AND BEYOND: FRACTURED, OR RESILIENT?

1996. A typical year, in a relatively calm decade. It was a year since the relief of the destructive 3-year siege of the host city of the 1984 Olympic Winter Games, Sarajevo, Bosnia; a year since the bombing of the Federal Building in Oklahoma City by Timothy McVeigh, killing 218; 3 years since the bombing of the World Trade Center in New York City; six were killed. On July 17, a Boeing 747, TWA Flight 800, exploded 28 minutes after takeoff over Center Moriches, Long Island, New York, killing 230. Some said it was destroyed by an American missile, and others said it was a terrorist attack (they remembered the spectacular bombing by Libyan extremists of a Pan Am 747 over Lockerbie, Scotland, in 1988), though it would eventually be shown to have resulted

185

from a spark in one of the fuel tanks. It was another Olympic year in the United States: During the event, on July 27, a bomb loaded with shrapnel would explode in Centennial Park in Atlanta, killing one. Atlanta police promptly pursued and publicly humiliated an innocent suspect.

In psychology, it was a prosperous year. It was 6 years since President George H. W. Bush signed a proclamation designating the 1990s as "The Decade of the Brain," and 4 years before the American Psychological Association (APA) would pronounce the succeeding decade "The Decade of Behavior." APA membership also reached its all-time high water mark. There were now 51 APA divisions represented at the Toronto convention August 9 to 13: the newest, Men and Masculinity. Since 1990, Peace Psychology (Division 48), Group Psychology and Group Psychotherapy (49), and Society of Addiction Psychology (50) had also been added. Although the North American Free Trade Agreement (NAFTA) was in force for 2 years, although the rate of immigration had not slowed, nor had the flow of manufacturing jobs to Central America and Asia, the APA still did not officially have an international division (it would appear within 2 years). Dorothy Cantor, PsyD from Rutgers University, 1976, was President of the APA. One of her presidential initiatives was aimed at establishing ground rules for access to psychotherapy in the face of restrictions aimed at it by health insurers. Another was her APA presidential miniconvention, "A Tale of New Cities: Psychology's Response to Urban America," including sessions on "Urban Children: Great Expectations or Limited Opportunities," "Psychology's Many Promises to Urban Schools," "The Changing Face of Work in Urban America," "Our Urban Neighborhoods and Our Mental Health," and "Building New Cities: Psychology's Blueprint for the Future." This coincided with the publication, also in 1996, of *The New Urban Frontier: Gentrification and the Revanchist City* by Neil

Neil Smith (1954–2012, Scotland–USA) Anthropologist and geographer; theorist of urban gentrification.

Smith, outlining the process by which inner-city neighborhoods were being recolonized by returnees from the suburbs, with little provision for those that would be displaced in the process.

The Human Genome Project was about halfway through the process of mapping the entire human genome. Within 15 years it would be common to refer to epigenetics, the influence of environment on the expression of genes—a real revolution in biobehavioral science. In February 1996, Ulric Neisser reported as chairperson on the results of the task force convened by the Board of Scientific Affairs of the APA in response to the 1994 publication of *The Bell Curve* by Richard Herrnstein and Charles Murray, a resurfacing of the long-standing debate about inequality determined by genetics (Neisser et al., 1996). This had, among other things, resulted in another signed letter, this time published in the *Wall Street Journal*, asserting the immutability of racial differences based on intelligence test scores (Gottfredson, 1997). A few of the signers had also signed the 1972 *American Psychologist* response. At its conclusion, Neisser and the committee wrote regarding the problem of differential scores between cultural groups on intelligence tests:

Richard Herrnstein (1930–1994, USA) American operant behaviorist.

Charles Murray (1943–, USA) Political scientist and libertarian social critic.

> In a field where so many issues are unresolved and so many questions unanswered, the confident tone that has characterized most of the debate on these topics is clearly out of place. The study of intelligence does not need politicized assertions and recriminations; it needs self-restraint, reflection, and a great deal more research. The questions that remain are socially as well as scientifically important. There is no reason to think them unanswerable, but finding the answers will require a shared and sustained effort as well as the commitment of substantial scientific resources. Just such a commitment is what we strongly recommend. (Neisser et al., 1996, p. 97)

J. P. Rushton (1943–2012) of Queen's University in Canada, long a strident proponent of the assertion of determinate and irreversible racial differences in intelligence, responded along with many others to the task force's report, and Neisser, responding to him in the letters section of the *American Psychologist* in January 1997, said,

I do not have the space or the stomach to reply to all the points raised by Rushton. His claim that the task force "sidestepped" many important pieces of evidence reflects his own evaluation of that evidence, which is by no means the only possible assessment.... It also reflects his own very peculiar perspective: for some reason, Rushton believes that ranking racial groups on various criteria is a matter of utmost importance. Happily, most of us do not share that priority. (Neisser, 1997, p. 81)

The Big 5 Personality Theory began to gather wide recognition and use at about this time. Dov Cohen of the University of Illinois and Richard Nisbett of the University of Michigan published their book on the Southern culture of honor (Nisbett & Cohen, 1996). They and their colleagues, Brian Bowdle of Northwestern University and Norbert Schwarz of the University of Michigan, followed this with an experimental demonstration of the difference in aggression exhibited by members of cultures of honor (Cohen, Nisbett, Bowdle, & Schwarz, 1996), reminiscent of the findings of Brady and Rapoport on the differences in perceptions of violence between civilians and combat veterans during the Vietnam War.

Dov Cohen (ca. 1950–, USA)
Sociocultural psychologist at the University of Illinois.

Richard Nisbett (1941–, USA)
Social psychologist with wide interests in cognition, decision and inference processes, and ethnography.

Tom Pyszczynski and colleagues were building Terror Management Theory. This theory, derived from the work of the psychologist Ernest Becker, centers around the idea that life is shaped by the consciousness of and reactions to and especially against death. A central idea of Becker's (expressed in a widely read and Pulitzer Prize-winning book, *The Denial of Death*, published in 1973) is that humans, confronted with death, adopt an irrational, illusion-grounded

Tom Pyszczynski (1954–, USA)
Social psychologist and developer, with colleagues, of experimental existential psychology.

Ernest Becker (1924–1974, USA)
Cultural anthropologist best known for his 1973 book The Denial of Death.

attitude that allows them to proceed in life as if they were invulnerable. In this, Becker followed his mentor, the psychiatrist Thomas Szasz (1920–2012), a radical critic of much of psychotherapy and indeed of the whole concept of mental health. Studies utilizing theoretical terms from Terror Management Theory began to

Thomas Szasz (1920–2012, Hungary–USA) Psychiatrist and critic best known for his contention that mental illness is largely a myth.

appear, suggesting that the closeness of death, or even the heightened thought or image of death (called mortality salience), could lead to irrational conformity, stereotype formation, dissociation, and increases in authoritarian attitudes toward self, others, and society. Along with this, mortality salience was shown to lead to increases in the ability to positively defend the self against existential threats and also led to increased consciousness of meaningfulness in life. Otherwise, the scholarly output of the coalition was very much in line with what would be recognized as concerns today. A Saturday afternoon (4:00–4:50 PM) sampling of posters, symposia, and addresses at the Toronto convention that year included Choichiro Yatani from SUNY College of Technology at Alfred, speaking on "Anti-Immigration Movements in the 1990s: A New Perspective on the Post Cold War"; Robert Spitzer, MD, from the New York State Psychiatric Institute speaking on "History and Philosophy of the *DSM*"; Alan I. Leshner from the National Institute on Drug Abuse, speaking on "Behavioral Science and Drug Abuse: A Half Century of Productive Partnership"; a poster presentation by Loraine Alderman, June Chisholm, and Florence Denmark of Pace University, "Psychological Experience of Miscarriage on Women and Their Families"; a symposium, "Privatizing Medicaid—Opportunities for Psychologists"; the Presidential Address for Division 5, Evaluation, Measurement, and Statistics, by Mark L. Davison from the University of Minnesota, "Multidimensional Scaling Interest and Aptitude Profiles: Idiographic Dimensions, Nomothetic Factors"; the address for the Leona Tyler Award for Division 17, Counseling Psychology (no speaker listed); and the Business Meeting and 10th Anniversary Celebration for Division 47, Sport and Exercise Psychology.

Mihalyi Csikszentmihalyi, now one of the best-known American psychologists after the publication of his book *Flow* in 1990, wondered in 1999, "Why is it that the crew on the flagship of capitalist affluence is becoming increasingly addicted to drugs for falling asleep, for waking up, for staying slim, for escaping boredom and depression? Why are suicides and loneliness such a problem in Sweden, which has applied the best of socialist principles to provide material security to its people?" (Csikszentmihalyi, 1999, p. 822). His question reflected the mid-'90s vogue for searching for the roots of happiness, another recurrence of the pleasure- and emotion-saturated psychologies of the late 1920s. One of the leading introductory textbook authors of the time, David Myers, was also the author of *The Pursuit of Happiness* (Myers, 1993) and, like Csikszentmihalyi and others, including the prolific Ed Diener, was assembling evidence to link the variables of social stability, family cohesiveness, religious faith, or passionate intellectual engagement to real, as opposed to artificial, happiness. The movement toward discovering the roots of the good life culminated, for the psychological coalition, in 1998 with the coinage of the term "positive psychology" by Martin Seligman and Csikszentmihalyi (Azar, 2011), a term that introductory textbook authors scrambled to add to their texts, now on a standard 3-year, and sometimes 2-year, revision cycle.

Arthur Reber (1940–, USA)
Specialist in implicit learning and consciousness; expert on all aspects of gambling.

In 1996, Arthur Reber, author of a well-regarded *Dictionary of Psychology* in 1986 and also several studies on implicit, unconscious cognitive processing, published *The New Gambler's Bible: How to Beat the Casinos, the Track, Your Bookie and Your Buddies* (Reber, 1996). On May 31, 1996, Timothy Leary, who said that you are only as young as the last time you changed your mind, died of pancreatic cancer. Two years earlier he had been welcomed back into the coalition's fold at a session on interpersonal personality theory at the 1994 APA meeting. He considered cryogenic preservation, but left specific instructions not to be brought back during a Republican administration. The next year, his cremains were shot into space.

I joined the coalition in March 2000 at age 46 because I thought that, since I was now tenured at my college, my students needed me to be connected to a large professional organization that could support their undergraduate psychology program with curricular direction and advice. Why I didn't join the American Psychological Society (soon to become the Association for Psychological Science) was dictated more by the idea of balancing out professional membership across our small faculty. My colleague, the other half of our permanent staff, was (and still is) an APS member as well as in the APA. Probably at some unconscious decision level I decided to go with the larger organization to balance out our rate of participation. Then, too, I have an affinity for all those things that are present in the coalition and not in a group of homogeneous psychological scientists: I like therapy, and I have wide cultural and literary interests that are represented in APA by divisions such as Aesthetics, Theoretical Psychology, and the Psychology of Religion.

At the time, the big issues in psychology were positive psychology and evidence-based therapy. Positive psychology, apparently a renascence of the Maslow "b" needs and behaviors from the '60s, promised at least an opportunity to focus study on some important and neglected aspects of human life such as courage, zest, spirituality, kindness, and active citizenship (some of the "character strengths" associated with the positive psychology movement). Evidence-based therapy seemed to be a further stage in the incursion of cost management into health care. The U.S. private health care system as well as the large public health administration systems of Medicare and Medicaid—more survivals from the '60s—were coming still more under the control of economic algorithms and profit-making (sometimes euphemistically recast as cost-restraining) strategies managed by economists and business specialists. The United States inaugurated its first MBA President in 2001, setting the tone for the next several years of economic instability. Regarding managed care and evidence-based therapy, I gave those little thought at the time, as I am about as far from caring about economic issues as any general psychologist and I am not subject to licensure, but when I was working on a biography of Paul Meehl a few years later I smiled to think that he had predicted that eventually people would come around to the idea that the prediction based on tests was in virtually all cases superior to the predictions of mere humans; prediction that had also been shown in 40 years of cognitive and social psychological research to be riddled with biases, internally generated and interpersonally influenced. Now I smile even more to think that the evidence, when it is in, will show what the data have shown for 80 years: that all therapy works; that it all works about equally well on average; that it has, collectively, a moderate base rate of success; and that it all takes more time than expected. But back to the history: In June 2001, the U.S. Senate passed, 91–8, the No Child Left Behind Act, actually a revision of the Elementary and Secondary Education Act of 1965 on the occasion of its reauthorization, which mandated that all American schoolchildren, without exception, meet grade-level standards based on test performance by 2014. The scientific basis for this initiative was the well-established and thoroughly empirically supported Congressional Theory of Education that the best incentive to learning is to increase the number of tests and to punish all failures. This seemed to me and to most educators at the time a hilarious parody as well as an impossibility, but from the perspective of psychology within the American economic system, it was entirely welcome in the areas of test development and test marketing. States began to race with each other to develop proprietary exams; predictable shortfalls were observed in meeting goals; goals were continually readjusted downward; test cheating episodes popped up; and multiple challenges to the law were raised, eventually leading to its effective gutting in 39 out of 50 states and the District of Columbia. It was a reassuring demonstration of the persistence of human nature.

I attended and presented at my first APA convention in August 2001, in San Francisco. I am a fan of fairs, expositions, and shows generally, whether of cats or cars, so seeing the vast array of psychology spread out all at once, for the first time, was a thrill. Of course, due to multiple concurrent scheduling, as I've tried to show, it was also positively impossible to see everything of interest and to take in the sights of San Francisco for the first time as well. Due to the sheer numbers involved, only a few cities can host APA conventions, and the organization tends to choose sites in the North American summer temperate zone, in a band from Montreal and Toronto down to San Diego. There may have been poor areas of the city and its surroundings, but on a 4-day stay, with every hour from 8:00 AM through 5:00 PM spoken for by presentations, displays, and impromptu meetings with colleagues, all taking place in the isolated city-within-a-city of a modern convention center, I did not see any directly. (The only time I directly saw poverty and want during an APA convention—other than stepping around the many homeless denizens of the San Francisco streets—was when my wife and I were taken on an impromptu tour of the 9th Ward of New Orleans one morning during the 2006 meeting, a year after Hurricane Katrina's devastating flood.) Two weeks after my return, on September 11, 2001, airliners flown by terrorists from Saudi Arabia crashed into the World Trade Center towers in New York, a wing of the Pentagon was leveled by an explosion, and the United States was effectively again at war.

The most memorable response to the terrorist attacks of 2001 was the misinterpretation of then-President George W. Bush's attempts to reassure Americans in the immediate aftermath, when Muslim citizens were indeed made afraid of carrying out daily tasks, such as shopping, by thoughtless and fearful fellow citizens. "This great nation will never be intimidated," Bush said on November 8, 2001 (Bush, 2001). "People are going about their daily lives, working and shopping and playing, worshiping at churches and synagogues and mosques, going to movies and to baseball games." Most commentators after that accused the President of telling people to shop, rather than to do some other alternative, which alternative those commentators did not make very clear. But the misinterpretation fit well with the patterns of a primarily consumption-driven society, which America had now fully become. For a short time great patriotic fervor was aroused by the official entry of the United States into combat in Afghanistan in 2001 and Iraq, on what turned out to be pretexts, in 2003. But this wore off, and it then became clear that many lessons have been learned since Vietnam about how to wage war and maintain a peacetime consumer economy at the same time. First, separate the military from the general population by making it a specialized trade rather than a shared public responsibility. Then, elevate that trade to an elevated social rank (though without necessarily increasing the wages and benefits paid to those who are employed in it). Send the troops off to fight in very distant places, so that what happens there is diffused by distance and time. Keep the military kill rate down to a level that will keep mass public protests and antiwar sentiment from spreading. Align the military with the civilian police and other public safety organizations in the civilian sector, and create a climate where both the military and the civilian police forces are immunized against public criticism. And keep the public focused on domestic issues, dividing them, if possible, so that they will be kept in check by periodic campaigns pitting one or another group against each other at home. Focus on the threats posed by immigration, by potential terrorist infiltration, and at the same time make employment, health care, and other aspects of domestic security uncertain, to promote competition for scarce resources rather than maintaining a common level at which needs are met. Agitate against social programs directed at redressing inequality. Strive to weaken affirmative action and gender equity at all points; resist any further progress toward gender equality; decrease membership in liberal religious organizations and increase the membership, visibility, and political activity (up to the borderline of illegal activity for tax-exempt organizations) of religious groups with a low commitment to science as a way of understanding and managing the world; and affirm religions that emphasize punishment and patriarchy. And if these policies are not written into law, disable the lawmaking bodies by thwarting, by parliamentary maneuvers or refusals to compromise, any forward progress on legislation. Of course this is not any official policy, but it is a sampling of the currents in an increasingly conservative political environment that grew stronger after the events of 2001, possibly in response to mortality salience, as future research may show.

Even though all of these forces were in play, they still could not stop a free press from uncovering the inevitable atrocities of war. A memorable picture of a hooded Iraqi prisoner standing on a box with electric wires attached to his extremities became iconic. This led, as did the revelations of atrocities during the Vietnam War, to prosecution of the soldiers involved and was well covered in the news, but not to any lessening of the conflict. Meanwhile, news also seeped out about the means being used in the interrogations of prisoners. The United States had collected, soon after the beginning of the wars, during its earliest days of the Afghanistan incursion, a number of individuals that it identified as terrorists and as prisoners of war. As such, they needed to be confined in a military facility, but public sentiment was such that the United States was forced to intern them at the remarkable prison it maintains in a socialist country. The last bit of Cuba that the United States retained after the Cuban revolution was a spit of land in the northwest of the country, on which was a military reservation and a fortified prison, Guantanamo. The prisoners held there were effectively rendered stateless and also outside any recognizable judicial process. The military could not sentence them to military prisons, because those are for U.S. military personnel. There are no prisons for foreign prisoners of war anywhere else. The U.S. government has to date resisted all congressional and executive proposals to induct the prisoners into the U.S. civilian legal system, try them, and either release them or imprison them in the United States. This state of empty uncertainty persists today, and the prisoners have been consistently ignored, by the government and the U.S. population at large. Early in the process, before the apparent official policy of letting them quietly expire in legal limbo took hold, it was thought that some, at least, of these prisoners would be able to provide intelligence about other terrorist networks. As the prisoners proved either resistant to become informants, or, what is more probable, simply unable to provide information, the U.S. government, military, and intelligence agencies began to introduce extreme interrogation procedures, including forms of physical torture (there is no good euphemistic word for it). It also became clear that psychologists, some employed by the military, had become involved as consultants about, and possibly as participants in, such interrogations.

Fast-forward to the 2007 APA convention, again held in San Francisco in August. By this time the organization had again become internally polarized, caught between the question of whether a scientific organization ought to engage in social advocacy and the question of the ethical responsibility of an organization to respond to the behavior of some of its members in what appeared to be a clear violation of the ethical principles of psychologists. For years, the sentiment in much of psychology, especially among the more senior members of the profession, was that—as Howard Kendler put it in a 1999 article—psychology could not scientifically prescribe correct moral behavior, and that psychologists should separate their scientific activity and their roles as private citizens, speaking out for social causes only outside of the official structure of the psychological coalition (Kendler, 1999). This reflection of a long-standing attitude among scientific psychologists, that psychology is properly value-free, tempered psychology's responses to all previous challenges to social orthodoxy, and once again there was internal conflict among APA members over what the organization's public response to psychologists' involvement in torture would be. Up to 2007, although the major medical and psychiatric associations had condemned their members' participation in interrogations involving torture, the APA had yet to make a public statement either way. I don't remember too much from that convention. I did circle a symposium on "Lying in Psychotherapy" as one that I would have liked to attend, though I did not. But one thing that I clearly remember is that one afternoon my wife and I stood with about a thousand other APA members in the gardens outside of the Moscone Center, demonstrating in favor of the resolution before the APA council to publicly condemn torture and psychologists' participation in it. To my mind this was not at all a question about the role of the organization's advocacy, but a question about its self-presentation as an ethical organization based on principles of humanity and decency. The response then by the council was ambiguous, but less so the next year when such a resolution passed—not unanimously, an important indication that psychology, at least as far as it is represented by the APA, is still not only a coalition of professions but also a coalition of fundamentally different sociopolitical philosophies.

Of all the sessions at that 2007 convention, the one that, in retrospect, I would have most liked to attend but did not was a morning session at which the featured speaker was A. Dean Byrd (1948–2012), then the President-Elect of the National Association for Research and Theory in Homosexuality (NARTH). Byrd, an evangelical Christian who converted to the Church of Jesus Christ of the Latter Day Saints, was unmistakably an advocate for therapies designed to change sexual orientation from gay to straight, and to conform gender identity to value systems. The session was titled "Reforming APA Advocacy—Association Leaders Debate the Issues." Also on the program were two psychologists, one a former APA president who had just edited a notable rebuttal to social advocacy in psychology, "Destructive Trends in Mental Health: The Well-Intentioned Path to Harm." One of the chief destructive trends in that book, which Byrd (2006) had just reviewed on the NARTH website, was, in its authors' views, the 1973 decision by the American Psychiatric Association to depathologize homosexuality. I don't know what was discussed at the session, scheduled at the same time as a symposium on "Improving Psychology Teaching and Learning Through International Experiences and Collaborations"; an invited address for Division 6, Comparative and Physiological Psychology, on "Cognitive Dissonance in Animals: Implications for Social Psychology"; a symposium on "Dissemination of Evidence-Based Psychological Treatments in the Veterans Health Administration"; and a symposium on "Roles of Emotion Regulation and Reactivity in Children's School Adjustment in the United States and China." I do remember that my wife and I were both happy to get home and witness, 11 days after the convention's end,

Mark Stringer, the minister of our church, First Unitarian Church of Des Moines, officiate in his front yard at the first legal gay marriage in Iowa, which took place during a very brief window between a court ruling favorable to the marriage and an injunction against it (eventually resolved in full favor of gay marriage by the Iowa Supreme Court, April 4, 2009).

Now, at the end of this tale, are there any heroes? Modern histories shy away from heroes and even from heroic characters. Their purpose is to show how individuals' actions are determined, or as Freud would say, overdetermined, by forces, events, and the actions of others, and above all to try, if not to trace the multiple streams of influence running under any historical surface to their ultimate sources, at least to convey some idea of the directions in which they flow. This is the way that the history of psychology is tending: may it continue. Still, histories are stories, and stories ought to have, if not heroes, then representative people and perhaps even morals—but how to select representative people? There are billions of people in the world, and hundreds of thousands of psychologists. Psychology sets out to study people, and I take it that means everybody. Everybody has the potential of interacting with, and thus shaping, and being shaped by, psychology. Singling out is hard, and yet somehow people are able to do it. I used to say without hesitation that D. O. Hebb was my hero, and you can probably tell that I hold him and Paul Meehl in high esteem as characters in this story. One answer to the heroes question is to say that anyone mentioned in this book was and is part of a heroic attempt to understand and make peace with ourselves as human beings. It is not the whole of that attempt, and in retrospect it seems hardly begun. Like Lindbergh's aircraft of 1927, psychology is airborne, but we are still wondering, sometimes, whether it can clear the wires at the end of the field.

First, though, in any list of representatives would have to be the characters in the billions of parallel stories of which the story of the Black family is an $n = 1$ example. In some quarters of psychology today the case study isn't in fashion, but I think it served Freud and Allport well. Ultimately, psychology's journey to wherever it ends up will happen only if there are enough people convinced by it to pursue it, to study it further. B. F. Skinner said that he was his own favorite subject. That is probably the case for everyone. It has been observed many times that many psychologists got their start by concerns over mental illness either in themselves or in others. Both Paul Meehl and Timothy Leary started their investigations, Meehl early in life and Leary later, by confronting suicide in close relatives. Both William James and John Vasconcellos chose psychological humanism to quell their youthful psychological distress. Others may recognize themselves because psychology gave them a framework in which to see themselves as human and worthy of study. I am betting that many generations to come will agree with what E. C. Tolman said about his life in psychology, and will call it fun. Never underestimate fun!

But if real heroes are necessary, then I have to tell how my personal view of heroism in the practice of psychology has evolved. I began studying the history of psychology in a place where the idea of "great psychologists" was conceived and taken to extremes. One of the first courses I taught in a university had that title—"The Great Psychologists." The original book about great psychologists was by Robert I. Watson, a clinical psychologist whose interest in the history of psychology got the best of him. The 1963 version, which in truth I found hard going, was *The Great Psychologists: From Aristotle to Freud.*

As you can see from what has gone on so far in my story in the present book and as I promised in the preface, the heroes in the story will probably not be found in Watson's book or on the frontispiece map (although, if I had to choose between Aristotle and Freud, I would unhesitatingly choose Freud). In structuring that course, in 1985, I chose some of the psychologists who I felt were the best and most interesting to me in my encounters with history to that time. The first one I included was not by anyone's estimation in the usual history of psychology even a psychologist—the biologist Karl von Frisch (1886–1982), who had made many discoveries about bees and their means of communication, which were crucially important to some aspects of the study of language, my main graduate advisor's interest and by association one of mine at the time. Another was Leon Festinger, but not the cognitive dissonance work mentioned in this book, but rather a very late essay about the place of humans in anthropological time and history. I still think that this is the real ground of study in the history of psychology and welcome all accounts of prehistoric as well as posthistoric and even future historic humans. Another was D. O. Hebb; another was B. F. Skinner writing about creativity. Another was Lucretius, the Roman poet philosopher of nature, whose writing on the perception of refraction is as limpid as the waters into which he observed the illusory bending of a stick while preoccupied with unrequited love 60 years before the A.D. era. This leads me to the individuals who for me sum up the state of heroism in psychology as it is now.

The first of these is Jennifer Freyd. Born in 1957, she studied at Stanford with Roger Shepard and began what I imagined would be a long and brilliant career as a psychological scientist specializing in perception. In 1986, I thought that her work on representational momentum, mentioned before in this book, was the best of all the experimental work I had encountered to that time in perception and cognition. I thought then, and still think now, that a representational momentum paradigm will ultimately be the best probe for finding the routes that thought takes through the brain. In that, I share that old dream of finding a visible mind. I included her in my Great Psychologists course as a great psychologist of the future, a woman to inspire the women who made up more than three fourths of my class, an impeccable scientist.

I went on to study history and pleasure and left the study of perception and memory to one side. When I returned later—15 years later—to Freyd's work, I found that in the interim something had happened that would change both her and me. In 1990, newly installed as a professor at the University of Oregon and a new parent, Jennifer Freyd experienced a state of mental uncertainty that led her to a course of therapy. During that therapy, she came to realize that she had experienced abuse as a child, abuse that led her to accuse her father of committing reprehensible, deviant acts with and upon her when she was in her preteen and early teenage years. This was a shock, but what was even more shocking to my scientific mind was that, while she still maintained a representational momentum lab, she also had formulated a theory of why she would not have recognized the source of her mental pain for so long. Her theory is betrayal trauma theory (Freyd, 2012). Briefly put, the theory states that the anguish of abuse is compounded when, as it is in many cases, the person who commits the acts is one who was trusted absolutely. The mind, the theory holds, has to massively reorganize itself to accommodate the enormity of the act, and this leads to the familiar psychic consequences of posttraumatic experience.

When I first encountered this new theory, she had been researching its dimensions with her graduate and undergraduate students for years. Frankly, I was at first dismayed, and saddened. This has to be seen in the context of the 1990s. In those years, the anorexia fad dissolved and the recovered memory fad took its place. Daycare was a focal problem in the '80s and '90s, as women went into the workplace in greater numbers to support the consumption-driven lifestyle so familiar to us now. Somehow, possibly maliciously, the idea of child abuse got connected to child daycare, and some celebrated legal cases brought the subject to national attention. Therapists were called to testify, and reported that the children that they had interviewed had undergone bizarre ritualistic abuse beyond what the extreme norms were in that situation. Daycare workers and proprietors went to prison based on this testimony. This led to an opening of the floodgates for persons to come forward, supported by memories supposedly regained during therapy, to accuse teachers, parents, and religious figures of abuse that had happened sometimes decades before. What appalled me was that the best scientific evidence, both from the legal side of the inaccuracy of eyewitness testimony (especially the work of Gary Wells at Iowa State, with which I was by then familiar) and from the side of humans' susceptibility to persuasion under pressure (which I had had personal experience with, briefly, as a youth), converged on a position that drew any report of recovered memory during therapy into grave doubt.

Jennifer Freyd's well-educated parents, also uncomprehending of the reason for and source of their daughter's accusations, gathered a legal and scientific team together to defend themselves. Their accusations and counteraccusations stained luridly what I had up to that time thought was a pristine scientific career, and I mourned its dissolution in such a tragic and, it seemed to me, unnecessary way. I still think that the scientific evidence against recovered memory is strong. Yet Jennifer Freyd has held to her alternative theory. I have since come to the position that this is a form of heroism, a particular form of psychological heroism akin to that held by saints and seers. The truth on which her new, plausible theory is based is one that resides in her mind and her conception of reality. It is, to my mind, heroic to hold to one's convictions, especially those that arise in the well-honed mind of a psychological scientist, and to attempt to find where they may fit into the universe. So I say that Jennifer Freyd is a heroine, but in an unexpected direction, and represents both courage in the face of hostile opposition and also the complexity of paths that psychological careers must take.

Another representative is Martin Seligman (1942–). I never met him—I saw him at a distance once at an APA convention—but I feel I know him by proxy. I was influenced by many undergraduate teachers, one of whom, Suzanne Miller, was my instructor in Abnormal Psychology. But as significant an experience as that was, equally meaningful was her agreeing to allow me to work in her laboratory at Temple University in 1980. This was in the fall and winter of 1980–1981. I worked under the direction of her then-graduate student Jeffrey Summerton, now a forensic clinical psychologist in New Jersey, in a human learned helplessness paradigm. We charted the verbal responses of student volunteers who either could escape or not escape unpleasant noise (delivered through headphones) by figuring out—operantly—a patterned push-button code. Ultimately, this research added to the learned helplessness literature, but by then Dr. Miller had begun to move away from strictly academic research and had gravitated to psycho-oncology, becoming a research psychologist at a cancer treatment and research center in Philadelphia. I benefited by having had the experience, along with other lab experiences that I took advantage of when I was a student, and while I can't say I owe it all to Seligman, it was his paradigm that introduced me to the actual mechanics and, as well, the ethical aspects of psychological research. Discussions among Dr. Miller, Jeff Summerton, other research assistants, and myself about the underlying philosophy of the experiments as well as more mundane matters of coding were enriching in unique ways, experience that was unobtainable except by experiencing it. My understanding of Seligman, gleaned from Dr. Miller, was that he was a genial, cultured, and funny man. When I encountered his theory of optimism in *Learned Optimism* (Seligman, 1991) and took the optimism test included in it, I was elated, although by my count I scored off the scale on the pessimistic end. For a time, if anyone had asked me what psychological theories I connected with most, I would have without hesitation said Csikszentmihalyi's "flow" (and his affirmative theory of adolescence as well) and Seligman's "learned optimism." In Seligman's conversion of the negative connotations of the helplessness paradigm to positive ones I saw a confirmation of a pattern of conversion I had observed earlier, in my graduate school days. Dr. Tony (John Anthony) Nevin (1933–), a student of William Schoenfeld (1915–1996), was, when I first met him, an exemplar of what seemed, in 1982, already an antique: thoroughgoing operant behaviorism. To me, schooled in phenomenology and clinical psychology with no formal training in behaviorism beyond my introductory textbooks, I found him at first incomprehensible. Later, as I came to understand why the cognitive-behavioral model had a behavioral lobe, and as I became more fascinated by Skinner's approaches to culture, which seemed eminently desirable and sound, I came a little closer to understanding Tony. But nothing prepared me for finding out that Tony's real love was peace studies and peace psychology. How could such a religious—I guess that would be the word for it—goal as peace link up with the gritty reality of the behavioral lab? Now I know that Schoenfeld himself, later in his career, authored a book on religion from a behaviorist perspective, and that Tony's conversion—as he explained it—to a theory of nonviolence stemmed from his rejection of earlier behavioral paradigms in which he had worked, which involved the direct delivery of aversive stimuli to the experimental organisms (shocking pigeons, in Tony's case).

I followed Seligman's elaboration of learned optimism into positive psychology in the late '90s and felt that it defined what I felt was a humane, Utopian direction for the field to follow. It answered, again, the earlier call to choose research wisely, and do little harm. Positive psychology seemed something that, problematical as it was in terms of its scope and the individual definition of its individual terms such as "kindness," represented the best that experimental psychology could do to articulate a comprehensive theory of prohuman behavior. But during the next decade, events occurred that rendered this picture less sunny. Seligman's consulting work with the U.S. military on resilience was seized upon and conflated with Guantanamo torture, and even though Seligman categorically condemned torture and disavowed any connection with it (Seligman, 2010), uncritical public opinion inside and outside psychology, ready to see psychology as an enemy, obscured the good he had been trying to accomplish. Seligman epitomizes to me the heroism of good people in bad situations. That description represents many psychologists today.

A third representative hero of the last 2 decades came to prominence in the Hudson River in New York City. No, he did not emerge like Venus on a shell, but he did emerge from an airliner door, standing on a wing of a jet, floating in the open expanse of water between New York and New Jersey in January 2009. A few minutes before, he was the chief pilot of U.S. Airways flight 1549 to Charlotte, North Carolina, when he and the passengers heard a "whoomp" followed by frightening silence. The airliner had hit birds on takeoff and both engines were dead. Quickly reviewing his options, he realized that he would not be able to reach the nearest emergency airport at Teterboro, New

Jersey. The options narrowed to one: ditching in an open patch of water on the river. This he did, according to films and eyewitness accounts, as deftly and precisely as it could be done. No rents had been opened in the fuselage. There, luck (an often unappreciated psychological variable!) played a role, as the plane remained afloat long enough for a well-disciplined evacuation to take place, saving all passengers.

The pilot, Chesley Sullenberger (1951–), was awarded, as might be expected, all the accolades of a hero. He was feted by the mayor of New York, Michael Bloomberg, who himself had a brief moment of health psychological heroism a few years later when he insisted on regulating the size of unhealthy beverages sold in the city. Sullenberger's deed electrified the country, often jaded by the Niagara of information arriving second by second in a now totally wired age. Do not let it be forgotten that luck was on the side of the passengers and crew of flight 1549 in another way. For Chesley Sullenberger was then, and is now, the best authority on the procedures for ensuring safe outcomes in panic emergency situations in flight. He followed a systematic procedure that he had evolved through years of reading and experience: Part of the reason that it was so automatic and ready for operation was that its parts connected systematically and predicted, in a stepwise successive fashion, the sequence of events and prescribed the behaviors to be performed contingent on reaching each step. We are not often in awe of systematic theories of learning and performance, though these have been around for 70 years or more, exemplified by the theoretical work of, among others, Robert E. Gagné (1916–2002), who structured complex learning procedures into logical systems modulating expert performance (Gagne, 1985). Chesley Sullenberger's graduate program in Industrial Psychology at Purdue (Sullenberger, 2014), where he obtained his Master of Arts (MA) after completing his basic studies at the U.S. Air Force Academy, celebrates him as an example of the benefits of study in that area (along with his other MA in Public Administration—another highly systematized profession—at the University of Northern Colorado). I contend that Chesley Sullenberger represents a dimension of heroism accessible to anyone who learns competence in the saving of life by the execution of a competent procedure. No more or less than a surgeon following a systematic procedure, or a practiced clinical psychologist working to direct a client off of a suicidal path, he exemplifies a way that psychology assisted in designing a system, one of many that allow individuals to perform small heroic acts that sum into a collective saving of lives. He is living proof, as are his passengers, that the influence of psychology is encountered everywhere now—that it has reached a level of permanent incorporation into culture.

Every history of psychology must be incomplete, and this one is no exception. At its close, I am reminded of the question implied in the title of the book by the Jungian therapist James Hillman (1926–2011) and novelist Michael Ventura (1945–), *We've Had A Hundred Years of Psychotherapy and the World's Getting Worse* (Hillman & Ventura, 1993). Is this so? Does the review of the last 87 years lead to the conclusion that we would have been better off not starting down the path that the psychological coalition has taken? To answer this, I think that first, it is necessary to realize and accept that psychologists themselves are human, no more or less than the individuals they study, advise, or try to help heal. They are just as fallible and just as biased as the people with whom they interact. There is no line that separates the psychologists from the rest of humanity, and as the rest of humanity goes, so must the psychologist—we are all in this psychology together. Perhaps the study of psychology, or any mental discipline at all, helps in resisting the worst of social and political pressures. I think the record shows that, for the most part, psychologists have endorsed the ideals that they have expressed in their organizational codes and in their public and private writings. To the extent that psychologists have not been able to resist the remarkably resistant forces of prejudice of all types and the drives to war, then to that extent the world has not gotten better through their efforts, though whether it is worse now than it was in 1927 is not clear. To the extent that psychologists have resisted these, then I think, yes, psychology has created a language in which prosocial policy can be constructed in ways that may lead to it being scientifically implemented and assessed, as Donald Campbell envisioned many years ago (Campbell, 1969). The extent to which this can be accomplished is limited by the vision and willingness of the people and their representatives to experiment.

Donald Campbell (1916–1996, USA) Theorist best known for his work with Julian Stanley on quasi-experimentation, he also advanced a theory of cultural evolution via blind variation and selective retention of ideas, and proposed a system of deriving public policy from macrosocial experimentation.

At another level I feel a great deal more optimistic after seeing how far we have come over the past 9 decades. In the particular area of experimental psychology that interests me, the relation of perception to thought, I think a great deal of theoretical progress has been made, and I have tried to trace that through this book. In 1927, Lashley was removing the cortex and correlating the degree of removal with quality of function. Today we understand, and are getting closer to visualizing, the exact interconnections in the brain that underlie mental states. Theoretically and also in terms of being able to actually view the brain, the difference is very large and very positive. I also think that progress in science is slow and incremental, and this process is active and productive in psychology today. Psychologists live long lives and change their focus throughout their careers. Irving Biederman (1939–), who started out in the 1970s researching object recognition in scenes, proposed, just before the 2007 APA meetings, a neural theory to explain the pleasures of seeing (Biederman & Vessel, 2006), in which the receptors for vision are wired into a parallel system of endorphin-based receptors that mediate a combined visual-pleasurable experience. This traces back to the very beginnings of psychology in philosophical aesthetics (What is beauty? And why does it excite us?), and forward through a series of theories of the aesthetic experience of pleasure that span the 20th century. I think this sort of theorizing is advanced compared to that available in 1927, the year after Leonard Troland pronounced the mind "a mystery" (Troland, 1926). It is still a great mystery but I think it is not impossible to solve. That is a source of my hope in psychology. Another is that good people in bad situations continue to conceptualize ways in which we can understand those situations and change them for the better. Craig Haney, whose life was individually changed by his participation in Philip Zimbardo's Stanford Prison Study, has now completed the theoretical works that serve as a starting point for future research on ways to reconceptualize punishment (Haney, 2006). This is another source of hope. Yet another source of hope is that people have, very recently, been willing to die for psychology, like Ignacio Martín-Baró, or Alharith Abdulhameed Hassan, murdered in Iraq while driving to work on ways to create peace and heal trauma (Eastern Mennonite University, 2007). Psychology is not the only way to understand experience, but it is a unique blend of science and art, a potentially powerful tool for reconceptualizing reality. It is unfinished, as is the end of a young branch.

Alharith Abdulhameed Hassan (1951–2006, Iraq) Professor of psychiatry at the University of Baghdad specializing in posttraumatic stress disorder and interfaith understanding.

THE FAMILY STORY: THE FIFTH GENERATION

The 1990s opened with Juana and her mother mourning the murder, on November 16, 1989, of Ignacio Martín-Baró and his Jesuit colleagues by a Salvadorean governmental death squad: The right-wing military government, predictably, blamed the murder of the country's chief intellectual on the Communists. The editors of Martín-Baró's *Writings for a Liberation Psychology* 4 years later noted that at the 1990 APA convention, studies about the type of men women find attractive got media attention; Noam Chomsky's tribute to Ignacio Martín-Baró did not. Helen retired at age 72. Still energetic, she independently set up a program, staffed with other retired volunteers and student interns from the University of California, Los Angeles (UCLA) and the University of Southern California (USC), to help poor people and immigrants navigate the California mental health care system. Carolyn continued to live and work in San Francisco. The company for which she was working during the 1970s and 1980s had become involved in the manufacturing of components for the printing industry. As the '90s began, Carolyn began to see that there was only a limited future for manufacturing in the United States, and she began to actively seek out other employment. Luckily, she was in the San Francisco area and she was able to catch the wave of the developing Internet at its very beginning: The .com startup company that hired her because of her general manufacturing background and her contacts in the printing industry was bought up by one of the largest deliverers of Internet content, and she, lucky that the manufacturing processes at her former company allowed her to develop substantial programming skills, adapted to the new digital environment easily. Lucky again that her new company was very large and was able to provide health care benefits, in 1999 she was diagnosed with early-stage breast cancer, which was successfully treated with a lumpectomy and radiation, one of the earlier examples of treatment of this kind. She is currently cancer free and taking various medications to remain so. In 2007 she retired at age 65, again lucky, since she had a good pension and some health care perks as well—a very fortunate American—and since she had always had a simple lifestyle, partly influenced by reading Philip Slater (Slater, 1970), she was and is still able to enjoy the good life in the Bay Area. She did not see Juana that often during the 1990s, since Juana was now finishing her doctorate at UCLA and had married.

Juana, in the meantime, had finished her doctorate in 1991 and had been appointed assistant professor at one of the state universities in California. She and her partner knew at the time of their marriage in 1991 that she would not be able to have children of her own, so they set out to adopt first Carlos, from Mexico, in 1992, and Anh Binh, from California, in 1996.

It was Juana who finally came to realize the importance of family: Her uncle Harry had been a loner, and her aunt Rosa independent. Helen, after being widowed, threw herself into work very much like Harry had, but she was not as reclusive as he was, and reached out to Harry and Rosa, though she was unable to make very much contact because of distance and her commitments in California. But now, in 1997, Rosa's partner Francine had been dead for 3 years—they had been a couple for 54 years and lived in the same apartment for 51, about the same length of time as Sigmund Freud and his wife Marthe, and some people had remarked on the consistency of their relationship in the context of a growing interest in gay marriage. Rosa had always been alternately pleased and bemused by the attention that she and Francine got. She was pleased because she knew that those who were interested in it were, like those who were attracted to racial cooperation or gender equality in earlier times, on the path to acceptance through familiarity. On the other hand, she was naturally shy and was awkward with attention. When Francine died, Helen made a trip to the funeral and visited with Rosa for a week. Returning, Helen realized how much a difference in environment widens the cultural differences between people, and yet at the same time she realized how much she loved Rosa, connected to her in the way that people from the same parents can be. Knowing that Rosa's health was failing, Juana arranged with mutual friends on Long Island to host a family reunion, to be attended by all of Rosa's family and as many friends of each of them as could be found and invited. Juana, her partner, and Carlos and Anh Binh were there: Helen, Carolyn, many friends of Francine and Rosa, many friends of Helen, and even Catherine, who had befriended and become close to Harry in assisted living. Catherine brought with her Harry's memoir and many photos and papers, of which the family had no idea: She gave them all to Helen, who brought them back to California on her return. Videotapes from the reunion can hardly be played anymore, since the technology has advanced so much, but the printed photos show a happy, smiling family and a galaxy of friends on a sunny summer lawn.

The 1990s were pronounced the Decade of the Brain by President George H. W. Bush, and the 2000s were pronounced the Decade of Behavior by the APA, but the real symbol for anyone in the United States, psychologist or not psychologist, is the smear of smoke on the face of one of the towers of the World Trade Center in New York before its collapse on September 11, 2001. This is the "flashbulb" memory for anyone of this time, and its repercussions in terms of social regression and repression have left what will be a lasting mark, as definitional of the current age as the protests in Birmingham and Selma, Alabama, in the 1960s were for Harry and Donald. On August 19, 2007, Juana, now a professor of cultural psychology and cultural studies and a recognized consultant on immigration issues for the U.S. State Department, stood with Carolyn, her partner, her children, and her mother on the plaza outside of the Moscone Convention Center in San Francisco, named after the San Francisco mayor who was assassinated on November 27, 1978, along with Harvey Milk. They stood to protest the APA's refusal, to that time, to disassociate the organization and the psychologists that it represents from the use of torture in the U.S. military prison at Guantanamo Bay, Cuba. That protest, and others within and outside the organization, was ultimately successful, resulting in a plurality—certainly not an unanimity—of members of the organization voting "against" and leading the Council of Representatives to issue a statement condemning psychologists' participation in such activities. Helen, by that time living with Juana and her family, was unable to travel, but gave everyone a good-luck kiss before they left and on their return. Before Juana left for San Francisco, a colleague asked her about the APA's position on torture. "They understand power," said Juana, "and they value truth. But right now they are having a hard time speaking truth to power."

Now it is 2014. Helen is 95, mind still sharp, but fragile. She is now in an assisted living center and receives frequent visits from her family and friends. Carlos, now 21, is a senior at UCLA. He became fascinated by the story, in Harry's memoir, of his great-uncle Donald, who came back from Vietnam psychically changed, and who relived that experience until his death. Carlos intends a graduate career in neuroscience: He just finished writing a junior honors paper on posttraumatic stress disorder (PTSD). So much more is now known about it. The *DSM–5* has just come out, and has put cognitive factors on par with the emotional and behavioral factors in the syndrome, lending credence to the idea that meditation, a form of cognitive entrainment, may have beneficial results in cases of postcombat stress, of which there is no shortage today. Carlos has the good luck of coming of military age when combat postings to Iraq and Afghanistan are winding down. It is likely he will be able to study in uninterrupted peace—his family hopes so, at any rate. And Anh Binh? Now 17, at her high school graduation, she said in her salutatory speech: "I'm Black and Vietnamese; I'm adopted. My mother is half-Ecuadorean. My grandmother, she's 71, is Irish and Yiddish. My great-grandmother is 95 and survived the Influenza Epidemic of 1918. My great-great-grandmother fled anti-Semitism in Russia. My great-Aunt Rosa, rest her soul, lived with her partner Francine for more than 50 years in a committed same-sex marriage in all but the legal papers. I come from a long line of strong, strong women. I am the past—and I am the future!"

Epilogue:
An Interview

Q. You end on a note of war and something like a feeling that psychology is in disarray. Why are you not more optimistic about the future?

A. Well, it does look bleak from some angles. But not every part of history has to be happy, and not every part of society or even every person has to be happy. I don't see this history as pessimistic or bleak as much as I see it as cyclic. It has a natural rise to 1970 and a fall thereafter, nicely split into two halves. I think that it's realistic and accurate to look at the recent history of psychology that way. It tracks the course of the Civil Rights Movement very well. In 1927, the momentum was building for civil rights. People all over the United States were realizing the criminality of the treatment of African Americans. Earlier they had been stimulated by reading Booker Washington and W. E. B. DuBois, and in New York in 1927 they were witnessing the Harlem Renaissance. True, it was still a bad time. Lynchings were common. There was a lynching right down the street from the office and the home of the head of the Psychology Department at the University of Missouri, in fact...

Q. When was that?

A. ...in 1923. The psychologist was Max Meyer. I briefly mentioned him as an early behaviorist, which he was, but

213

he was an irascible and brilliant German import whose real interests were hearing and music. To get back to the question of whether this is an optimistic history or not, through the 1930s the Depression brought new impetus for social justice for Blacks and Whites alike. Everyone suffered (except the very rich, of course) and some form of socialism or communism looked like a real possibility at the time. Humanitarians and intelligent people generally realized that something had to give, that socialism of some sort would have to be accommodated. The social programs of the 1930s were extremely effective in smoothing things out, though the Depression continued to linger for a long time until full employment could happen during the war. Then, during the '40s, more and more people became aware of the bad conditions among Blacks and it made them— Whites—conscious of the problem and willing to do something about it. The '50s and '60s had a lot of catalysts for change and it caught hold: The *Brown* decision, the Selma march, the "I Have a Dream" speech, the Civil Rights Acts, and all of the Great Society programs were a culmination of 60 years of work. And then, boom, it was all over. The momentum of the '60s was gone. It was done in by lack of foresight, by lack of planning, by simple greed, simple complacency—and that was on the left. The right was always waiting to undo equality and freedom. It always is, in my opinion. And now it is getting its way again. But sure as day follows night, there will be another swing upward. I have confidence in that. Abolition was followed by repression; establishment of civil rights, followed by repression. Look forward with hope to whatever new formulation of liberation happens next.

Q. The fight today seems to be more about health care rather than civil rights....

A. Someone ought to look into the relation between race prejudice and opposition to health care. They interact: The kinds of things that make health care more likely to take the form of a program that will provide mental health benefits at parity will also benefit the poor, and that means that any components of whatever new system is proposed will necessarily benefit the historically deprived populations in the United States, who are different and also poorer. In my experience, the opponents of universal health care managed as a government program hardly ever mention the actual practices or results of health care, but focus almost exclusively on who should and should not benefit from it. Very few, if any, opponents of the move toward single-payer coverage ever mention psychology or mental health care. For those who have private insurance, those who can pay, presumably it's fine to get whatever their money will buy. Buy more insurance, as my rightwing former Congressman said, when he was asked what to do about mental health care being paid for at lower rates by cost-shaving insurance plans. Those who don't have the money to pay—consign them to the nether darkness. "Those who don't work shall not eat" crops up eventually at some point in their arguments. The antiegalitarian wing of the power elite in the United States is always going to be resourceful in finding ways to demonize its opponents, who are most commonly either Black or Hispanic or, sometimes but rarely, Asian these days, until they all morph into socialists. In my opinion, it's all of a piece, all the same piece of prejudice. Of course it isn't that simple. There have been strong Black and Hispanic conservative voices in the past, and currently as well. Probably, ultimately it comes down to right versus left, with the disliked populations batted about between the two sides. The right is ahead now. The left will have to figure out what to do next.

Q. Is history always so political?

A. Isn't it? Most history of any sort is about war—politics carried out by other methods, Clausewitz called it. Look at the continual role that war has played in psychology's history. I started this story in 1927, partly to avoid looking at the First World War again. Most histories of psychology date psychology's beginning as a profession in the United States from

World War I's "putting psychology on the map," as the contemporary phrase had it. Freud noted, as have many others, that peace is a preparation for war. The United States has been actively at war from 1941 through '45; '50 through '53; '59 (the usual first date for Vietnam) through '75; a couple of brief flareups in the '80s, but nothing large; and in '90–'91. It intervened in Bosnia in '94–'95. Starting in 2001, it's been involved in fighting nonstop. So add it up: 36 of the past 72 years have seen some form of substantial military engagement. Throw in the periods of military buildup during the Cold War Period (1946–1991), and the continual military presence of the United States in Germany, Japan, the Philippines, and the periodic policing actions in the Middle East, and covert operations in Central and South America and otherwise—there hasn't been much of a war shortage. War is a stimulant for psychology: for those who help design the weapons, train the troops, manage the propaganda, advise on strategy, interact with prisoners, and counsel the survivors, as well as for those who theorize about and occasionally act for peace. If that's the only conclusion the readers of this history reach, then good. If they come to the conclusion that psychology's modern history is half reaction to war and half involvement with social activism for peace through politics, then even better.

Q. What continuities do you see in the recent history of psychology?

A. There are two ways to answer that...

Q. What's the first way?

A. The first way is to say that what I included in this history are issues, ideas, techniques, and even products that have continued to influence psychology through the present. Gestalt ideas permeated all of psychology, so much so that they inspired sharp resistance from some of the orthodox psychologists when they first appeared (an excellent sign of a productive idea). The study of emotion continued: in the 1930s some psychologists predicted it would disappear. They hoped. It never left and it accumulated theory after theory (e.g., emotion-focused coping), and more than a few good techniques as well (e.g., the Facial Action Coding System). Technicolor survived and evolved. J. J. Gibson's challenge to study perception in the context of the real world physical environment continues to stimulate research. The persistence of the issues raised by Milgram and Zimbardo's simulation studies. The persistence of the "cognitive-behavioral" formulation. The coalition nature of psychology combining theory, applied, and clinical psychology as an entity. All of those were in the works by 1940. B. F. Skinner was fond of saying that, until he came along, nothing had changed in psychology for 2,500 years. I don't think that's true, although the triumvirate "cognition-emotion-behavior" is the longest-running idea in all of psychology. I see a trend, which I've attempted to portray in the text, from a social psychology that is collective to one that focuses mainly on the effects of group-related events or actions on the individual mind. And I also see a trend in cognitive psychology toward focusing on mental illusions and their propensity to mislead thinking. These are two-edged swords. Psychology engenders self-perceptions. In leading us to conceive of ourselves as easily swayed from a rational course of action, both by our associates and by our own cognitive biases, psychology may lead us to take more care to think critically. But it may also be painting a picture of the human being as a generally irrational and unthinking person, which is, however, unintentional and the result of the direction of current research, somewhat demeaning, in my view. Freud at least provided some remedies for our basal irrationalities: a return to reality, to work, and to love. Our modern cognitive and social psychologies leave us in the position of being poorly functional computers. That, and a dearth of research on affirmative prosocial behavior, has not equipped us well to counteract the corrosive amoral reasoning of algorithms of profit embodied in our social and economic systems. In my opinion, of course!

Q. And the second?

A. Robert MacLeod (1907–1972), an eminent theorist and historian of psychology, wrote a book published posthumously in 1975 called *The Persistent Problems of Psychology* (MacLeod, 1975). It was meant to be a complete history of psychology, from its earliest beginnings to the present, that focused on ideas and the pattern of their development. A wonderful plan, but unfortunately he died halfway through writing it, right at the beginning of the 19th century.

The first half of MacLeod's book is, like many histories of psychology that begin with the Greeks, an undisguised history of philosophy. If you take a sample of the ideas there, there is continuity between the story I've told and the ancient bones of the field. Here's a short list of classic, ancient philosophical ideas that, MacLeod claimed, animate psychology today, drawn from the part of the book that he finished—I've put an idea or two from the 1927–2013 period in parentheses after each:

Materialism (Consumer psychology)

Idealism (The idea of mind, for one; the abstraction of mental health, for another)

Monism/dualism and the mind/body problem (Cognition versus behavior—Hebb insisted, in his 1974 article mentioned here and elsewhere, that the mind/body problem was the one problem that every student of psychology must wrestle with, above and before all others)

Teleology (Purposive behavior—Tolman)

The Higher Good (Social activism)

Causality (Operationism and the striving to make psychology scientific)

Cognition (The cognitive component of the "cognitive-behavioral" formulation)

Sensation (The persistence of "feelings" as central premises in psychology: self-esteem; "flow")

Reason versus unreason (abnormal and clinical psychology included in the coalition)

Freedom (Rogers versus Skinner, 1956)

Hedonism (Tolman versus Troland, 1932, as well as the myriad of implicit connections between pleasure and reinforcement, esteem, "positivity," etc.—and don't forget Tim Leary!)

For the modern period, I'd add my own list of persistent problems to his, as follows (some—many—of these are alluded to in MacLeod as well, either in his completed text or in the outline he left for the remaining chapters in the book):

Should psychology strive to be value free? Value neutral? Value centered?

How complicit are psychologists with social evils and individual injustice?

Who is psychology serving? (I'm alluding here to an excellent book by the cultural historian Loren Baritz from many years ago—1960—*Servants of Power*,

> Loren Baritz (1928–2009, USA) Historian and social critic, wrote on the social sciences, the meaning of success for the middle class, radical thought, and Vietnam.

which details the rise of applied psychology, especially as it developed as an arm of industry and commerce.)

Is psychology primarily proactive or reactive?

At its core, is psychology more individualist or collectivist?

Is psychology idiographic, or nomothetic? (This was Gordon Allport's favorite formulation, and he always returned to it in his thinking about personality. Should the individual be understood biographically, or instead in terms of behavior determined by general laws?)

Is psychology dependent on or independent of religion?

Is consciousness, as George Miller said, the "constitutive" problem of psychology? (Can there be a psychology without consciousness?)

What is the relation of psychology to law and the legal system? And how are legal counsel and psychological counseling similar and different?

What is the relation between psychology and medicine?

How necessary is political engagement for psychology?

What are the conceptual and theoretical relations between business and economics and psychology?

Will the relation between psychology and warmaking continue? Must it continue for psychology to survive?

Does (should) psychology promote creativity or conformity?

Does psychology guarantee, or even relate to, progress?

Which best defines psychology, learning or thinking?

Should psychology be descriptive, or predictive?

(The following three cluster together) *Should psychology, as science, take as its models theoretical, "pure" scientists, or "bench" scientists whose work is driven by practical problems? Should we be primarily theoretical or applied? Is psychology a science or a technology?* (Both pure and applied science are valid, and as Donald Stokes noted in his book *Pasteur's Quadrant* (1997), both are represented across the physical and social sciences. However, in psychology to date, our histories have favored the pure rather than the applied approach. E. G. Boring, the eminent first historian of the field, was the student of E. B. Titchener, who had no love of applied psychology and considered any applications "mere technology." It took until 1945 for an official recognition of coalition partnership for psychology's various technological applications. B. F. Skinner called for a "technology of behavior" to replace what he saw as ancient holdovers of mind philosophy and dualism in psychology, which may have made him less than welcome in many quarters.

Donald Stokes (1927–1997, USA) Political scientist and author of several works on voting behavior. His last work, Pasteur's Quadrant, *advanced the idea that applications are necessary and perhaps primary in the development of science.*

Is psychology one, or many? Unifiable, or necessarily a collection of sciences, technologies, or "studies?"

Where does psychology fit on the "revolutionary—evolutionary" spectrum?

That's my take on what seem to me to be new additions to the persisting problems in the coalition of psychology.

Q. Critics—you've mentioned critics of psychology. Is this history a kind of criticism of the field?

A. I think any history contains an implicit criticism of its subject by what it includes and leaves out. I'm sure that my biases could be pretty quickly gauged from what I've written. Like any great work, psychology has acquired many critics. Some are just ranters and hate it unreasonably, occasionally for religious reasons. Some persons feel that they have been harmed by therapy, or, alternatively, that therapy in its essence is harmful. Then there are the critics from other fields, either other social sciences or the humanities— rarely from mathematics or the physical and biological sciences, perhaps because psychology has to still make enough of a mark there to be critically engaged. Often critics from these fields proceed from an incomplete knowledge of psychology or a limited conception of it. The critics that I have had in the back of my mind while composing this history are those from within psychology itself. I'll limit myself to just listing and classifying them here and recommending a short taste of each. Also, I'll limit myself to the last 30 years or so. There are those psychologists who see psychology as, in the words of one of them, Seymour

Kenneth Gergen (1935–, USA) Social psychologist most often identified with the theory of social constructionism.

Nikolas Rose (1947–, Great Britain) British sociologist and social theorist who has written widely on the interpenetration of psychological science into culture.

Seymour Sarason (1919–2010, USA) Clinical psychologist who was one of the founders of community psychology. He wrote critical works about psychology's insularity and education schools' inefficiencies, and also wrote on the role of art in psychology.

David T. Lykken (1928–2006, USA) Experimental psychologist best known for his work debunking lie detection.

221

Sarason, "misdirected." They see psychology as divorced either from social or political or historical reality, and thus trivial and artificial and of little use for real humans in real social situations. For these, see Kenneth Gergen (1973), Nikolas Rose (1996), and Seymour Sarason (1981a, 1981b) in the reference list. Then there are those who see psychology as flawed science, incapable of rising above the "stamp-collecting" level (as one famous scientist called everything that was not physics). There are many of these, but the two Minnesotans, Paul Meehl (1978) and David Lykken, top the list for me. Lykken once memorably quipped, in his article, "What's Wrong With Psychology Anyway?" (Lykken, 1991), that psychology with regard to theories is like Douglas MacArthur's old soldier. MacArthur, a famous general of World War II and Korea, relieved of his command in 1951, closed his farewell address with the old Army song refrain that "old soldiers never die, they just fade away." For Lykken, theories in psychology not only never died—but many even forget to fade away! Finally, there are those who have criticized clinical psychology specifically. Among these, my favorite is George Albee. A simple man, more at home tending his vegetable garden than professing in a classroom, he had no compunction about calling out the profession when he detected it selling its soul to the corporate pirates, or worse. See Albee (1970, 2005). The reason I am recommending them is not only because they throw pepper in the pot, and not just because I think that they are all justified and so far unanswered, but because I sense keenly that they each wrote what they did out of respect and love for the field, which I share.

George Albee (1921–2006, USA) Clinical psychologist and community psychologist, and gadfly to the profession.

Q. You mention operationism at the beginning and then leave it. What gives?

A. Adopting operationism, psychology committed itself to a constellation of ideas, including a conception of science as a process of theory validation by observation, establishing causality by means of experiment, mathematizing what had up to that point been only verbal, and—more important philosophically in 1927 than now—ruling out illusions of language in the description of causal relations. That is, rather than asserting that the "mind" controlled behavior, psychologists would be held to a high standard of proof of first, the existence of "mind" and, second, of the precise mechanisms by which this "mind" carried out its activities. It's easy to see, from this perspective, why the development of cognitive science became so optimistic after the formulation of good mechanical descriptions of internal problem-solving processes in computers. In my view, operationism is still the best way to establish psychology as it now stands as a science. The ideas that techniques of psychotherapy, for example, should be validated by evidence, and that the goals of psychology are essentially the prediction and control of behavior, as Gordon Allport asserted in that 1939 address I quoted in the text, are the expected outcomes of rigorously defining input and output variables within a proper theoretical framework. The fact is, though, that a lot of psychology still has to deal with speculations based on phenomenology, and it has yet to link up to observations made by less mathematically precise and highly verbal observers. Probably, as is the case in the prediction of weather, mathematical precision and phenomenological observation are tunneling toward each other and will eventually meet. Meanwhile, any psychologies that are highly mathematized—a prerequisite for fitting into the operationalist system that is, after all, derived from physics— are hardly readable by most psychologists, who are typically more comfortable with verbal expression and logic than with mathematics. At present, psychologists—educational or motivational psychologists perhaps—are happy to say things like "the flow experience results in heightened creativity" and be applauded for that at conferences. We don't know, though, exactly how to find the flow experience in the brain (or mind, which operationism tends to force to be the same thing as the brain), and we can't make any predictions as yet of what the heightened creativity will consist. We could go back to rats in mazes and rat brains, and some do, but it's probably going to be at the level of cognitive science meeting neuroscience that significant predictions of thoughts are going to occur. Try this "thought" experiment: predict, if you can, what your next thought will be. If you can do that, fine, then show what in the brain produces that, and you will be able to live in luxury on your Nobel funds for the rest of your life. If you want to go further and show yourself how much of a mountain operationalism sets psychologists to climb, predict what your partner will say, and in what emotional state she or he will be, when next you meet. Or what the Chief Justice's opinion will be on whatever Supreme Court case is most interesting to you at present. I've written a history where operationism, in the sense of defining variables enough to get them in the laboratory door, is assumed in most cases of experimental psychology after 1927. For clinical work, all bets are off. It was Meehl (again!), a scion of the operational age, that demonstrated that superiority of test prediction over individual judgment many, many years ago. This mode of thinking, and the types of statistical procedures that support it, are still hard to establish in psychology. Here is another thought experiment. Look up the works of any mathematical psychologist or neuropsychologist. Read a selection of their publications, and compare those to your favorite example of psychology today. Should a basic history of psychology like this one center around individuals like this (i.e., mathematical psychologists or neuropsychologists)? It's a tough call for the historian who, like me, has a neuropsychological orientation.

Q. Where are the schools and systems of psychology? Where are structuralism and functionalism?

A. Here is a place where a direct reference to current history of psychology can answer your question. Christopher Green at York University in Toronto and his colleagues are engaged in a project to analyze the content of the major psychological journal of the early 20th century, the *Psychological Review*, by applying clustering algorithms to the mass of verbal data in all of the articles for every issue for 5-year blocks (Green,

Feinerer, & Burman, 2013). What they show is that terms such as, for example, "structuralism" and "functionalism" define communities of interest that had many subdivisions and intersected with several other language- and theory-sharing communities in the psychologies of their time. Functionalism, for one example, like a weather front, shifts shape and interconnections so often that one is forced to the opinion that whatever functionalism was, it was dynamic and was a term that entered into multiple areas of thinking, including emotion, neurology (as that was defined circa 1912), aesthetics, and other peripheral as well as central connections. There were central cores to some of these terms, around which a number of writers cohered, but each one of them had significant variation from the other—exactly as the dynamic and changing systems of definition in psychology do today. To provide a single definition of, again, say, functionalism pulled out of a particular period's intellectual equilibrium today and to try to apply it to current psychological thinking would be like trying to fit the piston rings for a 1904 Cadillac engine on the pistons of a 2013 Honda. It would at best make metaphorical sense, but, like a piston ring, it could not stretch enough to overcome its anachronistic irrelevance to the current exchange of ideas. By 1923, as Green's analyses show, functionalism and structuralism aligned with entirely different ideas and communities of psychologists than they did 20 years earlier, and by the '30s they existed as terms only in the minds of those who could preserve history in mental amber. I've tried to suggest, in what I've written about psychology's history post 1927, what the succession of new intellectual communities were, but a basic history can convey only the barest idea of the fine grain of ideas that went into making behaviorism, cognitive science, or humanistic psychology what they were when they started and what they are now, after years of evolution. In short, structuralism and functionalism are antique terms: Go to the historical sources to understand them—don't expect to encounter them in current discourse. If you do, find out from the context, current or past, exactly what was intended by the users of these terms. That will be fairer to the process of intellectual or cultural evolution.

Q. You have so much about homosexuality in this history—are YOU gay?

A. Interesting question! Answer: I don't know. Maybe. Some people have said so. I know it's a centrally important part of the history of psychology, but even more so, a centrally important part of recent U.S. history. There is no way to conceptualize the 1980s and beyond without reference to Stonewall, AIDS, and the recent aggressive attacks on individual lesbian, gay, bisexual, and transgender [LGBT] individuals, as well as on this whole segment of society as a group. Along with abortion, the issue of homosexuality, especially homosexual marriage, has been and continues to be a flashpoint for rallying conservative opposition to prosocial policies generally. The coalition's recognition of it was a marker in its continuing shift toward recognizing its diverse human constituency. Remarkably, in what I think is the strongest recent general historical presentation of the developments in psychology since 1950, homosexuality is mentioned exactly once, in conjunction with feminist support in psychology for removal of the term as a diagnosis in the *Diagnostic and Statistical Manual of Mental Disorders*, and entirely in the context of an able discussion of the range of developments across psychology in the 1970s directed toward the support of women. These were echoed in the pattern of development of support systems for LGBT in psychology, but at a later time, even though both feminist and LGBT liberation movements as such got their start at the same time, in the 1960s. In fact, as I alluded earlier in the text, it was a woman, Evelyn Hooker, who broke down the barriers surrounding the empirical study of homosexuality in psychology (Milar, 2011). There are numerous histories and personal testimonies of LGBT psychologists. At the very dawn of psychotherapy in this book's chronology, Harry Stack Sullivan, who was gay (Blechner, 2005), was one of the first persons to offer acceptance and support to other gay and lesbian individuals in the arts community, where he was a prominent supportive figure. Roger Brown (1925–1997), eminent psycholinguist, one of the most significant of the early systematizers and theorists of cognitive science and very open about his sexuality, wrote, describing himself, "I am certainly not gay: 'gay' is a rarefied state of consciousness attainable only by those born after 1960 or so, and I was born in 1925" (Pinker, 1998). Read Steven Pinker's full obituary of Brown in *Cognition* (Pinker, 1998) for a fuller picture of the life of an academic homosexual who lived through most of this period.

Q. What theories and individuals do you think you've missed?

A. I haven't mentioned much about disability, autism, or other developmental disorders, though they are interwoven into the history of psychology, both in terms of institutional care and psychotherapy. Reading over the first draft, I was struck that I had entirely neglected to mention evolutionary psychology, the intellectual focus that grew up around the time of the publication of E. O. Wilson's *Sociobiology* in 1975. Strangely, evolution is never the centerpiece of the history of psychology, even though Jastrow identified Darwin as one of the models of the future great psychologist. Skinner overtly linked operant behaviorism to evolution. Perhaps one reason for evolution's partial eclipse is bound up with the animosity between cognitive and behavioral camps in the 1970s, when evolutionary psychology came on the scene. Add along with this that evolution, in terms of behavior, is speculative, resting on postulates of kin support and group behavior that have to be assembled from various sources outside of psychology: anthropology; primatology; and history. Perhaps as theories of economics and also of the psychological dimensions of primitive society tunnel toward current evolutionary theories of human mate choice and behavior allocation, there will be more prominence for evolutionary theories in psychology, and in its history. I'd also like to put in a "plug" for those psychologists who are taking anthropology seriously and trying to extend the history of psychology back into prehistory, before the development of writing at least. The collective decision to start the historical account at around the Hellenic age rather than 50,000 years earlier is a serious shortcoming of the present-day conception of the history of psychology, in my opinion. And I haven't captured how psychology has spread around the world, and how, even among those countries who are in dialogue with American psychology or who have largely modeled their psychologies on U.S. lines, important regional differences exist.

Q. Why do women and minorities not have a larger place in this history?

A. They could, if identity psychology and politics were the only story. But in my opinion the general movement toward racial equality in society as a whole, and the reaction against it since 1970, are the dynamics that are essential to understand. I have tried to show that women and minorities have been involved in psychology throughout the period I've covered. I recommend searching the history of Divisions 35 and 45 of the coalition to see the range of contributors from Hispanic, Native American, and Asian/Pacific cultures. I've attempted to redress the balance with Juana's story, but like Anh Binh has said, real cultural integration is the future. That is why I said, at the beginning, that the most serious critiques of psychology are directed at its American form, which has been slow to change to become fully representative, and accepting, of all people.

Q. Will the coalition survive?

A. No historian ought to make specific predictions about the future, especially in the current sociopolitical context, absent the conditions necessary for an exact point prediction. But my feeling is this: Before 1945 there was a mainly theoretical/ scientific APA [American Psychological Association] and other organizations for applied psychology. Clinical psychology, as we now conceive it, was hardly visible at all. By 1985 the coalition appeared strong, reasonably well balanced across its elements, and more representative of its clientele, although hardly populist and still mainly a reflection of an academic and professional elite. The effect of the 1988

APA–APS [American Psychological Society] split on the coalition was slight. Now, since that time, the number of specialty organizations that can attract a psychologist has increased vastly. Even in the 1960s a psychologist had many organizations to choose from, some very well established and not mentioned here. A case in point is the Society for Research in Child Development, an offshoot of a Committee on Child Development housed in the National Academy of Sciences in the 1920s and chartered as an independent organization in 1933, which has long been the primary institutional and official organization of child development specialists. I chose the APA for this history as a representative example of organized psychology and as the primary example of the coalition of forces that have defined psychology to date. I think those forces will continue to define psychology, but institutionally there will probably be continual migration toward specialist societies, especially if, as I expect, neuroscience will begin to differentiate to capture the variety of psychological interests that are likely to stream toward it. Will psychiatry and psychology eventually merge? Probably not. The fields will have to come to an understanding, but numbers usually win battles. On the applied side, computing and information science will probably engulf cognitive psychology. It may be that information science will overtake education in terms of the delivery of information, leaving socialization, both within and between cultures, as psychology's primary application. B. F. Skinner once opined that, after automation had relieved humans of most of the tasks of providing products and services, nothing would be left but education and counseling. And art.

Q. Who, in your view, was the greatest psychologist?

A. Well, I don't know about the "greatest" psychologist. As Jastrow said, maybe the real great psychologist hasn't arrived yet—like the Savior? Just kidding. But I think it's true that psychology still hasn't got its Newton or Darwin yet. Maybe we're looking for the wrong person. Maybe we ought to be looking at people who make good recombinations of the material. Possibly the greatest psychologist is going to be some artificial intelligence (AI) program that is able to recombine ideas better than any human recombiner of ideas that we now have or that we'll ever have. As for great individual performances, I recall one of my art teachers—Italo Scanga, wonderful, giving, funny, human man—saying that he liked it all, he didn't care whether he saw Warhol, or Giacometti, or some kid making a plaster mask, he was open, he said; he was easy. I think that's a good way for psychologists to be. I had too many prejudices when I was younger.

Q. Who was the greatest one that you personally came in contact with?

A. Again, really hard to answer that question. I think that every psychologist that I've come in contact with has had something to offer. I've disliked only a very few, and even from them I think I've learned things. They're all human and they all have good and bad days, and it's easy to have disagreements with just about anyone. I have to say, I made a contact with a psychologist early in my life who means the world to me with what he taught me—unintentionally taught me. I felt moved one time to say to him that he was the reason that I had gotten into the field. And his response was to vigorously resist the idea that anyone but myself was responsible for myself. Wise man. Wise, wise man.

Q. Who was the worst one?

A. Ha, ha!

Q. What do you think of Freud? I've heard that he is dead.

A. I think the world of Freud. I'm quite Freudian: My interest in psychology began when I read Freud when I was 16 years old—*The Ego and the Id*; short book, lots of punch. Freud determined much of the shape, kind, ideas, directions, and ethos of modern psychology. Another way of writing this recent history would be to write it from the vantage point of all the ways Freud intersects with it. In the '80s people were always saying, Freud is dead, you only read about Freud in the English department, and on and on. There were scandals: There was an attempt to show that Freud was actively trying to hide the truth about the abuse suffered by his patients; there was the recent discovery that Freud may have had an affair with his sister-in-law. A story: When I was a graduate student, we had a yearly undergraduate conference, and one time a student got up and read this paper—a well-researched and well-presented paper—about Freud and cocaine; the whole tenor of which was to damn Freud for being a rotten drug abuser, basing that more or less on the *DSM-III* (which was the diagnostic manual at the time). To which I had to say, come on, it's Freud you are judging here. Is your arm long enough to box with him? As for "dead": No psychologist to date has come close to Freud's depth of treatment of the concept of death in all of its ramifications. Those who want to study revenge, survivor guilt, and the roots of killing are necessarily going to pass through his door. Eros and Thanatos, Love or Life and Death, are locked in a titanic struggle, and which will win? Freud asked that question at the end of one of his last works, *Civilization and Its Discontents*, published in 1930, 3 years before Hitler took over the government of Germany. Which one won? Which will win in the future, in their eternal struggle? Freud will never die.

Q. What projects in history does this story suggest to you? My professor says that I should choose a problem in history of psychology and work on it.

A. Sure, many. Here are a dozen, not at all complete, of historical questions I'd pursue based on this story:

1. Vietnam and the ways that the Vietnam experience resonated with psychology. There is an excellent starting point for this in Bonnie Strickland's (APA president, 1987) short memoir in the *American Psychologist*, March 2000.

2. A history of psychology and the managed care/health care system/health insurance system.

3. The personal activities of individual psychologists during the high points of the Civil Rights Era. Indeed, the personal activities of any psychologist anytime.

4. The fate of German psychology after World War II. There is an excellent work that describes how easily established psychology in Germany adapted to the Nazis (Ulf Geuter) for a starting point.

5. Following on the previous, histories of psychology in any region outside the United States and Canada, especially how they interacted with U.S. psychology.

6. Psychology and its interaction with the "service economy," "flat world," and other modern economic conceits. Psychology's role in downsizing and offshoring.

7. The relative stagnation of personality theory after 1980, and the difficulty with getting new theories (post-1980) into circulation.

8. The full range of effect of digital technology and psychology.

9. Psychology's role in setting drug policy in the United States.

10. The deterioration in the relations between psychiatry and psychology after 1960. (Hint: David Rapaport died in 1960.)

11. The history of the campaign in the APA against advocacy and social activism in psychology after 1945.

12. The pattern of funding of psychology after 1960.

    … and many, many others.

Q. What is the role of religion in psychology? You mention a division of Religion and Psychology—is there a role for religion?

A. Without religion I doubt there would have been any psychology, or any activism for the common good, and certainly no gains for civil rights. Religion was instrumental to psychology's origins in the United States, as the work of Eugene Taylor (1946–2013) makes clear. Modern psychotherapy has its roots in diverse religious movements at the end of the 19th century, including Christian Science and New Thought. As a member of a Unitarian Universalist congregation myself, I take note of the Unitarian Universalists I encounter in the history of psychology: Among those who were Unitarians were Jane Addams; George Stoddard, who as director of the Iowa Child Welfare Research Station and Graduate Dean, was instrumental in supporting Kurt Lewin; J. Raymond Cope, the Unitarian Minister who made members of his Berkeley congregation available to Hubert Coffey's graduate students, including Abel Ossorio and Timothy Leary, to conduct their analysis of group therapy dynamics; and Dalmas Taylor, one of the group of psychologists who established Division 45 of the APA (American Psychological Association) and after whom the APA's minority fellowship is named. There have been psychologists who were not themselves associated with particular religions who nevertheless contributed to the activity of liberal religion and aligned this with a view of a cognitive system that would promote tolerance. Gordon Allport wrote, in *The Individual and His Religion* (1950), of mature religion contrasted with "immature" religion. Immature religion, characterized by literalism, nonreflective attitudes, and fanatic, should change, in healthy development, to mature religion, leading to the practice of a consistent morality, the ability to differentiate, openness to new knowledge, and heuristic application of knowledge to new life situations. Wieman's theology was shaped by his encounters with the philosophy that engendered much of humanist psychology as well as humanist religion. It was this mixture that contributed to Martin Luther King Jr.'s cognitive and spiritual maturation, and to his activism as well. While in the surrounding culture the influence of liberal religion, in terms of numbers of individuals active in it, has declined, and the activity of various types of evangelical religion, often hostile to some of the collective solutions to inequality advanced through the 1970s, in psychology the forward movement toward inclusion and equality, appears to have been maintained. The role of more conservative religious views in shaping future psychological practice needs to be examined: there is not much to go on historically regarding this. There has been a Christian Association for Psychological Studies since 1956, which has coexisted with the rest of psychology: It affirms a statement of faith that is expressly Christian, and its ethics code, with the exception of affirming certain biblical principles as defining features of its membership, follows point for point the language and intents of the APA Ethics Code. Some ecumenical evangelicals have been very close to psychology and psychologists. In the recent past, Dr. Robert Schuller in California would solicit the advice of psychologists, urban theorists, and others at weekly breakfasts. Regarding other faiths, there are lively discussions about the role of Muslim psychology, although some of the same dangers that were mortal to Martín-Baró are present in radicalized Muslim countries as well. In the United States, the APA has been accepting and supportive of Muslim psychology, although this has inflamed opposition by some parts of the general public. The question of whether psychology is a safe haven for religious tolerance, and, if so, how safe and how secure it is, is unsettled, and is one of the aspects of why the question of the relation of religion and psychology remains on the list of the persistent problems of psychology.

Q. You say an awful lot about Meehl. What was so important about him?

A. People who knew him personally and worked with him—I didn't—say that he was the smartest psychologist they ever met. I picked a book of his off the library shelf at Temple University in 1981 and was hooked after a few sentences. It was his 1973 collection of essays, *Psychodiagnosis*, and if my memory is to be trusted (and why should it be? If psychology has discovered anything, it's that memory is a weak reed) I read his essay, "Why I Do Not Attend Case Conferences," which sends up the whole mental health establishment in fine style. I had just worked for a short time in a secure mental health facility and knew enough about the procedures to understand what frustrated him about that environment.

He evolved into a main character in the coalition side of the story. One reason is that he lived through virtually the whole era and was active all his life: Several of his papers were published posthumously. He was the modern equivalent of William James, in terms of him being a "triple threat." James's claim to be the primary ancestor of psychology in the United States stems from his ability to span and integrate three separate intellectual specialties: philosophy, psychology, and religion. He was also trained as an MD, but that was in 1869, so that while he had met Darwin personally while his family lived in England and had been "present at the creation" of modern biology, his appreciation of the importance of biology and physiology to psychology was more intuitive than actual. And he was interested in everything. All of this fits Meehl, with the exception that Meehl was a virtuoso in philosophy, psychology, and law, weaving in, like James, a kind of intuitive bioneurology and also in religion, for a time at least. Meehl once described psychology in terms of what he called its "five noble truths": **behavior theory**; **behavior genetics**; **psychometrics** (the theory of testing: Meehl and Lee Cronbach established the modern theory of construct validity in 1955); **psychodiagnosis** as well; **psychodiagnosis** and—brace yourselves—**psychoanalysis**. Later in life Meehl said he was a 30% Freudian, down from 50%. So in that way he personified the "bones" of the discipline of modern scientific psychology. One other thing about Meehl: He was incisively logical, and his favorite occupation was taxonomy, putting things in the right categories, "carving nature at its joints." So not only did he expose the skeleton, but because he specified this particular skeletal arrangement he also implied how its parts might interact. With his colleague, Kenneth MacCorquodale, he wrote an influential paper on the distinction between hypothetical constructs and intervening variables in 1948, which was instrumental in shaping experimental methodology in psychology; he advanced, as mentioned in this book, a theory of schizophrenia; he wrote cogently on the mind–brain problem and on law, especially on the concept of guilt—a rarity for any psychologist other than Freud.

A few other things make him useful for this history. One is that he connects directly to the Menningers from his earliest days and reinforces the idea that the coalition rests on the best, most complete and humane conception of mental medicine that psychiatry could deliver at the time. He was an incisive critic, especially of methodological flaws: My answer to the question above, about operationism, draws on his ideas about psychology's statistical shortcomings (which are shared by many other psychologists now, as well). Since the critics move history along, he's a propelling force. And he provides geographic centering to this U.S.-based story. Like Kant, Meehl stayed in the same place all his life. Born and bred in Minnesota, he entered the University of Minnesota in 1939 and never left—even after retirement he would walk to the campus from his home a few blocks away. He represented a kind of psychology of the 1930s that relied on data rather than speculation. People at the time saw this as typical of Iowa and Minnesota, called it "Dustbowl Empiricism," and the name stuck. The history of psychology, for a long time, centered on the Ivy League universities of the East. What I want to show in this history is how psychology spread out over the United States and Canada during the period: Meehl is an excellent representative of the contributions of the Midwest.

Q. You didn't say much about the actual practice of psychotherapy—Harry is a therapist, but we never see him in action.

A. He didn't leave any transcripts. Psychotherapy transcripts are, relative to the amount that could be available, among the rarest of archival materials. Occasionally, therapists dedicated to either getting the word out about psychotherapy, or empirically oriented with the intention to test theories about therapy content, have either filmed or recorded actual therapy sessions. One of the most heroic of these was the set of tapes made over 6 years by Hartvig Dahl, a psychoanalytic therapist who collected 219 sessions with a woman, "Mrs. C." These, along with many others, are available through an online library subscription service specializing in therapy transcripts (Alexander Street Press). Through the years, case studies of various types of psychotherapy have been published, for example, Burton (1959). Carl Rogers freely quoted from many cases in his own books. Freud is well known through his cases, but these are often incomplete, and at any rate are heavily redacted to read as literature rather than as the often boring and repetitive raw material of psychotherapeutic exchanges. Some of Harry's client sessions were as long as Dahl's, and unlike Dahl, Harry wasn't motivated to study the language that his clients were using. How could he do this for any more than a handful of them, even if he wanted to? Whatever notes that may have survived were destroyed either during his move to the care facility or after his death. Probably the closest approximation to Harry's style would be the demonstrations of therapy by Arnold Lazarus, demonstrating Multimodal Therapy; Everett Shostrom, demonstrating Actualizing Therapy; and Carl Rogers, demonstrating Client-Centered Therapy in sessions in 1977 with a young woman, "Cathy," intended as comparative illustrations of technique as well as for demystifying the process (Shostrom, 1977). The films, transcripts, and many studies based on them (e.g., Moreira, Gonçalves, & Matias, 2011) are available. Shostrom (1921–1992) was an advocate for making recordings and interviews of therapists and films with actual clients. He is pretty much forgotten today—he'd be a great subject for a biography of a serious apostle of psychotherapy. But in therapy, as everywhere else, close is "no cigar." Every therapist is unique, and techniques are like fingerprints. Even people who knew Harry probably could not imagine accurately what happened when he went into action behind his closed office door. The very brief information I've mentioned is all that's left of over 30 years of psychotherapy practice. Multiply the amount of therapeutic exchanges by the number of therapists who have practiced since licensure laws went into effect.

If transcribed, it would be one of the longest books in the world—most of it lost. Recently, there's been a good graphic novel [published on] the process of therapy, *Couch Fiction*, by Philippa Perry and Junko Graat (Perry & Graat, 2010). Worth a look.

Q. The family is often at variance with the story of the evolution of psychology. I thought you wanted to show how psychology affected lives for the good?

A. Yes, the family's story is a parallel history in many respects: It often seems as if the psychology of the times didn't penetrate into their lives. I never put these two histories together until now, so I can comment only on a series of first impressions of the linkage between the two. My first impression is that psychology, even today, is something of a luxury good. Sure, a lot of people will have encountered psychology as a formal set of ideas, as a school subject. True enough, but there it stops for many people as well. A person could go on to a career in food service or sales and rarely encounter psychology again. She might, for example, take diversity training at work, which might in some way be informed by psychologists. Or not— anthropology students, philosophy students, all sorts of students end up working in the diversity training system. It's possible that this hypothetical food service worker's diversity training might have psychological connections—but only distant ones. And after that? She might be among what William James called "the once born," those fortunate enough never to experience mental illness in themselves or others. She might only rarely contact psychology from the time she's 26 years old until she enters a hospital with symptoms of dementia at 66 or 76 or even 96 years old. She might have three direct contacts with psychology during her lifetime. I think that encounters of direct influence by psychology are crucially important, but that they happen irregularly. They contribute to a sort of "punctuate evolution" of every human.

I have a hard time imagining a person who might never ever encounter psychology, if only because virtually everyone who is born is evaluated with the Denver scale or something similar, sometime in their infancy. Even persons who hate and resist psychology from the first time they encounter it— Ayn Rand or L. Ron Hubbard libertarians or Scientologists (ironic, in my view), followers of religions that teach that psychology is not to be trusted, or persons who reject any idea of mental turmoil as weakness in themselves or others, or persons who see little use for health care of any sort and are committed to a campaign against psychology as doubly ineffectual: what of them? Are they engaging with psychology as an enemy, by establishing a relationship of distrust? And what of those individuals who concoct a very strange idea of psychology as a sort of paranormality, and use those ideas to craft an occult world of their own? Is a weird, homegrown psychology a psychology nevertheless? If drugs become involved, is a person who uses drugs inadvertently engaged in actual alteration of consciousness and a psychological process? Or is "contact with psychology" limited to contacts with "credentialed knowledge" delivered by "credentialed individuals," as Paul Meehl (again!) put it? As an exercise—an intentionally intended one—I invite the reader to think over her or his own life and cite the times when psychology was directly and usefully encountered. For myself, my first encounter was with Freud, whom I read when I was 16. Might I self-disclose? I was a difficult adolescent. I was forced to go to a counselor when I was a senior in high school because I quit in March, two months before graduation. That I stood 9th in a class of 360 might have had something to do with the forced encounter with a counselor. I experienced a psychologically traumatic event soon after that. It affected me for 5 years. I came into contact with psychologists—accidental mentors—and received wise counsel from them from the time I was 20 until I was 35. I came to study psychology and ultimately to write about its history. So I have had a heavy dose. Try it yourself and see, and then see whether the story I've told here about this hypothetical family has, if not predictive accuracy, at least the ring of statistical truth.

That's my answer to the first part of your question. To answer the second, I think that there was much that was good that happened with this family and that was directly due to its interactions with psychology. I think that psychology provided real opportunities for Rosa and Harry both to thrive when they might have had worse consequences when they were young. The recognition of Rosa's talent (and Juana's as well, 40 years later), and the second chance that Harry got from the Juvenile Justice Court were significant points of redirection in their lives. Harry's encounter with the potential for real change based on respect between equals in an industrial setting primed him to recognize the potential for change in nondirective Rogerian counseling, as well as in helping him devise strategies to make his interventions with rational-emotive, cognitive-behavioral, and even the small amount of psychoanalytic technique that he used accepted by his clients as realistic and promoting their autonomy. Connection with the Virginia Lewinians led to him seeing the potential for structured scientific intervention in human affairs generally, and made him aware of Rogers's scientific side and sensitive to his characterization of his approach as measurable and reproducible. His encounters with psychology through what he read as a soldier, as well as what he studied in his undergraduate and graduate psychology courses, especially the work of Hathaway and Meehl, developed his rationality and his ability to take logical perspective. Over the course of his career he helped thousands of clients to differing degrees of solving the problems that led them to consult him. When Harry ran on rough personal times himself, he was more aware than most of the availability and the skills needed on the part of a client to accept and understand treatment. He had few options regarding his son. This was a true tragedy for him.

For Rosa, Helen, and Carolyn, virtually all of the gains were psychology's from them, rather than advantages conferred on them by psychology. Rosa benefited from a network of dedicated early feminists—some were psychologically

240

adept, but not all. Helen was innocent of psychological knowledge until she was compelled to understand new things about herself and her capabilities during her work experience in the war. Carolyn was only indirectly influenced by psychology through her schooling: Her selection for the Peace Corps depended on psychology's participation. But her single pregnancy and her mother's adaptation to her father's sudden death were challenges [that] they had to meet on their own, with their own resources. Psychological theory, for them and for Rosa and Francine as well, had not noticed them. The lives they lived and the indomitability they each showed were the elements out of which modern feminism and modern feminist psychology evolved. Their lives were improved by the eventual effect of their lives on the thought of feminists and psychologists who added their voices to those which spoke against the pathologization of homosexuality and the exclusion of women from educational and economic restriction. The incidental benefits that enhanced Rosa's and Helen's lives as they aged were at least partly due to the activity of psychologists who developed philosophies of growth throughout the life span. Juana became a psychologist and benefited from all the things that everyone had done to provide her with a supportive professional structure and a framework in which to conceptualize doing good. Her adoptions had input from psychological professionals. Her adopted children's lives are better for the support provided by psychology as well as across society for persons of other cultures in the United States. For the most part, it is as optimal a story that can be told. It seems to say that the benefits of psychology stem from the applied and therapeutic parts of the coalition. But though those benefits are great, and often unremarked in people's lives, it's an illusion to think that theory doesn't significantly affect lives. The problem that Juana is working on, immigration and the accommodation of new cultures to each other, is going to take the combined efforts of theoreticians in psychology, economics, law, philosophy and ethics, and even religion to solve. I am optimistic enough

241

to believe that brains, especially in combination, will defeat ignorance. I am hopeful.

Q. You don't mention many historians of psychology in your story. Shouldn't there be more of them?

A. In my view, historians themselves ought to be, like theorists, in the background, working on the infrastructure of the field. Part of the reason for choosing to write this history is to see what the combined result of 50 years of intense scholarship; on feminism and minority involvement; on the relation between psychology and medicine and the law; on the interface between government and psychology; and on the intellectual status of the conception of psychology as a modern, applied science could look like. Much has been written: The citations and the recommended reading list are an acknowledgment of a great debt. More needs to be written: Perhaps you, the reader, will be one who adds to a story of humans helping themselves to understand each other better. If you want to quickly track where the current historians of psychology enter into the text, look in the references for those whose articles are in the journal *History of Psychology* or the *Journal of the History of the Behavioral Sciences* and the authors of the *Time Capsules* in the *APA Monitor.*

Q. I don't see too much developmental psychology in the story. You mention personality and social psychology—why not developmental psychology?

A. I notice this too, and I'm surprised, because I often recommend that the Intro Psych course be dropped from the curriculum and a Developmental course, possibly two semesters long, replace it. Especially, I notice that neither Jean Piaget nor Erik Erikson are mentioned, well Erikson is, a little. Sometimes they get mentioned not only in Developmental Psychology but in Personality Psychology as well. There were thousands of other psychologists who were active in all phases of the study of development. Regarding aging alone, Walter and Catherine Cox Miles, Wayne Dennis (also an early and important figure in writing the history of psychology), Jack Botwinick, Paul Baltes and his colleagues, and many others contributed to a positive view of aging that is becoming more and more my own concern. Every one of the subdivisions of Developmental Psychology and, really, each of psychology's specialty fields, has a detailed and rich history. Developmental is particularly rich because of the number of women that worked in it from the very beginning, since they had particular closeness to children and childrearing. I would estimate that half or more of those who would have called themselves developmental psychologists in the '20s were women. That is another history project. Piaget and Erikson were each inimitable originators in psychology. Piaget was the psychologist with [possibly] the widest vision of humanity of all. Erikson understood life at all levels and experienced great personal tragedy as well. I've tried, though, to redress this lack of specificity about Developmental Psychology by showing how psychology might have effects on individual lives across generations. I also note that Nicholas Hobbs, who was involved with starting the Peace Corps, was a comparatively unsung developmental psychologist (possibly because of the focus of his work), and Mihalyi Csikszentmihalyi (M. C.) and Reed Larson's *Being Adolescent* is a superb addition to our knowledge of what it's like to be teenaged, although M. C. is better known for his happiness and flow work now.

Q. What does the freeway system look like on this side, 1920 to now?

A. I haven't drawn it yet, because I haven't decided on the form it should take. This is something that you, the readers, can do for yourselves along with me. For my part, I think that there is, running right down the center, a cognitive freeway paralleled by a behaviorist "old road," like Old Route 66. By about halfway through the modern period the cognitive freeway eats up the old road, like I-80 has eaten up U.S. 6 around Des Moines. Occasionally you see it breaking away and running in a nearly parallel direction. Where they both are going, that's a good question! I see the philosophy and religion roads bending away from the psychology roads. I see a parallel psychotherapy highway, and a parallel scientific psychology highway (broken coalition?). Or, possibly psychology and the other social sciences are forming their own, interconnected cities out in the intellectual deserts: psychologists are self-sufficient. They drive to political science or philosophy for a weekend, like Angelenos to Las Vegas. Maybe air routes need to be incorporated. Maybe a map of air routes and frequency of flights to other places in the world would be a better model. Maybe the whole intellectual world is like what Freud imagined the mind to be: one city, with multiple layers, ancient to modern, like Rome or, less ancient, New York. Or one gated community? I hope not. Right now, it's what I like best—a blank canvas.

Any more? Thank you, and if you ever have any questions about this history, or the history of psychology generally, write me at devonis@graceland.edu, or care of the publishers.

Appendix I

Some Notes on the Characters

This history is not precisely an example of "new biography" or "psychohistory," although it has some connections to both. The form it approaches most closely is probably historical fiction. The intent was to show one example of the ways in which psychology could touch people in their individual lives across several generations. If Social Security and Medicare are considered, these are common connections for almost every American. The number of people who undertake psychotherapy is large: Probably every American family that has the means to do so has a member who has entered counseling or therapy at some point, for some reason. Families with older members have doubtless encountered various psychological interventions in health and rehabilitation. Thankfully, the number of families that have experienced a suicide is smaller, but it is not insignificant, and the gravity and repercussions of that act outweigh its relative rarity. The direct experience of war was something that loomed large in most people's lives, either as civilians or combatants, during and for many years after the Second World War and Korea. The transmission of those experiences, and the attitudes shaped by those experiences, are still unexamined with relation to psychology. Very few professors, applied psychologists, or therapists were or are Vietnam veterans: The influence on psychology of those who were is another gap in the historical record. Probably the most fictive of the characters is Juana: A lot of things would have had to break in the right direction for this combination of events and this life direction to transpire. The most improbable event in the series is Juana's encounter with the work of Ignacio Martín-Baró, while he was still alive. Persons who met and knew him in America would have to have been older, like Juana's professors in California, rather than students like Juana herself. They would also have had to be able to stay in contact with him, have access to his locally published writings in El Salvador, and able to read and, if necessary, translate Spanish (Juana had the advantage, like many students today, of bilinguality). Otherwise, though, the story contains many representative events. The readers of this book are invited to think over their own family histories and examine at how many points psychology had remarked and unremarked effects. I believe it will be a surprise for most to see that the number is not small.

THE CHARACTERS THEMSELVES

Their Family Name

Schwartz was not an uncommon name in the western Ukraine. Nor was it uncommon for whole villages' records to be incinerated along with their Jewish inhabitants by the Nazi occupiers between 1941 and 1944. Changes of name were also not uncommon on coming to America; there were various reasons for this. These included misspellings by immigration registration personnel (probably the fate of my own paternal ancestors); difficulty of pronunciation; and in some cases, as with the Blacks, the desire to make a break from the past. Jacob and Lyuba were actively involved in changing their cultural identity. As can be surmised from their story, their commitment to their religion was slight: They were not observant and did not teach the tenets of their religion to their children, although Jacob's cousin did manage to get Harry through his Bar Mitzvah ceremony before Harry's acute rebellious phase. Religious connection and observance varied widely among those, both immigrant and American-born, who became psychologists: This is a good area for future historical research, as the exact dimensions of childhood and adolescent religious experiences on individuals' psychological views, then and now, are not well documented. At any rate, the name change was their choice—it was a direct translation of the name from Yiddish to English. Some psychologists of similar cultural backgrounds shortened or respelled their names (e.g., Isidor Krechevsky, who shortened his to David Krech), sometimes because of anti-Semitic prejudices in psychology (Winston, 1996), but most others kept their original names. Kurt Lewin remained Kurt Lewin after his move to America, though after he came here he insisted that his family name be pronounced "Lou-in" rather than "Luhveen," as it was pronounced in the Poland and Germany of his youth and early adulthood. This, he said, was to assist his children in fitting into American society.

Rosa

I never knew a person with a personality exactly like this, although she is reminiscent of the wife of one of my early mentors, himself a first-generation son of Eastern European Jewish immigrants. I have known pacifists, some more active than Rosa. Her long-term relationship with Francine is not unusual. The plaintiffs in one of the 2013 Supreme Court decisions striking down federal restrictions on full marriage rights for lesbians and gays were together for 44 years. I personally know individuals in Iowa with relationships lasting well over 25 years who have been officially married only for 4, since 2009. In my experience I have encountered all shades and grades of being "out." To some extent, Rosa connects with another friend of mine, my oldest friend, who, with her sharp mind and her sensitive social conscience, has labored, not without happiness and fulfillment, as an editor over the past 40 years.

Harry and Donald

Harry is pretty directly modeled on another of my mentors, a clinician in Philadelphia. He obtained a Master of Arts (MA) from Temple University—my own undergraduate school—in 1950, studying psychology with, among others, James Page, one of the most prolific writers on mental hygiene and abnormal psychology at the time, and a proponent of logotherapy, the version of existential psychoanalysis championed by Viktor Frankl. Earlier, my mentor, child of immigrant Jewish parents (he himself was not religious, although his last rites—with traditional prayers and service—took place at Goldstein's-Rosenberg's-Raphael Sacks on North Broad Street), began to run with a rough crowd in his teens. After a car theft, he was offered the option of jail or the Army (it was 1943) and, choosing the Army, was sent to Lehigh University to study electronics and, incidentally, psychology as well. He shipped out for Europe in 1944 and just missed the disastrous practice run for D-Day, Operation Tiger, in which approximately 900 troops were killed, and the first wave of the D-Day invasion itself. He spoke hardly at all of his war experiences. During the 1950s and 1960s he practiced clinical psychology in all of its aspects: testing, guidance, and counseling; consulting at hospitals; and individual psychotherapy in an office in Center City Philadelphia. Next door, a psychiatrist colleague liaised with him to prescribe medications, when necessary. My mentor connected well with adolescent clients. One of these was a popular singer of the time, and he would often make "house calls" to her in New York. Others could be found camped out in his hallway waiting for him to make time for them—which he always did. Eventually, after several heart attacks, he closed his city practice and moved to a series of suburban homes where he maintained offices and his extensive, well-chosen psychological library. I have his copies of Freud's *Collected Papers*, Tolman's *Purposive Behavior in Animals and Men*, and Reich's *Character Analysis*. I got to know him through being friends with a friend of his son's, and eventually was invited to his home. Much of what I know about civilized American life I learned there, among his books and his extensive record collection. He and his wife were another family to me. In my youth and young adulthood, when things were hardly clear to me after the suicide of my mother, my mentor offered what I now recognize was therapy contained in the ordinary conversations we had. For this I am grateful now and forever—I never got a chance to thank him.

All this said, my mentor was a very private man and difficult to know. His son, my friend, was indulged. He had the best of everything. Given those advantages, he dissipated them. His father did not live to see his son's downward drift, the development of his drug addictions, and ultimately the natural social consequences of illegal acts he performed as a medical professional. Unlike Donald, though, he is still alive, and near 60—there's still hope.

One other thing occurs to me before I leave Harry's—my mentor's—home. It was there, though I thought little about it at the time, that I benefited from the cleanliness and order of the home that was the result of the work of Rosa, their maid, who cleaned twice a week and who for a long time was like a member of the family—a distant member, but still included. Although Philadelphia may have been 40% Black when I was growing up, my contacts with Black people were very limited, partly because my parents had opted to move away from the city to a suburb in which only a very few Black families, descendants of free Blacks who had lived there since Revolutionary times, were residents. All the prejudices of the time were in full view in my home town, even prejudices against Jews, which my parents at once shared, and yet detested enough to teach me that such attitudes were wrong. That race runs through this history is at least in part determined by my own ambiguous relation to it.

Helen, Carolyn, and Juana

Helen's wartime experience is modeled directly on that of Mable Gerken, whose remarkable memoir of her wartime work experiences, *Ladies in Pants: A Home Front Diary*, I discovered when reading Walter Kempowski's *Das Echolot* (1993), in which excerpts from it are interspersed with the other biographies that make up that tapestry of life. The various forms of independence portrayed are those I have encountered in the women I have met in my life. Helen's activities as a social worker are influenced by the feisty 70-year-old juvenile court social worker in Des Moines and the jaunty Jane Bibber, rest her soul, who conducted a clinical psychology practice in Des Moines well into her 70s. Carolyn's experiences as a single mom reflect those of many of my students and colleagues. I have purposely stayed away from including the life and lifestyles of professional colleagues in academia in describing Juana's later experiences, in order to keep the focus on the future as projected by her children. For all of them, Rosa, Harry, Helen, their children, and their children's children's children, I wanted to convey the spirit of service and sacrifice that comes with living life every day and doing a job. This, in contrast to the sorry show that our times sometimes hang on us as our legacy, is something not exactly heroic but not alien to it either.

The Places

There has been some discussion among historians of psychology over the past few years about the influence of place or cultural background in the creation of psychology. Some have held that New York is the center of psychological creativity, others Boston, others other places. In a similar way, symposia have been held on the contributions of, for instance, Italian Americans to psychology. If one is at all environmentalist, or even interactionist–environmentalist, then it is obvious that place has an effect: The way I understand place in this story is to see places as sources of nostalgic reactions and shared secret associations: those that Freud named "heimlich"—reminders of home. For everyone in this story, place is intended as a home, rather than simply an environment. Helen, Carolyn, and Juana are Californians: They are comfortable there, they understand its structure, know its joys, and know, intimately, its faults. Likewise, Rosa's affinity for Greenwich Village and Harry's development of an attachment for North Carolina, are highly personalized aspects of place that are implied and need to be taken into account to understand the people who lived in them.

Appendix II

Suggestions for Further Reading

The classic old history of psychology is E. G. Boring's 1929 *History of Experimental Psychology*. I cut my teeth on the 1950 edition (Boring, 1950). The most complete survey source through the 1970s and early 1980s is the magisterial work of E. R. Hilgard, *Psychology in America: A Historical Survey* (Hilgard, 1987). A very complete account of the modern period, which fleshes out much of the history covered in this book, is Wade Pickren and Alexandra Rutherford's *A History of Modern Psychology in Context* (Pickren & Rutherford, 2010). A rich source for the history of personality and humanistic psychology is the late Eugene Taylor's *The Mystery of Personality: A History of Psychodynamic Theories* (Taylor, 2009). The basic source for the history of clinical psychology and psychotherapy is the American Psychological Association's *History of Psychotherapy: Continuity and Change* (Norcross, Vandenbos, & Freedheim, 2011). Points of entry into the critical history of psychology are David Bakan's classic, *On Method: Toward a Reconstruction of Psychological Investigation* (Bakan, 1967), and Graham Richards's *Putting Psychology in Its Place* (Richards, 2010). Robert Val Guthrie's *Even the Rat Was White* (2nd edition, 2004) is indispensable for an understanding of the central social issues considered in this history. Beyond these, historical scholarship continues to expand the range and depth of psychology's history. An e-bibliography of essential sources is David Devonis's and Wade Pickren's *History of Psychology* in the *Oxford Bibliographies Online* series (Devonis & Pickren, 2013).

References

Albee, G. (1970). The uncertain future of clinical psychology. *American Psychologist, 25*(1), 1071–1080.

Albee, G. (2005). The decline and fall of the American Psychological Association. *The National Psychologist, 14*(5), 7.

Allport, G., & Postman, L. J. (1947). *The psychology of rumor.* New York, NY: Holt, Rinehart, & Winston.

Allport, G. W. (1940). The psychologist's frame of reference. *Psychological Bulletin, 37*(1), 1–28. Retrieved July 26, 2013, from http://psychclassics.yorku.ca/Allport/frame.htm

American Psychological Association. (1977). Sandra Lipsitz Bem: Early Career Award. *American Psychologist, 32*(1), 88–91.

American Psychological Association. (2013). APA amicus briefs by issue. Retrieved July 30, 2013, from http://www.apa.org/about/offices/ogc/amicus/index-issues.aspx

Azar, B. (2011). Positive psychology advances, with growing pains. *APA Monitor on Psychology, 42*(4), 32.

Bakan, D. (1967). *On method: Toward a reconstruction of psychological investigation.* San Francisco, CA: Jossey-Bass.

Baker, R. R. (1996). A history of Division 18 (Psychologists in Public Service). In D. A. Dewsbury (Ed.), *Unification through division, Vol. 1: Histories of the divisions of the American Psychological Association* (pp. 137–155). Washington, DC: American Psychological Association.

Ball, L. (2010). Catharine Cox Miles, 1890–1984. In A. Rutherford (Ed.), *Psychology's Feminist Voices Multimedia Internet Archive.* Retrieved July 29, 2013, from http://www.feministvoices.com/catharine-cox-miles

Bandura, A. (1986). *Social foundations of thought and action: A social cognitive theory.* New York, NY: Pearson.

Bandura, A., & Walters, R. H. (1963). *Social learning and personality development.* New York, NY: Holt, Rinehart, & Winston.

Barlett, D. L., & Steele, J. B. (1996, September 22). America: Who stole the dream? The have-mores and the have-lesses (Part 1). *The Philadelphia Inquirer.* Retrieved July 30, 2013, from http://www.barlettandsteele.com/journalism/inq_dream_1.php

Baumrind, D. (1964). Some thoughts on ethics of research after reading Milgram's *Behavioral Study of Obedience. American Psychologist, 19,* 421–423.

Behrens, R. R. (1994). Adalbert Ames and the cockeyed room. *Print, 48,* 92–97.

Berrien, F. K. (1944). *Practical psychology.* New York, NY: Macmillan.

Biederman, I., Glass, A. L., & Stacy, E. W. (1973). Searching for objects in real-world scenes. *Journal of Experimental Psychology, 97,* 22–27.

Biederman, I., & Vessel, E. A. (2006). Perceptual pleasure and the brain. *American Scientist, 94,* 249–255.

Blechner, M. (2005). The gay Harry Stack Sullivan: Interactions between his life, clinical work, and theory. *Contemporary Psychoanalysis, 41*(1), 1–18.

Boring, E. G. (1943). *Psychology for the fighting man.* New York, NY: Penguin Books.

Boring, E. G. (1946). Mind and mechanism. *American Journal of Psychology, 59,* 173–192.

Boring, E. G. (1950). *A history of experimental psychology* (2nd ed.). New York, NY: Appleton-Century-Crofts.

Boring, E. G. (1951). The woman problem. *American Psychologist, 6,* 679–682.

Botwinick, J. (1970). Geropsychology. In P. H. Mussen & M. Rosenzweig (Eds.), *Annual Review of Psychology, 21,* 239–272.

Boyd, W. S. (2004). *Juvenile justice in the making.* New York, NY: Oxford University Press.

Brady, D., & Rapoport, L. (1973). Violence and Vietnam: A comparison between attitudes of civilians and veterans. *Human Relations, 26*(6), 735–752.

Bridgman, P. (1927). *The logic of modern physics.* New York, NY: Macmillan.

Bronstein, P., & Quina, K. (1988). *Teaching a psychology of people. Resources for gender and sociocultural awareness.* Washington, DC: American Psychological Association.

Brown v. Board of Education, 347 U.S. 483 (1954).

Bruner, J. S., & Goodman, C. C. (1947). Value and need as organizing features in perception. *Journal of Abnormal and Social Psychology, 42,* 33–44.

Burton, A. (Ed.). (1959). *Case studies in counseling and psychotherapy.* Englewood Cliffs, NJ: Prentice-Hall.

Bush, G. W. (2001, November 8). President Bush on homeland security. *Washington Post.* Retrieved from http://www.washingtonpost.com/ wp-srv/nation/specials/attacked/transcripts/bushtext_110801. html

Buss, A. H. (1961). *The psychology of aggression.* New York, NY: Wiley.

Byrd, A. D. (2006). Review of N. A. Cummings & R. H. Wright (Eds.), *Destructive trends in mental health: The well-intentioned path to harm.* Retrieved July 30, 2013, from http://narth.com/docs/destructive. html

California Task Force. (1990). *Toward a state of esteem: The final report of the California Task Force to Promote Self-esteem and Personal and Social Responsibility.* Sacramento, CA: California State Department of Education.

Campbell, D. T. (1969). Reforms as experiments. *American Psychologist, 24*(4), 409–429.

Capshew, J. (1999). *Psychologists on the march: Science, practice, and professional identity in America, 1929–1969.* New York, NY: Cambridge University Press.

Chomsky, N. (1959). A review of B. F. Skinner's *Verbal Behavior. Language, 35,* 26–58.

Cialdini, R. (1984). *Influence: The new psychology of modern persuasion.* New York, NY: William Morrow.

Clark, K. B. (1963). Transcript of excerpts of interview (*Pageant Magazine* interviews Kenneth B. Clark, in "Notes and News"). *American Psychologist, 18,* 725–726.

Clark, K. B., & Clark, M. P. (1939). The development of consciousness of self and the emergence of racial identification in Negro preschool children. *Journal of Social Psychology, S.P. S. S. I. Bulletin, 10,* 591–599.

Coch, L., & French, J. R. P. Jr. (1948). Overcoming resistance to change. *Social Relations, 1,* 512–532.

Cohen, D., Nisbett, R. E., Bowdle, B. F., & Schwarz, N. (1996). Insult, aggression, and the Southern culture of honor: An "experimental ethnography." *Journal of Personality and Social Psychology, 70*(5), 945–960.

Collins, A. F. (2013). The reputation of K. J. W. Craik. *History of Psychology, 16*, 93–111.

Csikszentmihalyi, M. (1990). *Flow: The psychology of optimal experience.* New York, NY: Harper & Row.

Csikszentmihalyi, M. (1999). If we are so rich, why aren't we happy? *American Psychologist, 54*(10), 821–827.

Csikzentmihalyi, M., & Larsen, R. (1984). *Being adolescent: Conflict and growth in the teenage years.* New York, NY: Basic Books.

Csikszentmihalyi, M., & Rochberg-Halton, E. (1981). *The meaning of things: Domestic symbols and the self.* Cambridge, UK: Cambridge University Press.

Cutting, J. E. (1978). A program to generate synthetic walkers as dynamic point-light displays. *Behavior Research Methods and Instrumentation, 10*, 91–94.

Devonis, D. C. (2012a). Leonard T. Troland. In R. Rieber (Ed.), *Encyclopedia of the history of psychological theories.* New York, NY: Springer Publishing Company.

Devonis, D. C. (2012b). Timothy Leary's mid-career shift: Clean break or inflection point? *Journal of the History of the Behavioral Sciences, 48*(1), 16–39.

Devonis, D. C. (2013). Come Alfred Binet venne in America per rimanervi (How Alfred Binet came to America to stay.) In G. Ceccarelli (Ed.), *Alfred Binet e la misura dell'intelligenza (Alfred Binet and the measurement of intelligence).* Milan, Italy: FrancoAngeli.

Devonis, D. C., & Pickren, W. E. (2013). History of psychology (online bibliography). In D. Dunn (Ed.), *Oxford bibliographies online: Psychology.* Retrieved October 15, 2013, from http://www.oxfordbibliographies.com/view/document/obo-9780199828340/obo-9780199828340-0064.xml?rskey=ar1Au4&result=43&q=

Dodge, R. (1902). The act of vision. *Harper's Monthly Magazine, 104*, 937–941.

Eastern Mennonite University. (2007). Iraqi peace worker killed in Baghdad. *The Mennonite, 10*(3), 7.

Ehrle, R. A., & Johnson, B. G. (1963). Psychologists and cartoonists. *American Psychologist, 16*, 693–695.

El-Hai, J. (2005). *The lobotomist: A maverick medical genius and his tragic quest to rid the world of mental illness.* New York, NY: John Wiley & Sons.

Epstein, R., Kirshnit, C. E., Lanza, R. P., & Rubin, L. C. (1984). 'Insight' in the pigeon: Antecedents and determinants of an intelligent performance. *Nature, 308*, 61–62.

Eysenck, H. (1952). The effectiveness of psychotherapy: An evaluation. *Journal of Consulting Psychology, 16*, 319–324.

Finison, L. J. (1986). The psychological insurgency, 1936–1945. *Journal of Social Issues, 42*, 21–33.

Foucault, M. (1977). *Discipline and punish: The birth of the prison* (Tr. Alan Sheridan). New York, NY: Vintage.

Freyd, J., & Finke, R. (1985). A velocity effect for representational momentum. *Bulletin of the Psychonomic Society, 23*(6), 443–446.

Freyd, J. J. (2012). *What is a betrayal trauma? What is betrayal trauma theory?* Retrieved July 30, 2013, from http://pages.uoregon.edu/dynamic/jjf/defineBT.html

Froese, J., & Devonis, D. C. (2000). Florence Richardson Robinson, 1885–1936. *The Feminist Psychologist, 27*, 29.

Fromm, E. (1941). *Escape from freedom.* New York, NY: Farrar & Rinehart.

Gade, P. A., & Drucker, A. J. (2000). A history of Division 19 (Military Psychology). In D. A. Dewsbury (Ed.), *Unification through division: Histories of the Divisions of the American Psychological Association, Vol V.* Washington, DC: American Psychological Association.

Gagné, R. M. (1985). *The conditions of learning* (4th ed.). Fort Worth, TX: Holt, Rinehart, & Winston.

Garmezy, N., & Holzman, P. (1984). Obituary: David Shakow (1901–1981). *American Psychologist, 39*, 698–699.

Gergen, K. (1973). Social psychology as history. *Journal of Personality and Social Psychology, 26*(2), 309–320.

Gerken, M. (1949). *Ladies in pants: A home front diary.* New York, NY: Exposition Press.

Geuter, U. (1992). *The professionalization of psychology in Nazi Germany.* New York, NY: Cambridge University Press.

Gibson, J. J. (1929). The reproduction of visually perceived forms. *Journal of Experimental Psychology, 12*, 1–39.

Gibson, J. J. (1947). Motion picture testing and research. *Aviation Psychology Research Reports No.7.* Washington, DC: U. S. Government Printing Office.

Glass, I. (2002). This American life 204: 81 words. This American Life webpage, January 18, 2002. Retrieved from http://www.thisamericanlife.org/radio-archives/episode/204/81-words

Goodwin, C. J. (2003). An insider's look at experimental psychology in America: The diaries of Walter Miles. In D. Baker (Ed.), *Thick description and fine texture: Studies in the history of psychology.* Akron, OH: University of Akron Press.

Gottfredson, L. (1997). Mainstream science on intelligence: An editorial with 52 signatories, history, and bibliography. *Intelligence, 24*(1), 13–23.

Green, C., Feinerer, I., & Burman, J. (2013). Networking. *Psychological Review*, 1894–1898. Presentation at Cheiron, International Society for the History of Behavioral and Social Sciences, University of Dallas, June 2013.

Green, C. D., & Benjamin, L. T. Jr. (2009). *Psychology gets in the game: Sport, mind, & behavior, 1880–1960*. Lincoln, NE: University of Nebraska Press.

Greenfield, J. (1974). *Wilhelm Reich vs. the USA*. New York, NY: Norton.

Gurung, R. (2013). *Health psychology: A cultural approach* (3rd ed.). New York, NY: Wadsworth.

Guthrie, R. V. (2004). *Even the rat was white* (2nd ed.). New York, NY: Pearson.

Haney, C. (2006). *Reforming punishment: Psychological limits to the pains of imprisonment*. Washington, DC: American Psychological Association.

Haney, C., Banks, C., & Zimbardo, P. (1973). Interpersonal dynamics in a simulated prison. *International Journal of Criminology and Penology, 1*, 69–97.

Haney, C., & Zimbardo, P. (1998). The past and future of U.S. prison policy: Twenty-five years after the Stanford Prison Experiment. *American Psychologist, 53*, 709–727.

Hardin, G. (1968). The tragedy of the commons. *Science, 162*, 1243–1248.

Harris, B. (2013, July/August). Time capsule: Preparing the human machine for war. *APA Monitor on Psychology*, 80–82.

Hathaway, S. R. (1958). A study of human behavior: The clinical psychologist. *American Psychologist, 13*(6), 257–265.

Hathaway, S. R., & Meehl, P. E. (1951). *An atlas for the clinical use of the MMPI*. Minneapolis, MN: University of Minnesota Press.

Hebb, D. O. (1974). What psychology is about. *American Psychologist, 29*(2), 71–79.

Held, L. (2010). Leona Tyler, 1906–1993. In A. Rutherford (Ed.), *Psychology's Feminist Voices Multimedia Internet Archive*. Retrieved July 26, 2013, from http://www.feministvoices.com/leona-tyler

Hilgard, E. R. (1980). The trilogy of mind: Cognition, affection, and conation. *Journal of the History of the Behavioral Sciences, 16*(2), 107–117.

Hilgard, E. R. (1987). *Psychology in America: A historical survey.* New York, NY: Harcourt Brace Jovanovich.

Hillman, J. & Ventura, M. (1993) *We've had a hundred years of psychotherapy and the world's getting worse.* New York, NY: HarperOne.

Hobbs, N. (1963). A psychologist in the Peace Corps. *American Psychologist, 18,* 47–55.

Holmes, O. W. Jr. (1927). Opinion of the court. In Buck v. Bell, Superintendent of State Colony Epileptics and Feeble Minded (Va.), 274 U.S. 200 (May 2, 1927).

Houston, J. P., Bee, H., Hatfield, E., & Rimm, D. (1979). *Invitation to psychology.* New York, NY: Academic Press.

Hovland, C. (1960). Computer simulation of thinking. *American Psychologist, 15,* 687–93.

Hovland, C. I., & Morrisett, L. (1959). A comparison of three varieties of training in human problem solving. *Journal of Experimental Psychology, 58,* 52–55.

Hsueh, Y. (2002). The Hawthorne experiments and the introduction of Jean Piaget in American industrial psychology, 1929–1932. *History of Psychology, 5*(2), 163–189.

Huffman, R. E. (1970). Which soldiers break down: A survey of 610 psychiatric patients in Vietnam. *Bulletin of the Menninger Clinic, 34*(6), 343–351.

James, W. (1892). *Psychology: Briefer course.* New York, NY: Henry Holt & Co.

Jastrow, J. (1928a). *Keeping mentally fit: A guide to everyday psychology.* New York, NY: Garden City Publishing Company.

Jastrow, J. (1928b). Lo, the Psychologist! In M. L. Reymert (Ed.), *Feelings and emotions: The Wittenberg Symposium* (pp. 434–438). Worcester, MA: Clark University Press.

Jensen, R. (2006). Behaviorism, latent learning, and cognitive maps: Needed revisions in introductory psychology textbooks. *The Behavior Analyst, 29*(2), 187–209.

Johannson, G. (1973). Visual perception of biological motion and a model for its analysis. *Perception and Psychophysics, 14,* 201–211.

Joyce, N., & Baker, D. (2008). Time capsule: The early days of sport psychology. *APA Monitor on Psychology, 39*(7), 28.

Kamin, L. (1974). *The science and politics of IQ.* Potomac, MD: Lawrence Erlbaum Associates.

Kempowski, W. (1993). *Das Echolot. Ein kollektives Tagebuch. Januar und Februar, 1943.* 4 vols. München: Knaus.

Kendler, H. (2009). The role of value in the world of psychology. *American Psychologist, 54*(10), 828–835.

Klee, E., Dressen, W., & Reiss, V. (1988). *The good old days: The Holocaust as seen by its perpetrators and bystanders.* Old Saybrook, CT: Konecky & Konecky.

Koch, S. (1993). "Psychology" or "the psychological studies"? *American Psychologist, 48*, 902–904.

Koffka, K. (1925). *The growth of the mind: An introduction to child-psychology.* New York, NY: Macmillan.

Koppes, L. (1997). American female pioneers of industrial psychology: The early years. *Journal of Applied Psychology, 82*(4), 500–515.

Korzybski, A. (1941). *Science and sanity: An introduction to non-Aristotelian systems and general semantics.* Lancaster, PA: The Science Press Printing Company.

Krantz, D. E., Grunberg, N. E., & Baum, A. (1985). Health psychology. *Annual Review of Psychology, 36*, 349–383.

Lashley, K. S. (1929). *Brain mechanisms and intelligence: A quantitative study of injuries to the brain.* Chicago, IL: University of Chicago Press.

Lashley, K. S. (1951). The problem of serial order in behavior. In L. A. Jeffress (Ed.), *Cerebral mechanisms in behavior.* New York, NY: Wiley.

Leary, T. (1957). *The interpersonal diagnosis of personality: A functional theory and methodology for personality evaluation.* New York, NY: Ronald Press Co.

Lewin, K. (1917). Kriegslandschaft. *Zeitschrift für Angewandte Psychologie, 12*, 440–447.

Lewin, K. (1943). Forces behind food habits and methods of change. *Bulletin of the National Research Council, 108*, 35–65.

Lewin, K. (1946). Action research and minority problems. *Journal of Social Issues, 4*, 34–46.

Lewis, J. M., & Hensley, T. R. (1998). The May 4 shootings at Kent State University: The search for historical accuracy. *Ohio Council for Social Studies Review, 34*(1), 9–21.

Lindner, R. (1954). *The fifty-minute hour.* New York, NY: Holt, Rinehart, & Winston.

Lombrozo, T. (2013). Of rats and men: Edward C. Tolman. *13.7 Cosmos & Culture* (blog/website): National Public Radio. Retrieved July 26, 2013, from http://www.npr.org/blogs/13.7/2013/02/11/171578224/of-rats-and-men-edward-c-tolman

Lykken, D. T. (1991). What's wrong with psychology anyway? In D. Cichetti & W. M. Grove (Eds.), *Thinking clearly about psychology.*

Volume 1: Matters of public interest (Essays in honor of Paul E. Meehl). Minneapolis, MN: University of Minnesota Press.

MacLeod, R. B. (1975). *The persistent problems of psychology.* Pittsburgh, PA: Duquesne University Press.

Maital, S. (2013, July 17). Too many MBA's in the world? *TIMnovate (Technion Institute of Management, Israel) Innovation Blog.* Retrieved July 30, 2013, from http://timnovate.wordpress.com/2013/07/17/too-many-mbas-in-the-world

Marrow, A. J. (1970) *The practical theorist: The life and work of Kurt Lewin.* New York, NY: Basic Books.

Martín-Baró, I. (1984/1994). War and mental health (Tr. Anne Wallace). In A. Aron & S. Corne (Eds.), *Writings for a liberation psychology: Ignacio Martín-Baró.* Cambridge, MA: Harvard University Press.

Maslow, A. H. (1954). *Motivation and personality.* New York, NY: Harper.

McClelland, D. C. (1961). *The achieving society.* Princeton, NJ: D. Van Nostrand.

McClelland, J. L., & Rumelhart, D. E. (1988). *Explorations in parallel distributed processing: A handbook of models, programs, and exercises.* Boston, MA: MIT Press.

McFadden, R. D. (2002, February 18). John W. Gardner, 89, founder of Common Cause and advisor to Presidents, dies. *The New York Times.* Retrieved July 29, 2013, from http://www.nytimes.com/2002/02/18/us/john-w-gardner-89-founder-of-common-cause-and-adviser-to-presidents-dies.html?pagewanted=all&src=pm

McLuhan, M. (1964). *Understanding media: The extensions of man.* New York, NY: McGraw-Hill.

Mecca, A., Smelser, N., & Vasconcellos, J. (Eds.). (1989). *The social importance of self-esteem.* Berkeley, CA: University of California Press.

Meehl, P. E. (1954). *Clinical vs. statistical prediction: A theoretical analysis and a review of the evidence.* Minneapolis, MN: University of Minnesota Press.

Meehl, P. E. (1956). Wanted: A good cookbook. *American Psychologist, 11,* 263–272.

Meehl, P. E. (1962). Schizotypy, schizotaxia, schizophrenia. *American Psychologist, 17,* 827–838.

Meehl, P. E. (1966). The compleat autocerebroscopist: A thought-experiment on Professor Feigl's mind-body identity thesis. In P.K. Feyerabend & G. Maxwell (Eds.), *Mind, matter, and method: Essays in philosophy and science in honor of Herbert Feigl.* Minneapolis, MN: University of Minnesota Press.

Meehl, P. E. (1971). Law and the fireside inductions: Some reflections of a clinical psychologist. *Journal of Social Issues, 27,* 65–100.

Meehl, P. E. (1973). Why I do not attend case conferences. In P. Meehl (Ed.), *Psychodiagnosis: Selected papers.* Minneapolis, MN: University of Minnesota Press.

Meehl, P. E. (1978). Theoretical risks and tabular asterisks: Sir Karl, Sir Ronald, and the slow progress of soft psychology. *Journal of Consulting and Clinical Psychology, 46,* 806–834.

Menninger, K. (1930). *The human mind.* New York, NY: Alfred A. Knopf.

Meyer, M. (1933). That whale among the fishes: The theory of emotions. *Psychological Review, 40,* 292–300.

Milar, K. (2011). Time capsule: The myth buster. *APA Monitor on Psychology, 42*(2), 24.

Miles, W. R. (1934). Alcohol and motor vehicle drivers. In R. W. Crum (Ed.), *Proceedings of the Thirteenth Annual Meeting of the Highway Research Board.* Washington, DC: Highway Research Board.

Miller, G. A. (1956). The magical number seven, plus or minus two. *Psychological Review, 63*(2), 81–97.

Miller, G. A. (1969). Psychology as a means of promoting human welfare. *American Psychologist, 24,* 1063–1075.

Miller, G. A. (1985). The constitutive problem of psychology. In S. Koch & D. Leary (Eds.), *A century of psychology as science* (pp. 40–59). Washington, DC: American Psychological Association.

Miller, J. G. (1955). Toward a general theory for the behavioral sciences. *American Psychologist, 10,* 513–531.

Miller, N. (1941). The frustration-aggression hypothesis. *Psychological Review, 48,* 337–342.

Minow, N. (1964). *Equal time: The private broadcaster and the public interest.* New York, NY: Atheneum.

Moreira, P., Goncalves, O. F., & Matias, C. (2011). Psychotherapy and therapist's theoretical orientation: Exploratory analysis of Gloria's narratives with Rogers, Ellis, and Perls. *Journal of Cognitive and Behavioral Psychotherapies, 21*(2), 173–190.

Murphy, G. (Ed.) (1945). *Human nature and enduring peace: Third yearbook of the Society for the Psychological Study of Social Issues.* New York, NY: Houghton Mifflin.

Myers, D. (1993). *The pursuit of happiness.* New York, NY: Avon.

Myrdal, G. (1944). *An American dilemma: The Negro problem and modern democracy* (2 vols.). New York, NY: Harper & Brothers.

Nagel, T. (1974). What is it like to be a bat? *Philosophical Review, 83,* 435–450.

National Archives. (2013). Our documents: The Sixteenth Amendment. *Our Documents Initiative Website* (online). Retrieved July 28, 2013, from http://www.ourdocuments.gov/doc.php?flash=true&doc=57

Neisser, U. (1997). Never a dull moment. *American Psychologist, 52*(1), 79–81.

Neisser, U., Boodoo, G., Bouchard, T., Boykin, A. W., Brody, N., Ceci, S., . . . Urbina, S. (1996). Intelligence: Knowns and unknowns. *American Psychologist, 51*(2), 77–101.

Nicholson, I. (2007). Baring the soul: Paul Bindrim, Abraham Maslow, and "nude psychotherapy." *Journal of the History of the Behavioral Sciences, 43*(4), 337–359.

Nisbett, R. E., & Cohen, D. (1996). *Culture of honor: The psychology of violence in the South.* Boulder, CO: Westview Press.

Norcross, J. C., Vandenbos, G. R., & Freedheim, D. K. (Eds.). (2011). *History of psychotherapy: Continuity and change* (2nd ed.). Washington, DC: American Psychological Association.

Norman, D. A. (1988). *The design of everyday things.* New York, NY: Doubleday.

Olds, J., & Milner, P. (1954). Positive reinforcement produced by electrical stimulation of septal area and other regions of the rat brain. *Journal of Comparative and Physiological Psychology, 47,* 419–427.

Olson-Buchanan, J. B., Koppes Bryan, L. L., & Thompson, L. F. (Eds.). (2013). *Using industrial psychology for the greater good: Helping those who help others* (SIOP Organizational Frontiers Series). New York, NY: Routledge.

O'Shea, M. V. (1909). Progress in child and educational psychology. *Psychological Bulletin, 6,* 73–77.

Padilla, A. (2003). The origins of the *Hispanic Journal of Behavioral Sciences*: A personal memoir. *Hispanic Journal of Behavioral Sciences, 25*(1), 3–12.

Page, E. (1972). Behavior and heredity. *American Psychologist, 27*(7), 660–661.

Perry, P., & Graat, J. (2010). *Couch fiction: A graphic tale of psychotherapy.* Houndmills, Basingstoke, Hampshire (UK): Palgrave Macmillan.

Pfeiffer, M. B. (2007). *Crazy in America: The hidden tragedy of our criminalized mentally ill.* New York, NY: Carroll & Graf.

Pickren, W. E., & Rutherford, A. (2010). *A history of modern psychology in context.* New York, NY: Wiley.

Pinker, S. (1998). Obituary: Roger Brown. *Cognition, 66*, 199–213.

Portillo, N. (2012). The life of Ignacio Martin-Baro: A narrative account of a personal biographical journey. *Peace and Conflict: Journal of Peace Psychology, 18*(1), 77–87.

Pritchard, M. C. (1951). The contributions of Leta S. Hollingworth to the study of gifted children. In P. Witty (Ed.), *The gifted child* (pp. 47–85). New York, NY: D. C. Heath & Co.

Raimy, V. (Ed.). (1950). *Training in clinical psychology.* New York, NY: Prentice-Hall.

Reber, A. (1996). *The new gambler's bible: How to beat the casinos, the track, your bookie and your buddies.* New York, NY: Three Rivers Press.

Reich, W. (1949). *Character analysis* (3rd ed.). New York, NY: Orgone Institute Press.

Reymert, M. L. (Ed.). (1928). *Feelings and emotions: The Wittenberg Symposium.* Worcester, MA: Clark University Press.

Richards, G. (2010). *Putting psychology in its place: Critical historical perspectives.* London, UK: Routledge.

Richardson, J. T. E. (2011). *Howard Andrew Knox: Pioneer of intelligence testing at Ellis Island.* New York, NY: Columbia University Press. Retrieved from http://psychcentral.com/lib/howard-andrew-knox-pioneer-of-intelligence-testing-at-ellis-island/00012829

Roberts, S. (2003). Triangle fire: New leaders emerge. *The New York Times,* City Room Blog: 3/24/2011. Retrieved July 28, 2013, from http://cityroom.blogs.nytimes.com/2011/03/24/triangle-fire-new-leaders-emerge

Rogers, C. (1942). *Counseling and psychotherapy.* Boston, MA: Houghton Mifflin.

Rogers, C., & Skinner, B. F. (1956). Some issues concerning the control of human behavior: A symposium. *Science, 124*, 1057–1065.

Rose, N. (1996). Power and subjectivity: Critical history and psychology. In C. F. Graumann & K. Gergen (Eds.), *Historical dimensions of psychological discourse.* New York, NY: Cambridge University Press.

Rosenhan, D. (1973). On being sane in insane places. *Science, 179,* 250–258.

Rosenzweig, S. (1936). Some common implicit factors in diverse methods of psychotherapy. *American Journal of Orthopsychiatry, 6*(3), 412–415.

Rosner, R. (2012). Aaron T. Beck's drawings and the psychoanalytic origin story of cognitive therapy. *History of Psychology, 15*(1), 1–18.

Ross, E. A. (1909). Discussion: What is social psychology? *Psychological Bulletin, 6,* 409–411.

Sanford, N. (1976). Graduate education then and now. *American Psychologist, 31*(11), 756–764.

Sarason, S. B. (1981a). An asocial psychology and a misdirected clinical psychology. *American Psychologist, 36*(8), 827–836.

Sarason, S. B. (1981b). *Psychology misdirected.* New York, NY: Free Press.

Schofield, W. (1964). *Psychotherapy: The purchase of friendship.* New York, NY: Prentice-Hall.

Seligman, M. (2010, June 20). A letter to the editor by Martin Seligman. VoltaireNet.org website. Retrieved from http://www.voltairenet. org/article165964.html

Seligman, M. E. P. (1975). *Helplessness: On depression, development, and death.* San Francisco, CA: W. H. Freeman.

Seligman, M. E. P. (1991). *Learned optimism.* New York, NY: Knopf.

Seligman, M. E. P., & Schulman, P. (1986). Explanatory style as a predictor of productivity and quitting among life insurance agents. *Journal of Personality and Social Psychology, 50,* 832–838.

Shaffer, L. F. (1936). *The psychology of adjustment: An objective approach to mental hygiene.* Boston, MA: Houghton Mifflin.

Shakow, D. (1965). Seventeen years later: Clinical psychology in light of the 1947 Committee on Training in Clinical Psychology Report. *American Psychologist, 20,* 353–362.

Shepard, R. N., & Metzler, J. T. (1971). Mental rotation of three-dimensional objects. *Science, 171,* 701–703.

Sherry, J. (2012). *Carl Gustav Jung: Avant-Garde conservative.* New York, NY: Palgrave Macmillan.

Shostrom, E. (1977). *Three approaches to psychotherapy (II). (Film).* Orange, CA: Psychological Films.

Skinner, B. F. (1948/2009). *Verbal behavior: William James Lectures, Harvard University, 1948.* (Unpublished MS transcribed by David Palmer.) Retrieved July 28, 2013, from http://www.bfskinner.org/ bfskinner/PDFBooks_files/William%20James%20Lectures.pdf

Skinner, B. F. (1953). *Science and human behavior.* New York, NY: Macmillan.

Skinner, B. F. (1970). Creating the creative artist. In A. J. Toynbee et al. (Eds.), *On the future of art.* New York, NY: Viking Press.

Skinner, B. F. (1978). *Reflections on behaviorism and society.* Englewood Cliffs, NJ: Prentice-Hall.

Slater, P. (1970). *The pursuit of loneliness: American culture at the breaking point.* Boston, MA: Beacon Press.

Smith, N. (1996). *The new urban frontier: Gentrification and the revanchist city.* London, UK: Routledge.

Social Security Administration. (1979). Social Security history: Frances Perkins. *Social Security Administration History Online.* Retrieved July 27, 2013, from http://www.ssa.gov/history/fpbiossa.html

Sokal, M. (1994). Gestalt psychology in America in the 1920's and 1930's. In S. Poggi (Ed.), *Gestalt psychology: Its origins, foundations, and influence: An international workshop.* Firenze: Leo S. Olschke.

Sperry, R. (1968). Hemisphere deconnection and unity in conscious awareness. *American Psychologist, 23*(10), 723–733.

Starbuck, G. (1971). *Of late.* New York, NY: McGraw-Hill.

Starch, D. A. (1909). Review of "The Hearing of Primitive Peoples." *Psychological Bulletin, 6,* 146–147.

Strong, E. K. (1922). *Selling life insurance.* New York, NY: Harper & Brothers.

Sullenberger, C. (2014). Chesley B. "Sully" Sullenberger III. Retrieved from http://sullysullenberger.com/#/about

Takasuna, M. (2013, June). Important literature referenced in textbooks on the history of psychology: A preliminary citation analysis using 13 textbooks published after 2001. *Cheiron* (International Society for the History of Behavioral and Social Sciences), XLV, poster presentation, University of Dallas.

Taylor, E. (2009). *The mystery of personality: A history of psychodynamic theories.* New York, NY: Springer Publishing Company.

Tolman, E. C. (1932). *Purposive behavior in animals and men.* New York, NY: The Century Company.

Tolman, E. C. (1939). Prediction of vicarious trial and error by means of the schematic sowbug. *Psychological Review, 46,* 318–336.

Tolman, E. C. (1942). *Drives toward war.* New York, NY: D. Appleton-Century Company.

Tolman, E. C. (1948). Cognitive maps in rats and men. *Psychological Review, 55,* 189–208.

Tolman, E. C., & Honzik, C. H. (1930). Degrees of hunger, reward, and non-reward, and maze performance in rats. *University of California Publications in Psychology, 4,* 241–256.

Tolman, E. C., Ritchie, B. F., & Kalish, D. (1946). Studies in spatial learning: I: Orientation and short-cut. *Journal of Experimental Psychology, 36,* 13–24.

Troland, L. T. (1926). *The mystery of mind.* New York, NY: D. Van Nostrand.

Tversky, A., & Kahneman, D. (1986). Rational choice and the framing of decisions. *The Journal of Business, 59*(4), S251–S278.

Tyler, L. (1973). Design for a hopeful psychology. *American Psychologist, 28*(12), 1021–1029.

U.S. Department of Commerce, Bureau of the Census. (1943). *Patients in mental institutions, 1939.* Washington, DC: U.S. Government Printing Office.

U.S. National Archives. (2013). Our documents: The Sixteenth Amendment. *Our Documents Initiative Website.* Retrieved from http://www.ourdocuments.gov/doc.php?flash=true&doc=57

Valenstein, E. S. (1986). *Great and desperate cures: The rise and decline of psychosurgery and other radical treatments for mental illness.* New York, NY: Basic Books.

Vasconcellos, J. (2001). Foreword. In K. J. Schneider, J. F. T. Bugental, & J. F. Pierson (Eds.), *The handbook of humanistic psychology: Leading edges in theory, research, and practice.* Thousand Oaks, CA: Sage Publications.

Viteles, M. (1932). *Industrial psychology.* New York, NY: W. W. Norton.

Vrana, B. (1991). Senate Bill 43: A refinement of North Carolina's involuntary civil commitment procedures. *Campbell Law Review, 14*(1), 105–122.

Walters, E. T., Carew, T. J., & Kandel, E. R. (1979). Classical conditioning in Aplysia californica. *Proceedings of the National Academy of Sciences (USA), 76*(2), 6675–6679.

Watson, J. B. (1924). *Behaviorism.* New York, NY: People's Institute.

Wiener, N. (1948). *Cybernetics: Or, Control and communication in the animal and the machine.* New York, NY: John Wiley & Sons.

Wiener, N. (1950). *The human use of human beings: Cybernetics and society.* Boston, MA: Houghton Mifflin.

Wiener, N. (1964). *God and Golem, Inc.: A comment on certain points where cybernetics impinges on religion.* Cambridge, MA: MIT Press.

Weizmann, F., & Harris, B. (2012). Arnold Gesell: The maturationist. In W. Pickren, D. A. Dewsbury, & M. Wertheimer (Eds.), *Portraits of pioneers in developmental psychology.* New York, NY: Psychology Press.

Wells, F. L. (1927). *Mental tests in clinical practice.* Yonkers-on-Hudson, NY: World Book.

Williams, T. A. (1909). Mental causes in bodily disease: The most frequent cause of the origins of "nervous indigestion." *Journal of Abnormal Psychology, 3,* 386–390.

Wilson, W. J. (1987). *The truly disadvantaged: The inner city, the underclass, and public policy.* Chicago, IL: University of Chicago Press.

Winston, A. S. (1996). "As his name indicates": R. S. Woodworth's letters of reference and employment for Jewish psychologists in the 1930's. *Journal of the History of the Behavioral Sciences, 32*(1), 30–43.

Yerkes, R. M. (Ed.) (1921). Psychological examining in the United States Army. *Memoirs of the National Academy of Sciences, 15*, 1–890.

Yerkes, R. M., & Morgulis, S. (1909). The method of Pawlow in animal psychology. *Psychological Bulletin, 6*, 257–273.

Young, J. (2010). Augusta Fox Bronner, 1881–1966. In A. Rutherford (Ed.), *Psychology's Feminist Multimedia Archive.* Retrieved July 26, 2013, from http://www.feministvoices.com/augusta-fox-bronner

Zegarac, N. (2007). All the colors of the rainbow: A brief romp through Technicolor. *The Hollywood Art.* Retrieved July 27, 2013, from http://thehollywoodart.blogspot.com/2007_12_01_archive.html

Index